POPULATIONS, PUBLIC HEALTH, AND THE LAW

POPULATIONS, PUBLIC HEALTH, and the LAW

WENDY E. PARMET

Georgetown University Press
Washington, D.C.

Georgetown University Press, Washington, D.C. www.press.georgetown.edu
© 2009 by Georgetown University Press. All rights reserved. No part of this book
may be reproduced or utilized in any form or by any means, electronic or
mechanical, including photocopying and recording, or by any information storage
and retrieval system, without permission in writing from the publisher.

Library of Congress Cataloging-in-Publication Data

Parmet, Wendy E
  Populations, public health, and the law / Wendy E. Parmet.
    p. ; cm.
  Includes bibliographical references and index.
  ISBN 978–1-58901–261–5 (pbk. : alk. paper)
    1. Public health laws—United States.   I. Title.
[DNLM: 1. Public Health—legislation & jurisprudence—United States.
2. Delivery of Health Care—legislation & jurisprudence—United States.
3. Health Policy—legislation & jurisprudence—United States.   4. Health
Status—United States.   5. Population—United States.
WA 33 AA1 P254p 2008]
KF3775.P35   2008
344.73′04—dc22
                                                                    2008034759

⊗This book is printed on acid-free paper meeting the requirements of the
American National Standard for Permanence in Paper for Printed Library
Materials.

15   14   13   12   11   10   09   9   8   7   6   5   4   3   2
First printing

Printed in the United States of America

To Herbert and Joan Parmet

CONTENTS

ACKNOWLEDGMENTS

MANY PEOPLE HAVE HELPED make this book possible. I especially want to thank George J. and Kathleen Waters Matthews, whose support for scholarship at Northeastern University has made this book possible. I also want to thank my dean, Emily Spieler, for generous research support and a schedule conducive to writing. Many thanks are also owed to my wonderful colleagues at Northeastern University School of Law. In particular, I am grateful to Roger Abrams for insisting that I finally write *the* book, to Hope Lewis for showing me the connections between population-based legal analysis and human rights, and to Mary O'Connell for always providing encouragement and an open door.

Over the years I have had the great honor to work with and learn from many eminent scholars in public health and law. Among those with whom I have collaborated on projects that have informed this book are George Annas, Christopher Banthin, Richard Daynard, Richard Goodman, Patricia Illingworth, Peter Jacobson, Wendy Mariner, Anthony Robbins, and Jason Smith. Without their inspiration and insight this book could not have been written. I am also very grateful to those who have read all or part of the various drafts of the manuscript: Patricia Illingworth, Peter Jacobson, Hope Lewis, Wendy Mariner, Mary O'Connell, and Jason Smith. Any errors and misunderstandings in this work are my own and do not reflect on my collaborators and reviewers.

As always, Jan McNew provided unsurpassed secretarial support. The reference librarians at Northeastern University School of Law, especially Susan Zago and Kyle Courtney, helped me track down both readily accessible and obscure materials. Many students and former students at Northeastern University School of Law assisted me with research. Among them are Robin Ackerman, Tanya Booth, Marc Catalono, Julie Ciollo, Jeremy Cohen, Lisa Conley, Erik Heath, Dara Hefler, Sarah Klosner, Matthew McHugh, Siddhartha Mukherjee, Dan Perlman, Audrey Perlow, Golda

Philip, Kerry Tipper, Deborah Thorpe, Elena Vizvary, and Erin Wells. I regret if I have overlooked any of my fine student researchers.

Throughout this project Richard Brown, director of Georgetown University Press, provided wonderful advice and extraordinary encouragement. I had heard that *real* editors no longer exist; people who say that have not had the good fortune to meet him.

Finally, I want to thank my family, whose love and patience have made this work possible. My parents, Joan and Herbert Parmet, nurtured my appetite for scholarship and set an example that I can only strive to meet. My husband, Ron Lanoue, has always been there with love and encouragement, through good times and bad. My wonderful children, Daniel and Anna Lanoue, not only support Mom's work, they also remind me why the issues I write about matter.

ABBREVIATIONS AND ACRONYMS

ADA	Americans with Disabilities Act
AIDS	acquired immunodeficiency syndrome
BMI	body mass index
BSE	bovine spongiform encephalopathy, aka mad cow disease
CDC	Centers for Disease Control and Prevention
CON	Certificate of Need
DES	diethylstilbestrol
DRG	diagnostically related group
EU	European Union
EMTALA	Emergency Medical Treatment and Active Labor Act
EPA	Environmental Protection Agency
FDA	Food and Drug Administration
FSIS	Food Safety and Inspection Services
GAO	Government Accountability Office
GATT	General Agreement on Tariffs and Trade
GDP	gross domestic product
HAACP	Hazard Analysis and Critical Control Point Regulations
HIV	human immunodeficiency virus
ICCPR	International Covenant on Civil and Political Rights
ICESCR	International Covenant on Economic, Social and Cultural Rights
IFCTC	International Framework Convention on Tobacco Control
IHR	International Health Regulations
IOM	Institute of Medicine
IQA	Information Quality Act
MRSA	Methicillan-resistant staphylococcus aureus
MSA	Master Settlement Agreement
MSEHPA	Model State Emergency Health Powers Act
NAFTA	North Atlantic Free Trade Agreement

OED	Oxford English Dictionary
PHLA	Public Health Law Association
PHLP	Public Health Law Program
QALY	quality-adjusted life years
SARS	severe acute respiratory syndrome
TRIPS	Agreement on Trade-Related Aspects of Intellectual Property Rights
UDHR	Universal Declaration of Human Rights
USDA	United States Department of Agriculture
WHO	World Health Organization
WTO	World Trade Organization
XDR-TB	extensively drug-resistant tuberculosis

INTRODUCTION

Salus populi suprema lex.

—Common law maxim

THE VENERABLE COMMON LAW MAXIM, *salus populi suprema lex,* expresses a principle long noted, even if infrequently followed, by American law: the well-being of the community is the highest law. The maxim reminds us that law exists, at least in part, to serve the common good. To do so, law must be understood in light of that goal.

But what is the common good? In a diverse and complex society, such as our own, people disagree, often vehemently, about what constitutes the common good. Some citizens equate it with national wealth, others with military strength; some with godliness, others with secular tolerance. These disagreements rightly form the spark for public discussion and democratic engagement. In a democracy, even as imperfect a democracy as our own, conceptions of the common good are always subject to debate.

Still, there can be little doubt that public health is an important component of the common good. When a plague ravages a community, no other good can be realized until public health is restored. Even when the threat to public health is not catastrophic, when a society's survival is not on the line, the protection of public health remains vital to ensuring that individuals and communities are healthy enough to participate in civic life and pursue their own life's goals.[1]

Perhaps it is for this reason that the American polity has always presumed that public health protection is both an appropriate and an important goal, if not duty, of government. Indeed, whenever a new threat to public health appears or gains public salience, be it toxic chemicals or pandemic influenza, mad cow disease or autism, the public has always

1

demanded that government take some action, preferably sooner rather than later. More often than not, the action adopted relies on the law.

Yet, despite the public's implicit recognition of the importance of public health, as well as law's utility to public health, few scholars have explored public health's relationship to law.[2] Nor have many asked what legal reasoning would or could look like if it accepted that public health protection was a critical goal of law. Scholars have also largely failed to consider how legal analysis would change if it were to incorporate the methods and perspective of the discipline of public health.

This book asks those questions and answers them by offering a new approach to legal analysis, one that emphasizes the importance of public health and incorporates that discipline's methodology into the core of legal reasoning. This approach, which I call *population-based legal analysis*, takes as its starting point the fundamental recognition that law seeks, among other things, to protect and promote public health. In other words, public health protection is one of the rationales for law, an important but certainly not the only component of *salus populi*. Population-based legal analysis further asserts that to fulfill its public health function, law must acknowledge the critical importance of populations. Populations, as well as individuals, must be viewed as central targets of the law's concern. In addition, legal analysis must be open to and mindful of empirically gained knowledge as well as probabilistic reasoning.

As the chapters that follow demonstrate, population-based legal analysis provides a powerful critique of contemporary legal discourse. In addition, it can help the law fulfill the critical mission of protecting the public's health. And by placing populations at the center of the legal stage while emphasizing the importance of empirical evidence and probabilistic thinking, population-based legal analysis can enrich and expand legal discourse, offering an alternative to the individualism and formalism that is excessive in much of contemporary American law, especially contemporary constitutional law.

Going forward, however, a very real risk must be addressed. Historically, the cry of public health has frequently been used to justify draconian and oppressive state actions. All too often such measures, from detention to mandatory medical treatment, have fallen disproportionately on the shoulders of already vulnerable populations. In effect, the laudable goal of public health protection has often been misapplied, or even abused, to subvert other critical values held by our legal system, such as equality and due process. The chapters that follow offer many examples. For now, it should suffice to recall that eugenicists relied on the claim of public health, as well as the credibility of science, to justify the involuntary sterilization of thousands of poor, disenfranchised, young women. No less a judge than Oliver Wendell Holmes Jr. accepted that claim, infamously asserting in *Buck v. Bell* that the principle that justifies "compulsory vaccination [for smallpox] is broad enough to cover cutting the Fallopian tubes."[3]

With the distance of decades, Justice Holmes' words appear to be both ignorant and antiquated, a relic of a less-informed and less-enlightened era. Many in the public health community, and many public health law advocates, believe that with our greater understanding of human health and our increased sensitivity to civil rights, we need not worry that public health will overreach, or be misused, as it was in *Buck*. To many in the public health community, it seems self-evident that not only should public health be granted a central role in law, but that the claims of public health and their own expertise should also readily be accepted to trump individual rights. In effect, they suggest that *salus populi suprema lex* should be applied all too literally and all too simplistically.

Now, eight years into the war on terror, as the world plans for a possible influenza pandemic, trusting the intentions of public health experts seems vital yet risky. Human history teaches that even the loftiest of goals, such as public health protection, can always be and often are abused. For that reason, individualism and the legal rights it supports should not be casually discarded.

Thus the challenge for population-based legal analysis, and indeed for American law more generally, is an enormous one: to recognize the centrality of public health to and within the law without dismantling the critical safeguards that our legal system has developed to protect the vulnerable and limit the abuse of authority. In other words, population-based legal analysis must appreciate the importance of populations without overlooking the dignity and interests of individuals. It must emphasize the value and utility of empirical evidence without disavowing democratic principles and legal precedent. And population-based legal analysis must show how law can be constructed and construed with public health in mind, never forgetting that the protection of public health is not law's only legitimate goal.

This books meets these challenges, placing public health in the center of law in a way that enables law to promote public health without permitting public health claims to erode legal values. The argument proceeds as follows: chapter 1 defines public health, establishes its importance to human activity, and explores its insights, particularly the population perspective. Chapter 2 reviews public health's relationship to law, both historically and at the present time. Chapter 3 begins the exposition of population-based legal analysis and compares that approach to standard methods of legal decision making. Subsequent chapters further refine population-based legal analysis while focusing its critical lens on diverse legal fields. Chapters 4 through 7 apply population-based legal analysis to different areas of constitutional law. Chapter 8 applies the approach to health law. Chapter 9 moves the discussion to tort law, exploring the utility of population-based legal analysis to the domain of private law. Chapter 10 turns to international law and human rights. The book concludes with further thoughts about the promises and insights of population-based legal analysis and its central claim: that by recognizing the importance of public health to law, we cannot only use law to protect the public's health, but also enhance legal discourse itself.

NOTES

1. In this sense, public health may be seen as having special moral significance, as Norman Daniels uses the term, because of its importance to individual, not public, health. *See* NORMAN DANIELS, JUST HEALTH: MEETING HEALTH NEEDS FAIRLY 29–78 (2008) (discussing the moral importance of health in light of the work of John Rawls and Amartya Sen). *See also* DAN E. BEAUCHAMP, THE HEALTH OF THE REPUBLIC: EPIDEMICS, MEDICINE, AND MORALISM AS CHALLENGES TO DEMOCRACY 18–22 (1988) (discussing public health as a primary good in light of the work of John Rawls and Michael Walzer). For a more thorough discussion of these issues, *see infra* chapter 1.

2. As discussed in *infra* chapter 3, there has been a recent renaissance in public health law itself, though not in the broader recognition of public health's relationship to law.

3. 274 U.S. 200, 207 (1927).

CHAPTER 1

Public Health and the Population Perspective

The condition of perfect public health requires such laws and regulations, as will secure to man associated in society, the same sanitary enjoyments that he would have as an isolated individual.

—Lemuel Shattuck et al., *Report of the Sanitary Commission of Massachusetts*, 1850

P UBLIC HEALTH ISSUES are pervasive in the law. Every day in courtrooms throughout the United States, and indeed across the globe, courts hear cases that relate directly or indirectly to the public's health. Judges in constitutional law cases ponder the state's power to protect public health and the impact of that power on the rights of individuals. Administrative tribunals contemplate the meaning of statutes empowering them to regulate in the name of public health. Private parties contest the liability of individuals and firms that act in ways that endanger the health of others.

Yet, despite the ubiquity of public health issues in law, surprisingly little attention has been paid to public health's importance to law. Indeed, in field after field of American law, the centrality of public health issues has been overlooked by both courts and theorists. Cases are analyzed and decisions are made without a full appreciation of either the central role that public health has in the relevant legal field or the insights that public health, as a field, may bring to the legal question at hand. As a result, law's ability to serve as a positive force for public health is diminished. So, too, is legal discourse.

This book seeks to remedy the law's neglect of public health by offering an approach to legal analysis that I term population-based legal analysis. This approach affirms public health's importance as an appropriate goal or value to law and incorporates the perspectives and methodologies of public health into legal analysis. Most critical, population-based legal analysis validates the importance of populations as both subjects and objects of law.

As an approach to law, population-based legal analysis offers a powerful way of analyzing legal issues and critiquing contemporary legal discourse. It is not, however, and does not purport to be, either comprehensive or exclusive. It cannot resolve all legal issues or provide that elusive quest for determinacy. Nor do I claim that population-based legal analysis is the only appropriate way to think about and analyze legal questions. But I do claim and will demonstrate that it provides a valuable additional perspective on a wide range of legal issues.

The chapters that follow develop population-based legal analysis and apply its insight to myriad legal questions. The legal fields explored raise issues important to public health, but my analysis is neither organized by nor limited to traditional areas of public health law. Although population-based legal analysis is inspired by public health, and demonstrates public health's centrality to law, it is not applicable solely to public health issues. Nor is it an exposition of public health law.[1] Population-based legal analysis is instead an approach to legal reasoning that can be applied and offer insights to a wide range of legal issues.

To appreciate population-based legal analysis, however, it is first essential to understand what is meant by public health and why it is important to social organization and the law. Likewise, it is critical to consider the insights and methodologies of public health that form the building blocks of population-based legal analysis. Most essential is understanding public health's population perspective. This chapter reviews all these issues, thereby laying the groundwork for the subsequent discussion of population-based legal analysis.

The Myriad Meanings of Public Health

Issues of public health abound. When an emerging infection such as human immunodeficiency virus (HIV) or pandemic influenza appears, we know it is a public health threat. Likewise, most, but not all, observers would agree that smoking is a public health problem. But what about domestic violence? Global warming? Obesity? Drug abuse? Are they public health problems? What does it mean to call them as such? Indeed, what is public health?

Despite the frequent use of the term *public health*, the phrase is surprisingly difficult to define. According to *The Oxford English Dictionary* (OED) public health is "the health of the population as a whole, especially as monitored, regulated, and promoted by the state (by provision of sanitation, vaccination, etc.)."[2] A somewhat different and very influencial contemporary definition was the one proffered by the Institute of Medicine (IOM) in its 1988 report, *The Future of Public Health:* "public health is what we, as a society, do collectively to assure the conditions for people to be healthy."[3] As useful as these definitions are, they beg a critical question: what is meant by *health*? Unfortunately, this question is also not easy to answer.

The OED defines the noun *health* as "soundness of body; that condition in which its functions are duly and efficiently discharged."[4] Although this definition emphasizes the condition of the body, relating health to an organism's biological or corporeal state, the use of the term *functions* opens the door to a partially socially constructed notion of health. After all, how do we know what the body's functions are? The answer inevitably depends in part on the knowledge, norms, and expectations of a given society.[5] Thus the questions of whether the capacity to stay focused in a classroom or to see well at night are functions whose impairment is incompatible with health depends not only on human biology but also on what is expected in a given society of people and their interactions with their environment.

Recognizing the role social factors play in establishing health, the constitution of the World Health Organization (WHO) defines health more broadly as the "state of complete physical, mental, and social well-being and not merely the absence of disease or infirmity."[6] This definition demands that health be understood to require more than the capacity to perform vital bodily functions normally; it necessitates affirmative social well-being. As critics have noted, the WHO definition seems to equate health with the totality of human happiness.[7] If so, then public health, understood as what we do collectively to assure health, must necessarily encompass an extremely broad set of activities, including all collective actions undertaken to provide the conditions for human happiness. Given the broad claims made for public health below, the current discussion will rely on the narrower OED definition of health. If that is used, the IOM's definition of public health translates to what we as a society do collectively to ensure the conditions for people's bodies to be capable of performing their functions duly and efficiently.

Even restricted this way, the definition is expansive. It includes whatever we do collectively to ensure the conditions for people to be healthy. Presumably if an income tax cut improves the economy and thereby provides the conditions for more people to be left disease free, it is part of public health.[8] Public health therefore includes not only traditional core public health functions, such as those cited in the OED definition of public health, but also many other activities that are less obviously aimed at improving people's health. On the other hand, as Lawrence Gostin notes, the IOM definition implies that public health is the "collective responsibility of organized society to promote the health of the population."[9] From this perspective, tax cuts enacted for reasons that have nothing to do with the health of a group may not, after all, be a public health activity. In any case, the IOM definition suggests that public health applies to actions taken to promote the health of people, not individuals. The IOM thus concurs with the OED definition asserting that public health relates to the health of populations. This contrasts sharply with the practice of medicine, which generally focuses on the treatment of individuals qua individuals.[10]

Although instructive as an organizing principle for the activities to promote a population's health, several other potential meanings of the term should be noted. Consider the statement, "cigarettes are a public health problem." It does not refer to any activities society engages in collectively. Cigarettes are not a problem affecting activities that ensure healthy conditions; they are the source of harm to millions. In this sense, the term public health refers, as the OED definition suggests, not to what people do, but simply to the health of a group of people. As a result, in the absence of interventions, public health may be terrible, but it will still exist and require our attention. Public health, like death and taxes, is an inevitable aspect of the human condition.

Two additional connotations are also both commonly used and important to bear in mind. One is implicit in the definition offered in 1923 by the great public health scholar, C. W. Winslow. He stated that public health is "the science and art of preventing disease, prolonging life, and promoting physical health and efficiency through organized community efforts."[11] This definition is echoed in the second sentence of the OED definition, "the branch of medicine dealing with this (including hygiene, epidemiology, prevention of infectious diseases, etc.).[12] Similarly, the 1997 Acheson Report defined public health as the "the art and science of preventing disease, promoting health, and prolonging life through organized efforts of society."[13] These definitions concur with the IOM in viewing public health as relating to active and collective efforts undertaken to improve health. In contrast to the IOM and OED, however, both Winslow and the Acheson Report stress that public health is an art and science. In other words, public health is not simply the actions undertaken to improve health; it is a discipline, comprised of professionals, some of whom are physicians and most of whom are not, who work in a variety of settings, from state health departments to nongovernmental organizations, from large federal agencies to small community health centers.[14] What they share is their desire to understand and promote the health of one or more populations. Of course, any particular job they do, and any advice they offer, may or may not promote public health in the sense that the term refers to the health of a group. And it may or may not be based on the best evidence the field has to offer. Public health professionals can give poor public health advice, just as lawyers can make poor legal judgments.

Although these different uses of the phrase public health vary as to their parts of speech and their emphasis, they share certain features, critical to discussing the relationship of public health to law and the development of population-based legal analysis. Most important, these definitions each stress that the focus of public health is on the health or well-being of people, not individuals. This insight points to the so-called population focus that forms the foundation for the population perspective and its legal offshoot, population-based legal analysis.

THE HISTORY AND IMPORTANCE OF PUBLIC HEALTH

Philosophers have offered different arguments in support of a commonly accepted notion—health is, to use Norman Daniels's term, of "special moral importance."[15] According to Daniels, who attempts to build on and revise John Rawls's *A Theory of Justice*,[16] health is worthy of special moral consideration, and hence is rightly the concern of theories of justice, because it is essential to ensuring that individuals have their full range of opportunities.[17] In a slightly different vein, Amartya Sen emphasizes the importance of health to justice by noting that "health is among the most important conditions of human life and a critically significant constituent of human capabilities which we have reason to value."[18]

Although such arguments can provide support for the claim that public health (as opposed to individual health) is of special moral significance because public health is crucial to the maintenance of individual health, they envision individuals as the primary objects of moral concern.[19] In effect, they focus on the moral claims of individuals to health, and consider population health of value only insofar as it is essential to satisfying individual moral claims.

In contrast, some communitarian and social contract theorists focus on the moral claims of groups qua groups. For example, Dan Beauchamp contends that "public health stands for collective control over conditions affecting the common health—a very sturdy republican idea."[20] Applying such insights, scholars such as Emitai Etzioni have stressed the importance of public health as a communal value.[21] This approach resonates closely with public health's focus on populations but risks overstating the potential conflict of interest between individuals and the populations they form.[22]

Regardless of its philosophical underpinnings, the claim that public health, understood as the health of a group of people, or population, is of special importance is reinforced by humanity's historical experience with disease, especially infectious disease.[23] For most of human history, people have faced horrific epidemics. When an epidemic occurred, its impact fell not only on those individuals who were directly afflicted, but also on the community as a whole. Wars could be won or lost, governments empowered or deposed, economies strengthened or destroyed.[24] As a result, for most of human history, avoiding or mitigating epidemics was necessary for a society's survival. In this sense, public health, understood as the health status of a population, is not simply a preference or a question of taste. Rather, it is a precondition to social life, one of the goods a society must aim for and achieve if it is to survive and attain other ends.[25]

Moreover, infectious epidemics show that the health of an individual depends, to a great degree, on the health of others.[26] Although before the middle of the nineteenth century people did not understand the mechanisms of infection, and the theory of contagion was frequently disclaimed, people have known for millennia that some diseases tended to spread within and among villages, cities, and regions.[27] Likewise, humanity has long understood that an individual's ability to protect him or herself from disease was limited. An individuals' risk of becoming ill depended in uncertain ways on the steps that the community took and the environment and conditions in which the individual lived.[28]

Indeed, human experience with infectious diseases has long made clear the importance of collective action in preserving and protecting the health of populations. This became especially apparent as Europe confronted the Black Death. For example, recognizing that the plague traveled along trade routes (though not understanding how), fourteenth-century Italian city-states instituted quarantines that required ships to wait in port forty days before unloading.[29] Likewise, England responded to the plagues of the sixteenth and seventeenth centuries with "an elaborate public health policy involving quarantine and the cleansing of affected areas,"[30] as well as with laws providing for the care and treatment (such as it was) of the ill.[31] In colonial North America, governments also took many actions designed to prevent or mitigate the impact of epidemics.[32] These actions, which ranged from official days of fasting and prayer, to quarantines, the regulation of butchering, and laws providing for inoculation against smallpox, were all justifiable under the prevailing social contract theory, which insisted that governments were legitimated because they were necessary to secure the common good.[33]

The idea that the health of a population and the individuals within it are determined by conditions affecting the population and influenced by collective action became more broadly accepted and delineated in the nineteenth century, even before the advent of the germ theory, with the development of the sanitary movement. As cities grew, their sanitary conditions worsened and so did the health of their residents.[34] Early pioneers in the field of epidemiology, which studies "how often diseases occur in different groups of people and why,"[35] began to recognize the importance of health and mortality data.[36] They used that data and their analyses of it to study the causes of disease and discern the relationship between a population's health and its environment. For example, John Snow famously noted a relationship between the incidence of cholera and drinking water from the Broad Street pump.[37] Likewise, in 1850 Lemuel Shattuck studied the relationship between the sanitary conditions in Massachusetts and the health of the state's residents.[38] After surveying the data Shattuck concluded that laws and regulations were needed.[39] In effect, Shattuck's observation of an association between environmental conditions and health led him to advocate for legal and social change. This interrelationship between public health understood as a science and public health viewed as a form of collective action for a common good became a persistent feature of public health's population perspective.[40]

The late nineteenth century was the golden age of public health. It was when Oliver Wendell Holmes Jr. spoke of the man of statistics,[41] who could use newly developed quantitative methods to reveal the relationship between environmental conditions and a community's health. It was also the era when public health was institutionalized in the United States, as states, following Shattuck's advice, established standing boards of public health and empowered them to conduct a wide range of activities.[42] And it was the dawn of the germ theory that provided an empirically verifiable explanation for contagion and the interdependency of human health. To Progressive reformers, the germ theory highlighted why individuals must be concerned about the conditions and fate of others. For example, Cyrus Edson, a New York City health commissioner, spoke of the "socialism of the microbe, this is the chain of disease, which binds all the people of a community together."[43]

In the years since, the field of public health has not consistently held to that insight. Indeed, through much of the twentieth century public health often embraced a biomedical model of disease that, as Bruce Link and Jo Phelan suggest, emphasized "proximate risk factors, potentially controllable at the individual level."[44] According to Robert Beaglehole and Ruth Bonita, "much of modern epidemiology ignores the unique features of populations and, instead, isolates individual characteristics and risk factors from their social context."[45]

In recent years, however, numerous epidemiologists have returned their gaze to the role that social and environmental factors play in determining human health. One significant reason for this "return" to public health's social roots was the widespread recognition of what Link and Phelan describe as "the ubiquitous and often strong association between health and socioeconomic status."[46] Researchers have noted that there is a persistent and pervasive correlation between health outcomes and socioeconomic status (the so-called SES gradient) that appears across very different societies and exists despite the presence of universal access to health-care services.[47] Indeed, even as particular proximal causes of diseases are reduced or eliminated, the correlation between health and socioeconomic class continues, a phenomenon that has prompted social epidemiologists to search for more fundamental, distal causes of disease that may include socioeconomic status, as well as other social or environmental factors, such as social cohesion or even legal structures.[48] Some researchers contend that the slope of the distribution of income itself helps to determine the health of a population.[49] If so, even individuals placed high on the SES gradient may face greater health risks if they live in a society with an uneven distribution of income than they would in a more egalitarian society.

Whether this so-called relative income hypothesis proves true—and it is sharply debated[50]—research on so-called social determinants undeniably shows that the ways in which societies are organized, and the environment in which people live, can help determine human health.[51] Thus social determinants reinforce the ancient teaching that the health of individuals depends on social factors outside their own control.

THE POPULATION PERSPECTIVE

As public health developed as a discipline and activity during the nineteenth century, its proponents came to share (to differing degrees) several tenets that continue to inform the field. The first principle has already been noted—the health of individuals depends at least partly on social and environmental factors outside their control. This offers us a powerful selfish reason to care about public health: it often affects our own individual health.

Public health advocates, however, rely on more than self-interest to support their focus on populations. They also rely on a more fundamental moral interdependency, one that suggests a deeply communitarian ethic. For example, in his *Report of the Sanitary Commission of Massachusetts* in 1850, Lemuel Shattuck wrote: "No family,—no person liveth to himself alone. Every person has a direct or indirect interest in [every other] person. We are social beings—bound together by indissoluble ties. Every birth, every marriage, and every death, which takes place, has an impact somewhere; it may not be upon you or me now; but it has upon some others, and may hereafter have upon us."[52] Thus to Shattuck the health of others was both an indispensable and legitimate concern of a community.[53] Or, as John Donne so eloquently wrote: "No man is an island."[54]

Public health's assertion of both the empirical and ethical relationship between the health of individuals and the well-being of their communities helps underpin the so-called population perspective. As used here, that term connotes a particular vantage point that is heavily influenced by (though not necessarily identical to) the experiences and teachings of the field of public health, especially its subfield of social epidemiology. That perspective reflects and contains a set of normative, epistemological, methodological, and descriptive understandings that can be gleaned in public health scholarship and practice. As discussed in chapter 3, the population perspective forms the foundation for population-based legal analysis.

According to Dan Beauchamp and Bonnie Steinbock, the population perspective refers to "the effort to understand the occurrence of disease from a group or community perspective."[55] To public health scholars and practitioners, this emphasis on group or population health, a focus especially prominent in the field of social epidemiology and its search for social determinants, distinguishes public health from medicine, which focuses upon the treatment of individual patients.[56] The focus also distinguishes public health from much of contemporary legal discourse, which generally emphasizes the rights and interactions of individuals.[57]

Intrinsic to the population perspective is the normative claim that the health of populations qua populations is an important goal of social life. Historically, this assertion was first associated with the theological claim that epidemics resulted from a community's sin.[58] If that were the case, an unhealthy community could be viewed as one deserving divine wrath.

During the Enlightenment, support for the health of populations as a valid social goal was legitimated by social contract theory, which postulated that individuals willingly forgo the liberty of the hypothetical state of nature in favor of civil society where they can achieve, in the words of John Locke, "mutual *Preservation* of their Lives, Liberties and Estates."[59] According to historian Ronald Peters, although social contract theorists and adherents disagreed about many things, they concurred that "the only end of civil society is the common good. And the sine qua non of the common good is public safety, *salus populi suprema lex.*"[60] In other words, protection of public safety, which presumably included safety from deadly epidemics, was the highest good. Indeed, its attainment was the rationale for civil society.

By the nineteenth century a new theoretical construct, utilitarianism, offered a different but largely compatible justification for the population perspective's ethical assertions. According to nineteenth-century utilitarianism, maximizing utility, or well-being for the greatest number of people, was the highest good, the one that just societies should aim to achieve.[61] Utilitarianism, even more than social contract theory, would appear to provide a rationale for the population perspective's normative claim as to the importance of public health, as well as to the consequentialism inherent in a vantage point that gives normative value to social outcomes.

Despite the support that the population perspective would seem to derive from utilitarianism, the differences between it and that philosophical theory are significant. First, in contrast to utilitarianism, the population perspective is not a fully developed ethical theory. Rather, it is a perspective or approach that draws on the insights of numerous fields to interpret social and biological problems relating to human health. Second, also unlike utilitarianism, the population perspective seeks to maximize not overall happiness but instead a population's health, a good that can at least theoretically be measured by relatively objective health statistics, as opposed to the inherently subjective criteria of utility.[62] In addition, from the population perspective, the reference group is not the totality of human beings on the earth, as utilitarianism claims, but different populations of varying sizes.

The population perspective's focus on the health of groups also distinguishes it from other consequentialist neo-utilitarian constructs, such as welfare economics. From the perspective of welfare economics and its legal progeny, law and economics, overall utility is maximized when rational individuals exercise their so-called revealed preferences, which are measured in currency, and make choices in perfectly functioning markets.[63]

When such perfect markets achieve equilibrium, or Pareto optimality, individuals as an aggregate are as well off as they can be. Thus welfare economics seeks to maximize not the health of a population, which can partially be objectively determined, but the wholly subjective preferences of individuals.

Because of these distinctions, the population perspective offers a very different assessment than either welfare economics or law and economics about government's role in protecting public health. From the perspective of welfare economics, maximum utility (or the good) is best achieved when perfect markets are left to function freely. Hence governments should intervene in the name of public health only when there are market imperfections, such as an airborne infection, which cannot be subject to the rules of the market.[64] In effect, a public health problem warrants collective intervention only when markets do not work efficiently.

In contrast, because the population perspective seeks to maximize group health, it may support a health-improving intervention even if there is no obvious market failure. For example, laws requiring motorcycle riders to wear helmets may be justifiable because they reduce injuries and death in the population of motorcycle riders even if there are neither market failures preventing individual drivers from acting on the risks of riding without a helmet nor externalities that prevent riders from properly calculating the cost of not doing so.[65] In that situation, the welfare economics approach may argue that the public health intervention reduces overall welfare and inappropriately undermines the overall utility that an otherwise efficient market reaches. But to an adherent of the population perspective, the improvement in public health caused by the regulation (if there is any) may stand alone as an appropriate goal (which is not to say that there are not other reasons to limit particular government interventions).[66]

The population perspective also parts company from welfare economics in emphasizing the pervasiveness of the social and environmental determinants of health. The welfare economics approach presumes that preferences are endogenous[67] and that individuals can, for the most part, control their own health.[68] In contrast, the population perspective, steeped in the history of public health and influenced by the teachings of social epidemiology, questions whether that supposition is true. Indeed, the population perspective attempts to discern the factors that affect populations as a whole and influence an individual's preferences and risks, as well as the distribution of disease within a population. According to Scott Burris and colleagues, "from a public health perspective, individuals look much more constrained in their agency. Individual choice is limited by the options actually available to the chooser and, more deeply, by the way in which different options are socially constructed."[69] As a result, the population perspective emphasizes the environmental and social determinants of health and how they affect the health and well-being of populations.[70]

Several additional components of the population perspective deserve specific mention. First, influenced by the discipline of public health and its subfield epidemiology, the population perspective adopts the scientific method in which hypotheses are put to the test of observation and experimentation.[71] In contrast to traditional common law reasoning, the population perspective does not rely on deductive or analogical reasoning, though of course, experiences can form the basis for hypotheses. Rather, from a population perspective, hypotheses must be tested, either by the analysis of observational data or in the laboratory. The standard of proof is neither the persuasiveness nor the elegance of the reasoning; it is the fit between the hypothesis and empirical observations.[72]

Second, the population perspective generally adopts a probabilistic view. This aspect can be traced back to the early nineteenth century and the close relationship between the budding disciplines of statistics and epidemiology.[73] But the probabilistic approach was threatened for a time by the development of the germ theory and the institutionalization of the so-called Koch-Henle postulates, which provided a so-called test to determine when an organism caused a disease.[74] According to medical historian Allan Brandt, "statistical inference seemed a weak tool in comparison to the sophisticated biochemistry and microscopy of the laboratory."[75]

By the mid-twentieth century, however, statistical and probabilistic thinking in epidemiology reemerged. Brandt credits this change to a new focus on chronic diseases for which single causes could not be found.[76] According to Brandt, the 1964 Surgeon General's Report on smoking marked a decisive victory for probabilistic and inferential epistemology in public health.[77] By 1964 it was recognized that cigarettes did not cause cancer in the way that early adherents of the germ theory thought microorganisms caused infections. Not all individuals who smoked developed lung cancer and not all individuals who developed lung cancer smoked. Nevertheless, numerous population-based studies had demonstrated an irrefutable relationship between smoking and cancer.[78] The recognition of the importance of that relationship, and the decision by the U.S. Surgeon General in 1964 to issue a warning as a result, established the influence and power of population-based statistical analysis.[79] It also demonstrated the close association between public health as a discipline and as a collective intervention. The epidemiology of smoking helped lead to a series of (always contested) actions that sought to use statistical analyses to further the normative goal of improving public health.

Third, the concept of population in the population perspective is contingent, constructed, and relative. There is no doubt that the term *population* in common parlance usually refers to the residents of a particular geographical region (hence "the population of the United States").[80] But population as used in the population perspective refers more generally to any group or number of individuals (of any biological organism) sharing some common trait.[81]

The nature of the relevant trait may vary. Most often the common trait is one used frequently in lay discourse to identify people. Thus gender, age, or socioeconomic class can each serve as a trait that defines a population. Populations defined by such commonly described traits will be referred to below as "commonly identified populations," to highlight that the defining characteristic is one that is commonly used outside of the field of epidemiology. But, critically, the trait chosen need not be one typically used to define a group. One can speak of the population of individuals who smoke, the population of woman under thirty-five in Boston who smoke, or the population of women in Boston under thirty-five who smoke and drive SUVs. In each case, what constitutes the population is the set of traits (or variables) the individuals share, as highlighted by a public health researcher or practitioner, based on a hypothesis of the trait's relevance to a health issue in question. The defined population then is the entire group that has the shared variable.[82] Regardless of the nature of the trait, without reference to the defining variable, the term population is meaningless. Indeed, there is no such thing as *the* population, or, indeed, *the* public. Instead, population refers to any group that can be defined by the presence or absence of a given trait.

The contingent nature of populations is important to bear in mind for several reasons. First, it distinguishes (or should distinguish) the population perspective from nationalistic, ethnocentric, and many communitarian perspectives.[83] Public health's goal of improving population health does not require either reifying or privileging the health of any particular pre-set group of people. Commonly identified populations are not necessarily favored. Moreover, the constructed nature of populations demonstrates both the empirical and activist strands of public health within the population perspective. Populations are determined by the questions asked and the interventions taken to improve the health of a group of people.

The Ontology and Insights of the Public Health Perspective

The discussion thus far has identified five characteristics of the population perspective: its normative valuation of population health, its understanding of the interdependence of health within a population, its reliance on empiricism, its probabilistic stance, and its recognition that populations are contingent and constructed. The most central trait of the population perspective, however, is its focus on populations. But what exactly does that mean? Most simplistically, it might mean that the population perspective cares about and seeks to improve outcomes for populations qua populations as well as the health of individuals who comprise those populations. Thus populations, contingent and constructed, are the object of the population perspective's normative thrust.

Populations, however, are not simply objects for the population perspective. They are also its subjects. This factor is implicit in the idea that populations are constructed and contingent. Populations are artifacts empiricists use to test hypotheses and increase public health's understanding of the causes and distribution of disease and injury. But populations are also subjects in a more fundamental, ontological sense. Key to the population perspective is that human health is influenced at a population level.

By treating populations, contingent and constructed as they may be as a subject or agent, the population perspective parts company not only with contemporary utilitarian theories, such as welfare economics, but also with present-day liberal theories, all of which rely on and assert an essential, ontological individualism in which individuals, not populations, are the subjects and agents of human events. As discussed in later chapters, this ontological shift, from individual to population, creates significant tension both within the population perspective and between it and much of American law, which largely reflects the influence of liberal individualism. The chapters that follow explore and seek to reconcile these tensions. For now, it is helpful to observe what is gained when populations are treated as subjects. As noted earlier, social epidemiologists have recognized that social conditions, so-called social determinants, help to determine the health of an individual. This suggests that we cannot understand the causes of an individual's health status simply by looking at factors intrinsic or unique to that individual (that is, the individual's so-called risk factors). We need instead, or at least in addition, to focus on the individual's social environment. And, to see how the environment affects the individual and helps determine both the risk factors and their impact, we need to compare and contrast populations exposed to different social and environmental influences.

The work of English epidemiologist Geoffrey Rose provides a powerful example.[84] Rose explains that if we look only at the incidences (or cases) of a particular disease (he uses hypertension as his example) in a particular population, such as civil servants in London, epidemiologists may decide that the disease is caused by factors that vary between the individuals in the group, such as their genes or behavior.[85] These factors are commonly treated as individual risk factors. However, when epidemiologists compare the overall rate of disease in that population to the rate in another population (he chooses Kenyan nomads), they may uncover the fact that even those individuals in London with so-called normal blood pressures in fact have elevated rates compared to the Kenyans.[86] Thus, in comparing different populations, epidemiologists can uncover other factors that may work subtly, at an environmental or population level, to influence the health of populations, factors that may be missed when looking only at the clinical status of individuals or the health of people within one population.

"To find the determinants of prevalence and incidence rates," Rose says, "we need to study characteristics of populations, not characteristics of individuals."[87] Thus, the population perspective not only puts the health of a population at the center of the stage, it suggests that only comparisons between different groups can reveal health effects and determinants that may well be hidden at the individual level.[88] Moreover, Rose's work implies that subtle factors, operating at the social and environmental level and affecting a population writ large, can be responsible for a majority of cases of hypertension.

As Rose demonstrates, the population perspective points to different strategies of protection than does a more individually oriented analysis. To take again Rose's example of hypertension, if we look primarily at the blood pressures of individuals within a set population (London civil servants), we are apt to focus our attention on those individuals within the group who have the most significantly elevated blood pressure, to label them as at risk and to seek to remedy their condition through some combination of treatment or lifestyle interventions.[89] What this approach neglects, and what becomes clear only by comparing blood pressure levels of the group of London civil servants to that of another group such as the Kenyan nomads, is that the London civil service population as a whole may have a relatively elevated rate and that there may be many more people not viewed as at-risk in London who in fact may develop complications from coronary artery disease.[90] As a result, an intervention aimed only at the outliers in the London group may miss not only many, but perhaps the majority, of preventable cases of disease arising from hypertension in London. Conversely, a strategy that aims at altering the underlying (probably subtle) factors that affect a population as a whole may well prevent far more cases of disease, though it is less likely to benefit any single individual than would a treatment aimed directly at so-called high risk persons.[91]

By looking at multiple populations, public health researchers have observed the so-called prevention paradox: interventions (including legal interventions) that operate even slightly upon larger populations can, at times, reduce the overall incidence of disease more significantly than those that act more robustly upon high-risk individuals or narrowly defined groups.[92] For example, laws that require everyone in a car to wear a seat belt may save more lives than interventions (such as programs to suspend the licenses of drunk drivers) that effectively target at-risk drivers. Although the more targeted intervention may be very effective in getting bad drivers off the road, it may not save as many lives as the broader intervention that helps the vast majority of drivers who get into an accident (and aren't drunk) to survive a crash. On the other hand, as Katherine Frohlich and Louise Potvin have reminded us, interventions aimed at broad populations may have varied distributive impacts.[93] Particularly worrisome is that the interventions that lead to the greatest overall decline in cases of a disease may have less of an impact on the number of cases in vulnerable populations, and thus increase health disparities. Hence, in using the population perspective, keeping the multiplicity and diversity of populations in mind is always critical.

The population perspective can shed light on ways to improve the health of different populations. It can also provide new insights on legal and policy questions. It is important to bear in mind that, these strengths aside, the population perspective is simply a perspective that reflects a set of values and ontological assumptions. It uses a particular set of methodologies to understand and improve the health of groups of people. The population perspective is not an all-encompassing intellectual or moral theory. It neither provides nor promises determinative answers. Indeed, because it relies on empirical and probabilistic reasoning such offerings are impossible. Nevertheless, over the course of the past two centuries, studies and interventions influenced by the population perspective have taught the world much and have paved the way for collective actions that have saved millions of lives.[94] More often than not, these interventions have relied on law.

Notes

1. For several years the leading contemporary monograph on public health law in the United States has been LAWRENCE O. GOSTIN, PUBLIC HEALTH LAW: POWER, DUTY, RESTRAINT (2000). A second edition of this text has recently been released. LAWRENCE O. GOSTIN, PUBLIC HEALTH LAW: POWER DUTY, RESTRAINT (2d ed. 2008). For a further discussion of contemporary public health law, see chapter 2, *supra*.

2. OXFORD ENGLISH DICTIONARY, http://dictionary.oed.com (last visited Nov. 13, 2008).

3. INST. OF MED., COMM. FOR THE STUDY OF THE FUTURE OF PUBLIC HEALTH, THE FUTURE OF PUBLIC HEALTH 19 (1988).

4. *Health*, OXFORD ENGLISH DICTIONARY, http://dictionary.oed.com (last visited Oct. 10, 2008).

5. *See* René Dubos, *Health and Creative Adaptation*, in ETHICAL HEALTH CARE 19, 19 (Patricia Illingworth & Wendy E. Parmet eds., 2005).

6. World Health Organization, *Constitution of the World Health Organization 2*, http://www.who.int/governance/eb/who_constitution_en.pdf (last visited Oct. 10, 2008.

7. Daniel Callahan, *The WHO Definition of Health*, in ETHICAL HEALTH CARE, *supra* note 5, at 25–28.

8. *See* Wendy E. Parmet, *The Impact of the Law on Coronary Heart Disease: Some Preliminary Observations on the Relationship of Law to a Normalized Condition*, 30 J. L. MED. & ETHICS 608, 612–615 (2002).

9. LAWRENCE O. GOSTIN, PUBLIC HEALTH LAW AND ETHICS: A READER xix (2002).

10. *See* Anthony Robbins & Phyllis Freeman, *Public Health and Medicine: Synergistic Science and Conflicting Cultures*, 65 PHAROS 22 (Autumn 2002).

11. ROBERT BEAGLEHOLE & RUTH BONITA, PUBLIC HEALTH AT THE CROSSROADS: ACHIEVEMENTS AND PROSPECTS 174 (2d ed. 2004) (quoting C. W. Winslow).

12. OXFORD ENGLISH DICTIONARY, *supra* note 2.

13. BEAGLEHOLE & RUTH BONITA, *supra* note 11, at 174.

14. *See* PUBLIC HEALTH FUNCTIONS PROJECT, U.S. DEP'T HEALTH & HUMAN SERVS., THE PUBLIC HEALTH WORKFORCE: AN AGENDA FOR THE 21ST CENTURY (1997), http://www.health.gov/phfunctions/pubhlth.pdf.

15. NORMAN DANIELS, JUST HEALTH: MEETING HEALTH NEEDS FAIRLY 17–21 (2008).

16. JOHN RAWLS, A THEORY OF JUSTICE (1974).

17. DANIELS, *supra* note 14, at 29–64. For Daniels' earlier version of the argument, see NORMAN DANIELS, JUST HEALTH CARE 1–17 (1985).

18. Amartya Sen, *Why Health Equality*, in PUBLIC HEALTH, ETHICS AND EQUITY 21, 23 (Sudhir Anand, Fabienne Peter, & Amartya Sen eds., 2004).

19. *See* DANIELS, *supra* note 15, at 141–44.

20. DAN E. BEAUCHAMP, THE HEALTH OF THE REPUBLIC: EPIDEMICS, MEDICINE, AND MORALISM AS CHALLENGES TO DEMOCRACY 17 (1988).

21. Amitai Etzioni, *Perspective: Public Health Law: A Communitarian Perspective: The Attacks on America's Homeland Clearly Demonstrate the Need to Trim the Individual Excesses of the Previous Generation and Make Room for the Public Interest*, 21 HEALTH AFFAIRS 102, 102 (2002). *See also* Ronald Bayer and Amy L. Fairchild, *The Genesis of Public Health Ethics*, 18 BIOETHICS 473, 488 (2004) (emphasizing that the core of public health ethics is the common good).

22. *See* James F. Childress & Ruth Gaare Bernheim, *Beyond the Liberal and Communitarian Impasse: A Framework and Vision for Public Health*, 55 FLA. L. REV. 1191, 1194–95 (2003). For a further discussion of this issue, *see* chapter 5, *infra*.

23. Barry S. Levy, *Creating the Future of Public Health: Values, Vision, and Leadership*, 88 AMER. J. PUBLIC HEALTH 188, 188–92 (1998).

24. J.N. HAYS, THE BURDENS OF DISEASE: EPIDEMICS AND HUMAN RESPONSE IN WESTERN HISTORY 2 (1998); WILLIAM H. MCNEILL, PLAGUES AND PEOPLE *passim* (1976).

25. *See* DANIELS, *supra* note 15, at 29–64.

26. *See* Keith Thomas, *Health and Morality in Early Modern England*, in MORALITY AND HEALTH 15, 17–18 (Allan M. Brandt & Paul Rozin eds., 1997).

27. For a discussion of early theories of contagion, as well as competing theories of the etiology of disease, see Chris Collins, *IBMS History Zone, Causes of Fevers:*

Miasma versus Contagion, http://www.ibms.org/index.cfm?method = science
.history_zone&subpage = history_fevers (last visited Jan. 25, 2008).
28. Thomas, *supra* note 26, at 17–18.
29. Beaglehole & Bonita, *supra note* 11, at 109.
30. Thomas, *supra* note 26, at 18.
31. Wendy E. Parmet, *Health Care and the Constitution: Public Health and the Role of the State in the Framing Era,* 20 Hastings Const. L.Q. 267, 287 (1993).
32. *Id.* at 286–302.
33. *Id.* at 312–13.
34. Theodore H. Tulchinsky & Elena A. Varavikova, The New Public Health: An Introduction for the 21st Century 16–25 (2000).
35. D. Coggon, Geoffrey Rose & D.J.P. Barker, Epidemiology for the Uninitiated 1 (4th ed. 1997).
36. *Id.* at 21.
37. *Id.* at 26.
38. Lemuel Shattuck et al, Report of the Sanitary Commission of Massachusetts 1 (1850).
39. *Id.* at 71–72.
40. *See* Tulchinsky & Varavikova, *supra* note 34, at 22–27. *See also* Elizabeth Fee, *The Origins and Development of Public Health in the United States, reprinted in* Gostin, *supra* note 9, at 27, 28–29.
41. Louis Menand, The Metaphysical Club 346–47 (2001).
42. Richard Shryock, *The Origins and Significance of the Public Health Movement in the United States,* 1 Annals of Med. Hist. 645 (1929).
43. Cyrus Edson, *The Microbe as a Social Leveller, quoted in* Nancy Tomes, *Moralizing the Microbe: The Germ Theory and the Moral Construction of Behavior in the Late Nineteenth-Century Antituberculosis Movement, in* Morality and Health, *supra* note 26, at 271–84.
44. Bruce G. Link & Jo Phelan, *Social Conditions as Fundamental Causes of Disease,* 35 J. Health and Soc. Behavior, Extra Issue: Forty Years of Medical Sociology: The State of the Art and Directions for the Future 80, 80 (1995).
45. Beaglehole & Bonita, *supra* note 11, at 145. *See also* Milton Terris, *The Development of Cardiovascular Disease Risk Factors: Socioenvironmental Influences,* 20 Preventive Medicine S11, S11–12 (1999).
46. Link & Phelan, *supra* note 44, at 81.
47. *Id.* (citing studies). *See also* Daniels, *supra* note 15, at 83–92 (citing studies); Michael G. Marmot, *Understanding Social Inequalities in Health,* 46 Perspectives in Biology & Med. Supp. S 9, S 10 (Summer 2003).
48. Scott Burris, Ichiro Kawachi, & Austin Sarat, *Health, Law, and Human Rights: Exploring the Connections, Integrating Law and Social Epidemiology,* 30 J.L., Med. & Ethics 510, 511–13 (2002). For further discussion of the field of social epidemiology, see Social Epidemiology 3–12 (Lisa F. Berkman & Ichiro Kawachi eds., 2000). For a critique of the *proximal* and *distal* terminology, see Nancy Krieger, *Proximal, Distal,*

and the Politics of Causation: What's Level Got To Do With It?, 98 Am. J. Pub. Health 221, 221–30 (2008).

49. Ichiro Kawachi, *Income Inequality and Health*, in Social Epidemiology, *supra* note 48, at 76–94.

50. *E.g.*, Jennifer M. Mellor & Jeffrey Milyo, *Reexamining the Evidence of an Ecological Association between Income Inequality and Health*, 26 J. Health Pol'y Pol. & L. 487 (2001) (disputing the claim that inequality itself influences health).

51. World Health Organization, Comm. on Social Determinants of Health, *Closing the Gap in a Generation: Health Equity through Action on the Social Determinants of Health passim* (2008), http://whqlibdoc.who.int/publications/2008/9789241563703_eng.pdf (last visited Dec. 3, 2008); World Health Organization, Comm. on Social Determinants of Health, *Action on the Social Determinants of Health: Learning from Previous Experiences* 23 (2005), http://www.who.int/social_determinants/resources/action_sd.pdf (last visited Oct. 10, 2008). *See also* David Mechanic, *Who Shall Lead: Is There a Future for Population Health*, 28 J. Health Pol'y Pol. & L. 421, 421–22 (2003).

52. Shattuck, *supra* note 38, at 190.

53. *Id.* For contemporary articulations of the view, see Lawrence O. Gostin, *When Terrorism Threatens Health: How Far Are Limitations on Personal and Economic Liberties Justified?*, 55 Fla. L. Rev. 1105 (2003).

54. John Donne, *Meditation* XVII (1624).

55. Dan E. Beauchamp & Bonnie Steinbock, New Ethics for the Public's Health 25 (1999).

56. Lawrence O. Gostin, Public Health Law: Power, Duty, Restraint 11–12 (1st ed. 2000) (quoting Elizabeth Fee).

57. *See* Wendy E. Parmet & Anthony Robbins, *Public Health Literacy for Lawyers*, 31 J.L., Med. & Ethics 701, 706, nn.74–76 (2003) (citing sources).

58. Thomas, *supra* note 26, at 17.

59. John Locke, The Second Treatise of Government at 15–34, §123 *reprinted in* Two Treatises of Government 368 (Peter Laslett ed., 2d ed. 1967).

60. Ronald Peters Jr., The Massachusetts Constitution of 1780 103–104 (1978).

61. John Stuart Mill, Utilitarianism 10 (Oskar Piest ed., 1957). *See also* Marc Lappé, *Values and Public Health: Value Considerations in Setting Health Policy*, 4 Theoretical Med. 82 (1983) (noting that "an ethic for public health has generally been described as strictly utilitarian").

62. *See* Daniels, *supra* note 15, at 38 (distinguishing health claims as relatively objective claims). For a further discussion of this distinction, see Wendy E. Parmet, *Liberalism, Communitarianism, and Public Health: Comments on Lawrence O. Gostin's Lecture*, 55 Fla L. Rev. 1221, 1225–30 (2003).

63. *See generally* Jules L. Coleman, *The Economic Analysis of Law*, in Law, Economics, and Philosophy 102, 102–08 (Mark Kuperberg & Charles Beitz eds., 1983).

64. *See* Richard A. Epstein, *Let the Shoemaker Stick to His Last: A Defense of the "Old" Public Health*, 46 PERSP. IN BIO. & MED. S. 138, S. 142–43 (2003).

65. *E.g.*, Love v. Bell, 465 P. 2d 118, 121 (Colo. 1970). *But see* State v. Lee, 465 P. 2d 573, 576–77 (Haw. 1970) (upholding state motorcycle helmet law not because of its economic impact on others but because the state has the authority to act to prevent injuries and death).

66. For a further discussion of the role of individual rights as limits to public health interventions, see chapters 5 and 6, *infra*.

67. *See* Samuel Bowles, *Endogenous Preferences: The Cultural Consequences of Markets and Other Economic Institutions*, 36 J. ECON. LIT. 75 (1998).

68. *See* Richard A. Epstein, *What (Not) To Do about Obesity: A Moderate Aristotelian Answer*, 93 GEO. L.J. 1361, 1368 (2005).

69. Scott Burris, James Buehler, & Zita Lazzarini, *Applying the Common Rule to Public Health Agencies: Questions and Tentative Answers about a Separate Regulatory Regime*, 31 J.L. MED. & ETHICS 638, 643 (2003).

70. *See* SOCIAL EPIDEMIOLOGY, *supra* note 48 *passim*.

71. *See* TULCHINSKY & VARAVIKOVA, *supra* note 34, at 114 (defining epidemiology as the "study of health events in a population" and then defining study to include "surveillance, observation, hypothesis testing, analytic research and experiments").

72. On the distinctions between legal reasoning and scientific reasoning, see Jonathan Fielding et al., *How Do We Translate Science into Public Health Policy and Law*, 30 J.L., MED. & ETHICS 22, 25–26 (Supp. 2002); Joelle Anne Moreno, *Beyond the Polemic against Junk Science: Navigating the Oceans that Divide Science and Law with Justice Breyer at the Helm*, 81 BOSTON U. L. REV. 1033, 1034–36 (2001).

73. BEAGLEHOLE & BONITA, *supra* note 11, at 111–17.

74. *See* TULCHINSKY & VARAVIKOVA, *supra* note 34, at 32.

75. Allan M. Brandt, *Behavior, Disease, and Health in the Twentieth-Century United States: The Moral Valence of Individual Risk, in* MORALITY AND HEALTH, *supra* note 26, at 53, 60.

76. *Id.*

77. *Id.* at 61.

78. *E.g.*, TULCHINSKY & VARAVIKOVA, *supra* note 34, at 257.

79. *Id.*

80. *See Population*, Merriam-Webster's Online Dictionary, http://www.merriam-webster.com/dictionary/population (last visited June 1, 2008) (the first definition of *population* is "the whole number of people or inhabitants in a country or region").

81. *Id.*

82. *See* Valerie J. Easton & John H. McCall, *Population*, Statistics Glossary, vol. 1, http://www.stats.gla.ac.uk/steps/glossary/basic_definitions.html# popn ("A population is any entire collection of people, animals, plants or things from which we may collect data") (last visited June 1, 2008). The Oxford English Dictionary defines *population* as "a totality of objects or individuals under consideration." 12 OXFORD ENGLISH DICTIONARY 127 (2d ed. 1989).

83. *See* ELIZABETH FRAZIER, THE PROBLEMS OF COMMUNITARIAN POLITICS: UNITY AND CONFLICT 209–17 (1999).

84. Geoffrey Rose, *Sick Individuals and Sick Populations*, 30 INT'L J. OF EPIDEMIOLOGY 427 (2001).

85. *Id.*

86. *Id.* at 428.

87. *Id.*

88. *See also* WORLD HEALTH ORG., SOCIAL DETERMINANTS OF HEALTH 3 (Richard Wilkinson & Michael Marmot eds., 1999) (stressing the need to consider differences in risk between populations).

89. Rose, *supra* note 83, at 431.

90. *Id.* at 428.

91. *Id.* at 431.

92. For a fuller discussion of this paradox and its implications for public health law, see Lawrence O. Gostin, Scott Burris, & Zita Lazzarini, *The Law and the Public's Health: A Study of Infectious Disease Law in the United States*, 99 COL. L. REV. 59, 66–76 (1999).

93. Katherine L. Frohlich & Louise Potvin, *The Inequality Paradox: The Population Approach and Vulnerable Populations*, 98 AM. J. PUB. HEALTH 216, 219–20 (2008).

94. For a discussion of public health successes, see SILENT VICTORIES: THE HISTORY AND PRACTICE OF PUBLIC HEALTH IN TWENTIETH CENTURY AMERICA (John W. Ward & Christian Warren eds., 2007); Stephen L. Isaacs & Steven A. Schroeder, *Where the Public Good Prevailed: Lessons from Success Stories in Health*, 12 AM. PROSPECT 26, 26–30 (June 4, 2001).

CHAPTER 2

Public Health and American Law

For the rational study of the law the black-letter man may
be the man of the present, but the man of the future is the
man of statistics and the master of economics.

—Oliver Wendell Holmes Jr., *The Path of the Law*

I T HAS BEEN MORE than 100 years since Oliver Wendell Holmes Jr.
declared that the future of the law lay not in legal doctrine but in the
insights and understandings garnered by other disciplines. Since that
time, lawyers, jurists, and legal scholars have become acquainted with,
embraced, and sometimes abandoned a broad array of nonlegal disciplines. The teachings of sociology, psychology, literary theory, critical theory, and most frequently economics have all been applied, with varying
degrees of influence and success, to criticize and augment American
jurisprudence.

One perspective now largely absent from this interdisciplinary buffet is
public health. This absence from legal consciousness is surprising because
until relatively recently public health played a pivotal role in the development of several fields of law. But the deficit is also problematic because
issues relating to the health of populations are pervasive throughout the
law. Lawyers, legislators, and judges continually confront questions with
profound implications for the health of a community. Hence, lawyers
must understand the teachings of public health not only because the law

profoundly affects the health of populations, but also because an understanding of the field is necessary to appreciate the roots and nuances of multiple legal doctrines.

This chapter explores the critical and reciprocal relationship between law and public health in the United States, saving for a later chapter the discussion of this relationship on a global level.[1] The chapter begins by examining the differences between the perspectives of law and public health and then explores the ways in which law can affect population health. The chapter concludes by discussing public health's impact on American legal doctrine.

THE MEANING OF LAW

What is law?[2] Despite the ubiquity of the term, philosophers, jurists, scholars, and advocates have debated and expounded on the meaning of the word *law* for thousands of years. There is no easy answer.

Still, it is clear that law, like public health, has numerous common meanings. Most narrowly, the early positivists viewed it as the rules or commands that are enforceable by the state or sovereign. Since H. L. A. Hart, positivists have described law more broadly to include norms that garner legitimacy under an authoritative "rule of recognition."[3] These norms may include not only the statutes and regulations that purport to govern a matter, but also case law, constitutions, treaties, and other sources of authority so long as they are recognized as law pursuant to a valid rule of recognition. But, in contrast to natural law theorists, positivists deny that the commands of morality standing alone, regardless of their provenance, constitute law or that rules of a state that depart from moral norms are not in fact law merely because of that departure.[4]

For our purposes, it is not critical to enter the jurisprudential debate between positivists, natural law theorists, and scholars from other jurisprudential schools. It is enough to observe that in common parlance law is a broad concept, subject to multiple meanings and that it includes, at the very least, most rules that are enforceable by the state.[5] In addition, at least in the U.S. legal system, these commands come in multiple, explicit, and not-so-explicit forms. Thus, as Ronald Dworkin has argued, deeply held principles not only influence the law, in some circumstances they can be considered law.[6] In addition, practicing lawyers as well as legal scholars often apply the term law to the modes of analysis and argumentation, or ways of reasoning, that are used to decide which rules or principles are applicable to a given situation.[7]

However we define it, law helps organize and shape a society.[8] Thus law provides not only the organizational structure for government (e.g., constitutional law), but for the economy and civil society itself (e.g., contract and family law). Law also helps enforce and give legitimacy to social norms, such as the norm against discrimination on the basis of race, or the norm of free speech.[9] Law thus helps form and is a part of the social environment. Indeed, we can identify and define populations by their varied exposure to or interaction with different legal rules or regimes.

One final point deserves note. Law, like public health, is a discipline. In contrast to public health, law is one of the ancient professions, and as such it has its own traditions, norms, and ways of viewing the world. To a significant extent the legal perspective contrasts dramatically with public health's population perspective. For example, where the population perspective prizes health, the legal profession purports to cherish that abstract ideal known as justice. Likewise, where public health focuses on the interests of populations, lawyers are expected to represent the interests of individual clients, because the legal profession assumes that the common good will emerge from the clash of individual interests in an adversarial system. And where the public health perspective relies on empirical and probabilistic reasoning, legal reasoning, at least traditionally, has been primarily deductive and analogical. However, as the Oliver Wendell Holmes Jr. quote suggests, critics have long recognized that legal reasoning cannot rely solely on analogy or the deductive application of rules to facts.[10]

Despite the many differences between law and public health, the two fields are in many ways interdependent. Much of what public health seeks to accomplish requires the support of the law. At the same time, despite its commitment to an adversarial system that relies on a contest between individual interests, the furtherance of the common good remains a core goal of our legal system.[11] Because of these commonalities, public health's population perspective provides the field of law with an acute and powerful way of understanding myriad legal issues.

How Law Affects Public Health

Law affects public health in multiple ways. First, law forms the basis for organizing, empowering, and limiting the collective interventions that the IOM defines as public health.[12] But law does more than that. By establishing the social framework in which populations live, face disease and injury, and die, law forms an important social determinant of population health.[13]

Discussions of the relationship between law and public health typically focus on so-called public health powers or authorities, the laws that directly create and authorize the activities of public health boards and agencies.[14] These are the positive laws, such as those that empower a board of health to institute quarantines or inspect a restaurant, that explicitly and directly make possible the organized, collective governmental interventions that occur in the name of public health. At the same time, other laws set boundaries on public health interventions, often to protect individual interests such as claims to property or privacy. It is for this reason that Lawrence Gostin aptly subtitled his leading treatise on public health law with the phrase *Power, Duty, Restraint."*[15]

To be sure, not all public health interventions require explicit legal authorization or initiation. As a recent IOM report emphasizes, many public health activities take place in the private sector or within civil society.[16] These actions may not require any direct legal imprimatur, though law affects them too, by helping shape the institutions of civil society. For example, laws enabling the chartering of corporations or the favorable tax treatment of nonprofit organizations help make it possible for individuals in civil society to come together and organize interventions that promote population health.[17] Likewise, constitutional protections for speech help ensure that advocacy groups can spread their message regarding controversial approaches to protect public health, such as the distribution of condoms.

The complex relationship between law and public health can be illustrated by envisioning a series of concentric circles. In the innermost circle are so-called public health powers, laws that create and authorize government actions about or addressed to the health of a population. These include the laws that establish boards of health, authorize quarantines, or mandate vaccinations. Further from the center, in the next ring, are other laws that are highly relevant to public health but that do not directly address organizing and implementing public health activities. For example, laws pertaining to the civil liability for the production of toxic products are relevant to public health but they do not pertain to public health in as direct and explicit a manner as the laws that establish administrative agencies that regulate products that threaten public health.[18] Even further from the center, in an arbitrarily selected circumference, is the set of all the laws known as public health laws, a set that may include not only the laws that establish public health agencies, but also those that limit the authority of those agencies, for example, by providing protections for individual privacy. Immediately on the other side of the circumference are those laws that influence public health only indirectly, for example, the laws determining the tax status of hospitals and health care organizations.[19] Further away still are the untold number of laws that help shape the social environment by influencing the distribution of property, wealth, and power, the meaning and impact of race, gender, disability, and sexual orientation, as well as the nature and scope of the economy, and the rules that govern access to the legal system itself.[20]

Of course, there is no precise way to map where different laws or legal rules belong or to quantify their impact on different populations. Nor is it clear where the circumference line should be drawn between those laws that are called public health laws and those that are not. But the image of concentric circles helps illustrate both that there are an infinite number of laws that relate to public health and the obvious point that some laws are closer to the core than others. Not surprisingly, the impact of the laws nearest the center is more readily observed and better understood than that of those furthest from the center. But even laws outside the core may have a profound effect on a population's health.

THE IMPACT OF PUBLIC HEALTH LAW

Without question, many populations in the United States experienced enormous gains in their health status in the past hundred and fifty years. In the late nineteenth century, during the so-called golden age of public health, mortality from infectious diseases declined dramatically and life expectancy increased. According to Herman Biggs, the general medical officer of the New York Department of Health at the start of the twentieth century, between 1866 and 1903 life expectancy in New York climbed from twenty-five years to forty-two years.[21] In 1921, Frederick Hoffman noted that cholera deaths had been common in Chicago before 1860; after 1873 no more were recorded.[22] Likewise, by the early 1900s, once common killers of children like typhoid, diphtheria, and smallpox ceased to take many lives.[23]

The dramatic gains in the health of the general American population continued into the twentieth century, although not all populations experienced equal benefits. Indeed, the disparities in health between populations within the United States remain a pressing challenge for both public health and law.[24] Nevertheless, that advances in population health in the last hundred years were significant is undeniable. For example, at the start of the twentieth century the crude death rate in the United States stood at 17.2 per thousand, but by the end of the century it was 8.7 per thousand.[25] During the same period infant mortality in the United States declined from 120 to 6.9 per thousand.[26] Life expectancy increased by more than thirty years.[27]

Although many factors undoubtedly played a role in facilitating these advances, including improvements in nutrition,[28] population-based interventions aimed at improving population health deserve a large share of the credit.[29] The dramatic gains made in the nineteenth century against infectious disease, for example, occurred before antibiotics and effective medical treatments against infection were developed. The declines in incidence of infectious disease occurred instead as cities began to build sewers and provide clean drinking water[30] and states enacted food safety laws.[31] In the twentieth century, improvements in population health have been tied to such notable achievements as near universal childhood vaccination rates, reduction in workplace injuries, family planning and safer childbirths, improvement in motor vehicle safety, and a decline (in the second half of the twentieth century) in tobacco use.[32] In contrast, although curative medical services have received the lion's share of health dollars and are commonly assumed to be responsible for increases in life expectancy, researchers estimate that their contribution has been relatively modest.[33]

Laws helped create the conditions that made public health achievements possible. Laws were used to create boards of public health, establish clean water supplies, ensure the pasteurization of milk, require the vaccination of children, and inspect workplaces to ensure safe conditions. Laws also were required to gather the data (by collecting vital statistics and reporting communicable diseases) necessary to perform the epidemiological research that could inform public health actions (whether public or private).

The importance of law to improving population health remains true today. In a 2001 article, *Where the Public Good Prevailed*, Stephen Isaacs and Steven Schroeder describe four notable public health successes of recent decades: the reduction in blood lead levels among children, the reduction of dental cavities in children, the decline in the rate of motor vehicle injuries per mile driven, and the decline in the percentage of adults who smoke.[34] Laws or legal developments, Isaacs and Schroeder write, were critical to each of these happy public health stories: "Law and regulation, often at the federal level, have been critical elements in focusing Americans' attention on health concerns, providing policy direction, and setting standards that have led to improvement in the public's health. Despite all the criticism they have received, federal laws and regulations have vastly improved people's health. They have been—and continue to be—the underpinning that protects the health of the American public."[35]

Isaacs and Schroeder are not alone in their assessment. Although the efficacy and value of many laws enacted to improve a population's health is unknown, other researchers have connected legal interventions to many public health improvements.[36] For example, in a recent paper, Anthony Moulton and colleagues reviewed gains made in the areas of motor vehicle safety, dental health, and the control of infectious disease.[37] After finding that law was critical to each of the studied gains, they concluded that law can make a "powerful contribution" to public health.[38] Likewise, the Task Force on Community Preventive Services, convened by the CDC, reviewed twenty-five studies of the effectiveness of different child safety laws.[39] The studies reviewed determined that child safety laws led to a reduction in fatal motor vehicle injuries among children that ranged from 25 percent to 57.3 percent.[40] Studies have also credited workplace safety laws with helping to reduce the incidence of occupational injuries,[41] and tobacco control litigation and regulations with helping reduce cigarette smoking.[42]

None of this is to say that law is always or even usually beneficial to a population's health. To the contrary, law can often undermine a population's health. Most obviously, laws can authorize unnecessary wars that kill and maim untold numbers of people. More subtly, courts sometimes strike down laws that have the potential to improve a population's health.[43] Laws may also impose policies that on their face have no obvious relationship to health but in fact threaten a population's health. Recent studies, for example, have suggested a relationship between zoning laws and the concentration of hazardous pollutants in certain (particularly minority) communities,[44] as well as between zoning laws and asthma and obesity.[45]

Critically, the population perspective suggests that the laws with the greatest impact, for good or bad, on the health of a given population may not be those that most obviously pertain to public health.[46] Rather, the greatest impact may come from laws that lie far from the core of public health laws yet touch on large numbers of people and influence their health, even modestly. Thus, laws that affect the population broadly, such as by requiring universal education or clean air, may actually have a greater overall impact on a population's cardiovascular health than those that authorize public health interventions or that target so-called high-risk individuals.[47] Zoning laws may therefore have a greater impact on obesity than laws requiring insurers to pay for weight reduction surgery. Similarly, laws that modestly alter the sexual practices of a large population (perhaps by regulating the portrayal of sex in the media) may prevent more cases of HIV than would laws that directly target a few individuals who knowingly infect their sexual partners.[48] Moreover, given the increasing evidence that income and perhaps inequality are important social determinants of health, it would not be surprising if laws with a broad effect on the distribution of wealth have a more substantial impact on the health of large populations than so-called core public health laws.[49]

Although our understanding of the public health impact of law remains in its infancy and far more rigorous research is needed, it is beyond doubt that law plays an important role in shaping the health of populations.

Public Health's Influence on the Development of American Law

The influence of public health on the law is not always easy to discern but it is nevertheless profound. Both the health problems populations have faced and the responses communities have made to those threats have helped shape the fabric of our jurisprudence.

The impact of public health on law can be seen in numerous private and public fields. Consider tort law, the area of private law that deals with the liability of individuals (or entities) for civil harm done to others.[50] A quick perusal of a torts casebook or treatise quickly reveals that most cases discussed concern personal injuries. Closer examination reveals a striking correlation between the activities plaintiffs allege as the cause of their injury and activities that at the time of the case posed a significant threat to the health of large populations. In effect, tort law showcases the most salient activities or agents of disease and injury in an era. Thus, in the nineteenth and early twentieth centuries, courts faced numerous tort claims that arose from railroad accidents.[51] By the start of the twentieth century, tort law confronted the carnage caused by the automobile.[52] In the closing decades, toxic chemicals that increase the potential for disease began to occupy a large share of the tort law docket.[53] In each case, tort law necessarily responded to and changed as a result of its encounter with the new public health problem.

As subsequent chapters explore more thoroughly, public health has also influenced constitutional law.[54] For example, many of the leading cases decided under the so-called dormant commerce clause, which limits the ability of states to burden interstate commerce, have concerned state laws that purport to protect the health of the state's population.[55] In the middle of the nineteenth century, this jurisprudence relied heavily on the notion that the states had an inherent right, known as the police power, to protect the health of their citizens.[56] The Supreme Court then used this understanding of the police power to interpret the post–Civil War Fourteenth Amendment in the *Slaughter-House* cases.[57] In recent years, of course, the public health controversies that have given rise to constitutional cases are different. Noteworthy contemporary constitutional litigation has concerned pharmaceutical regulation,[58] physician-assisted suicide,[59] and cigarette marketing.[60] These cases and others demonstrate the impact of public health problems on the continued evolution of constitutional law.

Public health threats and the interventions aimed at them have also had an enormous influence upon the development and content of administrative law.[61] In the early nineteenth century, for example, when there were few federal administrative agencies, local boards of health were created to organize a locality's response to epidemics.[62] The actions of these boards,

including quarantine and isolation[63] and the abatement of public nui-
sances,[64] provided courts with an early exposure to the critical questions
of judicial review and administrative process that lie at the core of administrative law.[65]

More recently, administrative law has focused much of its attention on,
and has been largely shaped by, the federal government's attempts to
impose or loosen regulations designed to protect public health. Public
health threats such as air pollution,[66] motor vehicle injuries,[67] and occupational exposure to carcinogens[68] are among the mainstays of contemporary
administrative law. As a result, it should not be surprising that much of
the academic legal literature about administrative law has turned to risk
assessment and how government should regulate diffuse and complex
risks to health and safety.[69] Hence, as with constitutional law and torts,
legal doctrine and debate in administrative law are significantly affected
by the problems and even methodological issues central to public health.

Many other examples are available, and will be discussed in subsequent
chapters, to demonstrate the importance of public health to the evolution
of American law. For now, three points should be emphasized. First, the
public health threats of an era have always found their way before the
courts and lawmaking bodies of the time.[70] As a result, public health problems are a major part of the facts to which the law responds. Second, myriad legal doctrines reflect the tensions between society's organized efforts
to tame threats to population health and countervailing interests and values. Third, the relationship between law and public health is both pervasive and reciprocal. The law helps shape or constitute the social, economic,
and cultural environment, which in turn affects the health of the population exposed to that environment. But the health status of a population
affects its politics, economy, and perceptions of the world, shaping in turn
both the agenda before lawmaking bodies and the tone and tenor of
the law.

THE RISE OF PUBLIC HEALTH IN AMERICAN LEGAL DISCOURSE

Despite the intimate and important nature of the relationship between law
and public health, recognition of public health as either a central issue
or critical perspective in contemporary American legal consciousness is

surprisingly lacking. This was not always so. During the nineteenth century, jurists and commentators cited public health, sometimes along with the common law maxim, *salus populi suprema lex* (the well-being of the public is the highest law) as if those references provided a sufficient basis for deciding a case.[71] Thus nineteenth-century treatise writers Leroy Parker and Robert Worthington wrote that the preservation of public health was a "legitimate and [one of the] most important functions of government."[72] They added: "a proper presentation of the law relating to public health and safety should be of highest interest both to those who interpret that law in the courts, and to those who are entrusted with its execution."[73]

Perhaps not surprisingly, public health's influence on American law was at its zenith during the Progressive era. Enormous changes occurred in life expectancy, infant mortality, and death by infectious diseases.[74] Public health departments were professionalized and great strides were made in taming once fearsome infectious diseases.[75] An epidemiological transition in which the chronic diseases such as cancer and coronary heart disease replaced infections as the major cause of death was under way.[76] Public health officials were understandably confident about the importance of their mission and their capacity for success. In 1904, Herman Biggs boasted that the sanitary reforms undertaken in the previous forty years had saved some fifty thousand lives per year in New York alone.[77]

It was in this atmosphere, in which infectious diseases remained familiar yet health officials were confident about their ability to vanquish the threat, that the United States Supreme Court decided by a vote of 7–2 its most important case concerning a core public health law, *Jacobson v. Massachusetts*.[78] The *Jacobson* case arose from a smallpox epidemic that struck the Northeast in 1902. In the midst of the epidemic, the Cambridge Board of Health relied on a state statute to enact an ordinance requiring all adults who had not been vaccinated since 1897 to be vaccinated or revaccinated during a smallpox epidemic. A local pastor, Henning Jacobson, and several others refused to be vaccinated and were charged with violating the ordinance. The state courts and ultimately the United States Supreme Court upheld the ordinance.

In its *Jacobson* opinion the Supreme Court issued its most explicit and influential analysis of the law's relationship to public health and individual rights. Justice John Marshall Harlan's majority opinion offers an elegant testament to the importance of public health and its role in the law.

Justice Harlan began his discussion by noting that the state's authority to enact a mandatory vaccination statute derived from the state's police power. Relying on an earlier opinion by Chief Justice Marshal, Justice Harlan stated that "although this court has refrained . . . from any attempt to define the limits of that power, yet it has distinctly recognized the authority of a State to enact quarantine laws and 'health laws of every description.'"[79] He added that the police power of a state "must be held to embrace, at least, such reasonable regulations established directly by legislative enactment as will protect the public health and the public safety."[80]

Justice Harlan then turned to whether the state could use its police power to compel Reverend Jacobson to be vaccinated or pay a $5 fine. In finding that the state had such power, Justice Harlan expressed perhaps more fully than the Supreme Court has ever done before or since the view that public health is a fundamental objective of government and may, at times, take precedence over the interests of individuals:

> The liberty secured by the Constitution of the United States to every person within its jurisdiction does not import an absolute right in each person to be, at all times and in all circumstances, wholly freed from restraint. There are manifold restraints to which every person is necessarily subject for the common good. On any other basis organized society could not exist with safety to its members. . . . This court has more than once recognized it as a fundamental principle that "persons and property are subjected to all kinds of restraints and burdens, in order to secure the general comfort, health, and prosperity of the state; of the perfect right of the legislature to do which no question ever was, or upon acknowledged general principles ever can be, made."[81]

Justice Harlan's opinion in *Jacobson* not only extolled the importance of public health and the state's power to protect it, but also endorsed some of the methods and techniques of public health, as they were then understood. For example, in upholding the local vaccination ordinance, the Court accepted that collective interventions were necessary. And in affirming the state's power to delegate to the board of health the authority to determine whether to adopt mandatory vaccination, the Court implicitly accepted that public health experts had specialized knowledge about how to protect a population's health.[82] Perhaps most important, the Court's opinion contained extensive citations to historical and statistical data affirming the efficacy of vaccination.[83] Thus, the Court effectively endorsed the use of epidemiological evidence to determine the appropriateness of the state's action.

The Court's opinion in *Jacobson* also acknowledged the significance of both the tension between individual interests and protection of population health and the potential that government could abuse its public health powers. To ensure some constitutional check on the government's actions, the Court made clear that there had to be evidence that mandatory vaccination had a "real or substantial relation to the protection of public health and the public safety."[84] Moreover, in dicta the Court opined that mandatory administration of vaccination might in some cases be "cruel and inhuman in the last degree."[85] According to the Court, the exercise of the police power would be unconstitutional if it was "so arbitrary and oppressive" in an individual case.[86] But in finding that the state courts had not acted unconstitutionally in denying Jacobson's proffer of evidence, the Court was willing to defer to public health authorities and require Henning Jacobson to be vaccinated, or pay the fine.[87]

Two months after it decided *Jacobson*, the Supreme Court decided one of its most infamous cases, *Lochner v. New York*.[88] At issue in *Lochner* was a New York law setting maximum hours for bakeshop workers. On its face the Court's opinion, which was written by Justice Peckham, who dissented in *Jacobson*, appears to differ dramatically from its opinion in *Jacobson* with respect to the constitutionality of public health laws and the value of public health evidence. No doubt Justice Harlan, who authored *Jacobson* and dissented vigorously in *Lochner*, thought that the Court's opinion in *Lochner* did just that. To Harlan, the New York law was constitutional because, like the Cambridge ordinance in *Jacobson*, it was a police power regulation aimed at protecting public health. The difference between the two laws was that Cambridge directed its law against smallpox and the New York law aimed to reduce the risk of tuberculosis and other respiratory diseases believed to be associated with working in bakeshops.[89] In addition, as he stated in *Jacobson*, Justice Harlan believed that the Court should defer to legislative bodies and give consideration to empirical evidence, which New York had submitted to demonstrate the public health dangers addressed by the maximum hours law.[90]

The majority of the Court, however, did not agree. It refused to accede to the scientific evidence not because of its inadequacy but because the

Court simply did not believe there could be anything uniquely dangerous or unhealthy about the occupation of bakeshop worker.[91] Writing for the Court, Justice Peckham discounted the relevance of epidemiological evidence: "In looking through statistics regarding all trades and occupations, it may be true that the trade of a baker does not appear to be as healthy as some other trades, and is also vastly more healthy still others. To the common understanding the trade of a baker has never been regarded as an unhealthy one."[92]

More fundamentally, the majority did not view the state's measure as a true public health law. Justice Peckham observed that "it might be safely affirmed that almost all occupations more or less affect the health."[93] As he saw it, a health risk to a particular population, such as bakeshop workers, that did not traditionally require the protection of the law, could not be viewed as a public health problem justifying a limitation of liberty.

Despite the majority's rejection of the state's public health claim and evidence, the *Lochner* majority affirmed not only the state's right to protect public health as the Court defined it, but also public health's pivotal role in constitutional law. Indeed, in one sense, public health's importance to American law reached its apogee in *Lochner* as the majority held that the question of whether a state law was in fact a real public health measure was essential to determining the law's constitutionality. To put it simply, the *Lochner* Court continued *Jacobson's* placement of public health at the center of constitutional analysis.

The *Lochner* Court departed from *Jacobson*, however, in reading public health narrowly and in failing to consider empirical and statistical evidence. Relying instead on analogical reasoning and a formalism that placed maximum hours laws outside the circle of public health laws, the *Lochner* majority ignored Oliver Wendell Holmes Jr.'s earlier admonition that the future of the law lay with the man of statistics. [94] In effect, the justices who voted for the state in *Jacobson* and against the state in *Lochner* seemed to accept that smallpox was a public health problem because it affected everyone and had always been viewed as such, whereas occupational health laws were viewed as benefiting only one population and not the public. To the Court in 1905, *salus populi* was *suprema lex*, but only when the threat at hand and the intervention proposed to meet it were traditional and did not depend on either epidemiological evidence or the recognition of and concern for the health of multiple and distinct populations.

THE DECLINE OF PUBLIC HEALTH'S ROLE IN LAW

In both *Jacobson* and *Lochner*, the Supreme Court asserted the value and importance of public health to constitutional law. Yet public health's triumph in 1905 marked the beginning of its departure from the forefront of American law. Perhaps this was because the very success of public health interventions undermined the perception that public health laws were supported by necessity. As the dreaded epidemics of previous centuries began to fade from memory, the necessity of public health interventions became less obvious and the limitation of individual liberty in the name of public health became less readily accepted. At the same time, with less fear of contagious diseases, public health became less salient to both the culture and the law.[95] Indeed, following *Jacobson*, the Supreme Court would not again face a question that so starkly and directly related to a community's response to an imminent epidemic.

Another reason for the lowering of public health's visibility in the law may have been the rise of medicine in the early twentieth century.[96] As clinical medicine became more effective, it began to dominate discussions about health. Increasingly, the legal system focused on questions relating to the delivery of medical services to the detriment of population-based interventions. That health care law should eclipse the law's interaction with public health should not be surprising; health care was where the money and clients were. But, as John Jacobi has noted, and chapter 8 will more fully recount, health care law is quite distinct from public health law.[97] Legal discussions about health care typically disregard the population focus so central to a public health perspective.

Public health may also have lost its former salience because of its increasing complexity and specialization. In *Lochner*, the majority treated public health as if it were a clear, fixed category of activities; a category readily identifiable by tradition rather than by empiricism, and that could be used in deductive and analogical reasoning. Thus to Justice Peckham a maximum hours law for bakers was not a public health law simply because it did not look like the familiar public health laws aimed at infectious diseases and there was no readily available, a priori principle by which to distinguish the population of bakers from that of lawyers or other professionals.[98] In effect, Justice Peckham could enthrone public health as a central constitutional principle precisely because he could apply it as a fixed and easy-to-identify category.

As the epidemiological transition progressed, the infectious diseases and traditional public health measures that Justice Peckham could identify as matters of public health and therefore as appropriate objects of the police power became less important to the health of American populations.[99] At the same time, the discipline of public health expanded its vista and increasingly focused on new and more subtle population-based threats, including occupational hazards (such as that the workers in *Lochner* faced) and the health problems associated with poor housing.[100] In effect, as infections declined in importance, epidemiology took public health in new directions and toward a deeper understanding of the broader, social determinants of health.

This evolution in the field of public health, however, meant that public health was no longer grounded in tradition. It had become instead a broad and indefinite category, guided by epidemiology. As such, it could no longer serve as an obvious, self-evident category that could delineate, as it did in *Lochner,* the lines between appropriate and inappropriate uses of the police power. Simple maxims, such as *salus populi,* no longer appeared to justify the holding of a case. Instead, if public health was to continue to play a central role in law, it would have to do so in a more complex and less formal way, more in line with the complex, empirical reasoning of the population perspective than with the formal, deductive reasoning of *Lochner.*

At the same time, the formalism that *Lochner* has come to epitomize also came under assault from legal realism. With roots going back to Holmes, legal realism called for the recognition of experience and the incorporation of the social sciences into legal analysis. Legal realists also assailed the formalism that was so evident in *Lochner* and notably absent in *Jacobson.*[101] According to Gerald Wetlaufer, legal realism was "part of the early twentieth-century 'revolt against formalism' that manifested itself in a wide range of disciplines, as incorporating into the law the insights and instincts of American philosophical pragmatism, and as an attempt to bring to bear on the law a wide range of social sciences."[102]

The legal realist movement, which was closely aligned with Progressivism, inserted public health research and public health aims into legal discourse, as was evident in *Jacobson* itself.[103] A more famous and more influential example of the realist approach to constitutional advocacy, and the realist reliance on public health research, comes from a brief written by future Supreme Court Louis Brandeis and his colleague Josephine Goldmark in *Muller v. Oregon*.[104] Brandeis and Goldmark used public health evidence extensively to distinguish an Oregon law prohibiting women from working more than twenty hours a day in laundries from *Lochner*. The Supreme Court cited this brief approvingly in upholding the Oregon law in *Muller*, noting that the states' brief included extracts from more than "ninety reports of committees, bureaus of statistics, commissioners of hygiene, inspectors of factories, both in this country and in Europe, to the effect that long hours are dangerous for women, primarily because of their special physical organization."[105]

Thus the Court appeared to endorse using public health research to help determine the appropriate boundaries of the police power.[106] Of course, the use of such evidence in *Muller* to support the now widely discredited view that women need to be protected because of their "special physical organization" demonstrates the danger that can result when courts are overly credulous about public health evidence. As we shall see in subsequent chapters, population-based legal analysis reduces that risk both by resisting an unsophisticated and overly deferential stance to public health evidence and by reconciling public health protections with important legal safeguards.[107]

Ironically, the empiricism and pragmatism of legal realism evident in the Brandeis and Goldmark brief in *Muller* ultimately helped reduce public health's visibility and importance in American law. During the New Deal, realist-inspired jurists followed in Brandeis and Goldmark's path and discarded the formalistic police power jurisprudence of *Lochner*.[108] In so doing they granted greater deference to legislative and regulatory actions that sought to protect the health of different populations.[109] Yet, as the Court made it easier to uphold public health interventions from constitutional attack, public health itself became less crucial to determining whether a law was constitutional.

In the years following the New Deal, legal realism "quickly played itself out"[110] as it came under assault from competing schools of legal thought.[111] Some of these, such as the legal process school, argued that the realists had gone too far in undermining what was distinctive and important about law.[112] Other critics, including those within the law and economics and the critical studies movements, derided the realists for their lack of a clear normative stance.[113] Despite this criticism and the recent reemergence of formalism,[114] realism left its mark on American law. As Joseph Singer noted almost two decades ago, "the terms of legal discourse have shifted from the deduction of consequences from abstraction to the attempt to justify the law in terms of policy, morality, and institutional concerns."[115]

Nevertheless, since the end of the golden age of public health and the decline of the realist movement, public health has ceased to maintain its once central role in American legal consciousness.[116] This neglect makes it more difficult to use law successfully, in all of its myriad forms, to preserve and protect the health of populations. It also diminishes legal theory because a crucial rationale for law—the promotion of population health—is largely overlooked. Population-based legal theory seeks to address those shortcomings.

NOTES

1. *See* chapter 10, *infra*.

2. The discussion in this section builds on that in Wendy E. Parmet, *Introduction: The Interdependency of Law and Public Health*, in LAW IN PUBLIC HEALTH PRACTICE xxvii, xxvii–xxxvii (Richard A. Goodman et al. eds., 2d ed. 2007).

3. H. L. A. HART, THE CONCEPT OF LAW 3, 25 (1961).

4. For a review of the debate between positivists and natural law theorists, see MARK C. MURPHY, PHILOSOPHY OF LAW 17–43 (2007).

5. I say *most* to bracket the question of whether rules of the sovereign that violate morality are indeed law. In U.S. constitutional law, this question was most famously aired in the debate between Justices Chase and Iredell in *Calder v. Bull*, 3 U.S. (3 Dall.) 386, 387–89 (1798) (majority opinion by Chase, J.); *Id* at 398, 399 (Iredell, J., dissenting).

6. Ronald Dworkin, *The Model of Rules, reprinted in* READINGS IN THE PHILOSOPHY OF LAW 160–170 (John Arthur & William H. Shaw eds., 3d ed. 2001). Likewise, some theorists assert that widely shared norms can be viewed as law. *E.g.*, Scott Burris, *Introduction: Merging Law, Human Rights, and Social Epidemiology*, 30 J.L. MED. & ETHICS, 498, 501–02 (2002); A. Sarat & T.R. Kearns, *Beyond the Great Divide: Forms of Legal Scholarship and Everyday Life, in* LAW IN EVERYDAY LIFE 27–33 (A. Sarat & T.R. Kearns eds., 1993).

7. Parmet, *supra* note 2, at xxvii, xxviii.

8. *E.g.*, Kathryn Abrams, *The Constitution of Women*, 48 ALA. L. REV. 861, 861 (1997).

9. *See* Sarat & Kearns, *supra* note 6, at 27–33.

10. For a discussion of the role of deductive reasoning in the common law, see Frederick Schauer, *Williard H. Pedrick Lecture: The Failure of the Common Law*, 36 Ariz.

St. L.J. 765, 773 (2004). For a discussion of the role of analogical reasoning in the law, see Emily Sherwin, *A Defense of Analogical Reasoning in Law*, 66 U. CHI. L. REV. 1179 (1999).

11. MURPHY, *supra* note 4, at 9–11.

12. *See* chapter 1, *supra*.

13. This discussion draws heavily on Scott Burris, Ichiro Kawachi, & Austin Sarat, *Integrating Law and Social Epidemiology*, 30 J.L. MED. & ETHICS 510 (2003).

14. *E.g.*, Georges C. Benjamin & Anthony D. Moultin, *Public Health Legal Preparedness: A Framework for Action*, 36 J.L. MED. & ETHICS 13, 14–15 (Spec. Supp. 2007).

15. LAWRENCE O. GOSTIN, PUBLIC HEALTH LAW: POWER, DUTY, RESTRAINT 25–41 (2d ed. 2008).

16. INST. OF MED., U.S. BOARD ON HEALTH PROMOTION AND DISEASE PREVENTION, THE FUTURE OF THE PUBLIC'S HEALTH IN THE 21ST CENTURY 22–23 (2003).

17. *E.g.*, 26 U.S.C. 501 (setting conditions for corporations to be tax exempt).

18. *See* chapter 9, *infra*.

19. For further discussion, see Wendy E. Parmet, *The Impact of Law on Coronary Artery Disease; Some Preliminary Observations on the Relationship of Law to Normalized Conditions*, 30 J.L. MED. & ETHICS 608, 614–17 (2002).

20. *See* Burris, Kawachi, & Sarat, *supra* note 13, at 515–16.

21. Herman Biggs, *Preventive Medicine, Its Achievements, Scope, and Possibilities*, 65 MEDICAL RECORDS 954, 955 (1904).

22. Frederick Hoffman, *American Mortality Progress During the Last Half Century*, *in* A HALF CENTURY OF PUBLIC HEALTH 94 (Mazyck P. Ravenel ed., 1921).

23. Wendy E. Parmet, *From Slaughter-House to Lochner: The Rise and Fall of the Constitutionalization of Public Health*, 40 AM. J. LEGAL HIST. 476, 476–505 (1996).

24. For a discussion of health disparities, see Mary Anne Bobinski, *Health Disparities and the Law: Wrongs in Search of a Right*, 29 Am. J. Law & Med. 363, 365–70 (2003); Centers for Disease Control and Prevention, Office of Minority Health, *Eliminating Racial and Ethnic Health Disparities*, http://www.cdc.gov/omhd/About/disparities.htm (last visited Nov. 13, 2008).

25. John W. Ward & Christian Warren, *Preface, in* SILENT VICTORIES: THE HISTORY AND PRACTICE OF PUBLIC HEALTH IN TWENTIETH CENTURY AMERICA v (John W. Ward & Christian Warren eds., 2007).

26. *Id.*

27. *Ten Great Public Health Achievements—United States 1900–1999*, 48 MORBIDITY & MORTALITY WEEKLY REP. 241, 241 (1999).

28. THOMAS MCKEOWN, THE ROLE OF MEDICINE: DREAM, MIRAGE OR NEMESIS? 75 (1973).

29. *Ten Great Public Health Achievements—United States 1900–1999*, *supra* note 27, at 241.

30. George M. Korber, *The Progress and Tendency of Hygiene and Sanitary Science in the Nineteenth Century*, 36 JAMA 1617, 1620–21 (1901).

31. George H. Rohe, *Address in State Medicine, Recent Advances in Preventative Medicine*, 9 JAMA 1 (1887).

32. *Ten Great Public Health Achievements—United States 1900–1999*, supra note 27, at 241–43.

33. John F. Bunker, Howard S. Frazier, & Frederick Mosteller, *Improving Health: Measuring Effects of Medical Care*, 72 Milbank Quart. 225, 225–58 (1994).

34. Stephen L. Isaacs & Steven A. Schroeder, *Where the Public Good Prevailed*, 12 AM. PROSPECT (June 2001), http://www.prospect.org/cs/articles?article = where_the_public_good_pr evailed (last visited Oct. 10, 2008).

35. *Id.* (emphasis omitted).

36. *See* Don C. Des Jarlais et al., *Improving the Reporting Quality of Nonrandomized Evaluations of Behavioral and Public Health Interventions: The TREND Statement*, 94 AM. J. PUB. HEALTH 361, 361 nn. 4–5 (2004) (noting lack of evidence for many public health interventions).

37. Anthony D. Moulton, Richard A. Goodman, & Wendy E. Parmet, *Perspective: Law and Great Public Health Achievements*, in LAW IN PUBLIC HEALTH PRACTICE 3, 4–13 (Richard A. Goodman et al. eds., 2007).

38. *Id.* at 18.

39. Stephanie Zaza et al., *Reviews of Evidence Regarding Interventions to Increase Use of Child Safety Seats*, 21 AM. J. PREVENTIVE MED. 4S, 31, 33 (2001).

40. *Id.* at 38.

41. *Achievements in Public Health, 1900–1999: Improvements in Workplace Safety—United States, 1900–1999*, 48 Morbidity & Mortality Wkly Rep. 461, 461–69 (1999).

42. *See* George A. Mensah et al., *Law as a Tool for Preventing Chronic Diseases: Expanding the Spectrum of Effective Public Health Strategies*, 1 CHRONIC DISEASE 1, 4 (2004). *But see* Robert L. Rabin, *The Tobacco Litigation: A Tentative Assessment*, 51 DePAUL L. REV. 331, 350 (2001) (concluding that litigation had an uncertain or at best modest impact on tobacco usage).

43. *E.g.*, Boreali v. Axelrod, 517 N.E.2d 1350 (N.Y.Ct. App. 1987) (finding that New York Public Health Council acted beyond its authority in promulgating regulations prohibiting smoking in public areas).

44. *See* Juliana Maantay, *Zoning Law, Health and Environmental Justice: What's the Connection*, 30 J.L. MED. & ETHICS 572, 583 (2002).

45. Richard J. Jackson & Chris Kochtitzky, *Creating a Healthy Environment: The Impact of the Built Environment on Public Health*, Sprawl Watch Monograph Series, at 5–10, http://www.sprawlwatch.org/health.pdf (last visited Oct. 10, 2008).

46. *See* Parmet, supra note 19, at 617.

47. For a discussion of the link between education, particularly literacy, and health, see Rima E. Rudd, Barbara A. Moeykens, & Tayla C. Colton, *Health and Literacy: A Review of the Medical and Public Health Literature*, ANN. REV. OF ADULT LEARNING AND LITERACY 1999 (John Comings, Barbara Garners, & Cristine Smith eds., 1999), at chapter 5. *See also* Wendy E. Parmet & Anthony Robbins, *Public Health Literacy for Lawyers*, 31 J.L. MED. & ETHICS, 701, 707 (2003).

48. For a discussion of laws targeting high-risk individuals, see Kim M. Blankenship & Stephen Koester, *Criminal Law, Policing Policy, and HIV Risk in Female Street Sex Workers and Injection Drug Users*, 30 J.L.MED. & ETHICS 548, 549–51 (2002); Zita Lazzarini & Robert Klitzman, *HIV and the Law: Integrating Law, Policy and Social Epidemiology*, 30 J.L.MED. & ETHICS 533, 537–38 (2002).

49. See John Lynch & George Kaplan, *Socioeconomic Position*, in SOCIAL EPIDEMIOLOGY 13–35 (Lisa Berkman & Ichiro Kawachi eds., 2000) (discussing what is known about the relationship of socioeconomic status and health).

50. For further discussion of tort law, see chapter 9, *infra*.

51. *E.g.*, Pokora v. Wabash Ry. Co., 292 U.S. 98 (1934); Baltimore & Ohio R.R. Co. v. Goodman, 275 U.S. 66 (1927); Railway Co. v. Stevens, 95 U.S. 655 (1878); Railroad Co. v. Varnell, 98 U.S. 479 (1879).

52. *E.g.*, MacPherson v. Buick Motor Co., 111 N.E. 1050 (N.Y. 1916); Tedla v. Ellman, 19 N.E.2d 987 (N.Y. 1939).

53. Santiago v. Sherwin Williams Co., 3 F.3d 546 (1st Cir. 1993) (lead paint); Goldman v. Johns-Manville Sales Corp., 514 N.E.2d 691 (Ohio 1987) (asbestos).

54. *See* chapters 4–7, *infra*.

55. *E.g.*, Kassel v. Consolidated Freightways Corp., 450 U.S. 662 (1981); City of Philadelphia v. New Jersey, 437 U.S. 617 (1978); H.P. Hood & Sons, Inc. v. Du Mond, 336 U.S. 525 (1949); Baldwin v. G.A.F. Selig, Inc., 294 U.S. 511 (1935).

56. *See* Parmet, *supra* note 23, at 478–80.

57. The Slaughter-House Cases, 83 U.S. (16 Wall.) 36 (1873); RONALD M. LABBE & JONATHAN LURIE, THE SLAUGHTERHOUSE CASES, REGULATION, RECONSTRUCTION AND THE FOURTEENTH AMENDMENT passim (2003) (providing a complete history of the public health context for *Slaughter-House*).

58. Abigail Alliance for Better Access to Developmental Drugs v. Von Eschenbach, 495 F.3d 695 (D.C. Cir. 2007) (en banc) (finding FDA regulations barring access of unlicensed drugs to terminally patients does not violate Fifth Amendment's due process clause).

59. Washington v. Glucksberg, 521 U.S. 702 (1997) (finding no right under the Fourteenth Amendment to physician-assisted suicide).

60. *E.g.*, Lorillard Tobacco Co. v. Reilly, 523 U.S. 525 (2001) (finding that state regulations of tobacco marketing violate First Amendment).

61. Eleanor D. Kinney, *Administrative Law and the Public's Health*, 30 J.L. MED. & ETHICS 212, 213 (2002).

62. For an overview of the laws and legal principles that regulated boards of health in the nineteenth century, see LEROY PARKER & ROBERT H. WORTHINGTON, THE LAW OF PUBLIC HEALTH AND SAFETY AND THE POWERS AND DUTIES OF BOARDS OF HEALTH 82–196 (1892).

63. *E.g.*, Wendy E. Parmet, *AIDS and Quarantine: The Revival of an Archaic Doctrine*, 14 HOFSTRA L. REV. 53, 58–66, 77–79 (1985).

64. *E.g.*, PARKER & WORTHINGTON, *supra* note 62, at 199–285.

65. *See* Edward P. Richards, *Public Health Law as Administrative Law*, 10 J. HEALTH CARE L. & POL'Y 61, 61 (2007).

66. *E.g.*, Whitman v. American Trucking Ass'ns, 531 U.S. 457 (2001); Chevron U.S.A. v. Nat'l Res. Def. Council, Inc., 467 U.S. 837 (1984).

67. *E.g.*, Motor Vehicle Mfrs. Ass'n v. State Farm Mut. Auto. Ins. Co., 463 U.S. 29 (1983).

68. *E.g.*, Industrial Union Dep't, AFL-CIO v. American Petroleum Inst., 448 U.S. 607 (1980).

69. *E.g.*, Kinney, *supra* note 61, at 218–20; Richard B. Stewart, *Administrative Law in the Twenty-First Century*, 78 N.Y.U. L. REV. 437, 447–52 (2003).

70. *Cf.* Jacob D. Fuchsberg, *Introduction, Law, Social Policy, and Contagious Disease: A Symposium on Acquired Immune Deficiency Syndrome (AIDS)*, 14 HOFSTRA L. REV. 1, 1 (1985) (noting how in "but a twinkling of time" after its initial appearance, AIDS had "confront[ed] the legal system" with difficulties).

71. *See, e.g.*, Seavey v. Preble, 64 Me. 120 (1874); Segregation of Lepers, 5 Haw. 162, 166 (1884).

72. PARKER & WORTHINGTON, *supra* note 62, at 1.

73. *Id.* at xxxvii.

74. *See* text accompanying notes 20–26, *supra*.

75. *See* Hoffman, *supra* note 22, at 101–12.

76. T. KUE YOUNG, POPULATION HEALTH: CONCEPTS AND METHODS 41–43 (1998).

77. Herman Biggs, *supra* note 21, at 955.

78. 197 U.S. 11 (1905). For a further discussion, see Wendy E. Parmet, Richard A. Goodman, & Amy Farber, *Individual Rights versus the Public's Health: One Hundred Years after Jacobson v. Massachusetts*, 352 NEW ENGLAND J. MED. 652–54 (2005).

79. 197 U.S. at 25 (citing Gibbons v. Ogden, 22 U.S. (9 Wheat.) 1 (1824)).

80. *Id.*

81. *Id.* at 26 (quoting Railroad Co. v. Husen, 95 U.S. 465, 471 (1878)).

82. *Id.* at 25.

83. *Id.* at 25 n.1.

84. *Id.* at 31.

85. *Id.* at 38.

86. *Id.*

87. *Id.* at 36–37. The Court found that Jacobson's offer of proof "invited the court and jury to go over the whole ground gone over by the legislature" and "did not offer to prove that, by reason of his then condition, he was in fact not a fit subject of vaccination." *Id.* at 36.

88. 198 U.S. 45 (1905).

89. *Id.* at 65, 70–72 (Harlan, J., dissenting). Justice Harlan's dissent was joined by Justice Holmes who authored his own, more famous dissent. In contrast to Justice Harlan, Justice Holmes did not emphasize the need to defer to the state concerning public health problems, rather he concluded that the liberty protected by the Constitution did not apply to the matters at hand. 198 U.S. at 74 (Holmes, J., dissenting).

90. 198 U.S. at 68 (Harlan, J., dissenting).

91. *Id.* at 59.
92. *Id.*
93. *Id.*
94. Oliver Wendell Holmes Jr., *The Path of the Law*, 10 HARV. L. REV. 457, 469 (1897).
95. Wendy E. Parmet, *Legal Rights and Communicable Disease: AIDS, the Police Power and Individual Liberty*, 14 J. HEALTH POL. POL'Y & L. 741, 749–51 (1989).
96. *See* chapter 8, *infra.*
97. John V. Jacobi, *Book Review—Lawrence O. Gostin's Public Health Law, Power, Duty, Restraint*, 31 SETON HALL L. REV. 1089, 1089 (2001); chapter 8, *infra.*
98. 198 U.S. at 60–64.
99. There are some notable exceptions. *See* Edwin D. Kilbourne, *Influenza Pandemics of the 20th Century*, 12 EMERGING INFECTIOUS DISEASES 9 (2006), http://www.cdc.gov/eid (last visited Oct. 10, 2008) (discussing the 1918 influenza epidemic).
100. Parmet, *supra* note 56, at 489–92.
101. WILLIAM W. FISHER III, MORTON J. HORWITZ, & THOMAS A REED, AMERICAN LEGAL REALISM 232–37 (1993).
102. Gerald B. Wetlaufer, *Systems of Belief in Modern American Law: A View from Century's End*, 49 AM. U. L. REV. 1, 18 (1999) (citations omitted).
103. *Id.* at 17–21.
104. Brief for Defendant in Error, Muller v. Oregon, 208 U.S. 412 (1908).
105. 208 U.S. at 419 n.1 (1908).
106. *Id. But see* David L. Faigman, *"Normative Constitutional Fact-Finding," Exploring the Empirical Component of Constitutional Interpretation*, 139 U. PA. L. REV. 541, 560 (1991) (questioning the Court's use of empiricism in *Muller*).
107. *See, e.g.*, chapter 6, *infra* (discussing the role of the courts when governments seek to restrict individual liberty in the name of public health).
108. West Coast Hotel Co. v. Parrish, 300 U.S. 379 (1937) (overruling Adkins v. Children's Hosp., 261 U.S. 525 (1923)).
109. *E.g.*, Williamson v. Lee Optical, 348 U.S. 483 (1955); United States v. Carolene Products Co., 304 U.S. 144 (1938).
110. John Henry Schlegel, *American Legal Realism and Empirical Social Science: From the Yale Experience*, 28 BUFF. L. REV. 459, 459 (1978–79).
111. *See* Joseph William Singer, *Review Essay, Legal Realism Now*, 76 CAL. L. REV. 467, 505–41 (1988).
112. Jack M. Balkin & Sanford Levinson, *Law and the Humanities: An Uneasy Relationship*, 18 YALE J.L. & HUMANITIES 155, 169–70 (2006).
113. Singer, *supra* note 111, at 533.
114. Daniel Farber, *The Ages of American Formalism*, 90 NW. U. L. REV. 89, 95 (1995).
115. Singer, *supra* note 111, at 475.
116. For a discussion of signs of change, see chapter 11, *infra.*

CHAPTER 3

Toward a Population-Based Legal Analysis: The *Supreme Beef* Case

The population perspective constructs a new story.

—Dan E. Beauchamp and Bonnie Steinbock,
New Ethics for Public Health

FTER DECADES IN THE SHADOWS, public health law has begun to reemerge as a vibrant field within American law, albeit one that remains largely in the margins of legal discourse and education.[1] In the wake of AIDS, the anthrax attacks on the U.S. mail, and the decades-long battle against tobacco, practitioners and scholars have come to appreciate both the importance and richness of public health law. Both ancient questions, such as the government's power to quarantine, and new questions, such as the admissibility of epidemiological evidence in mass tort litigation, have become the subject of research, debate, legislation, and litigation.

Population-based legal analysis draws from this revival but goes beyond it in some critical ways. First, recognizing that the protection of population health is a goal of law itself and not simply of public health law, population-based legal analysis extends its reach beyond those topics and questions that have traditionally been viewed as falling within the boundaries of public health law. In other words, population-based legal analysis does not limit its scope to core public health laws or the law's response to perceived public health threats. Second, although public health law typically applies standard methods of legal analysis to legal questions pertaining to public health, population-based legal analysis seeks to alter legal analysis itself by incorporating public health's population perspective into legal discourse. Thus, in contrast to public health law, population-based legal analysis offers a public health-inspired approach to law.

As this discussion will demonstrate, the population perspective offers a powerful tool for critiquing contemporary legal doctrine and theory. It also opens the door to new ways of analyzing myriad legal problems. That said, it is important to underscore that population-based legal analysis is not a comprehensive theory of law. Nor is it a traditional form of doctrinal analysis that purports to explain and demonstrate correct results for a discrete area of the law. Indeed, given its reliance on empirical and probabilistic reasoning, and its insistence on the importance of both facts and context, population-based legal analysis can never provide the determinacy that formalism promises, even if that promise has always been more illusory than real.[2] Rather, following the pragmatic and interdisciplinary footsteps of legal realism and its many heirs, from law and economics on one side of the political spectrum to critical legal studies on the other side, population-based legal analysis simply attempts to articulate a set of values for and approaches to legal reasoning.[3] These values and approaches offer a way to critique legal decisions. They can also guide a decision maker. But they do not necessarily provide a firm answer to any particular question.

Population-based legal analysis is composed of three core elements. Not surprisingly, these elements parallel the attributes of the population perspective identified in chapter 1. Perhaps most critical is the recognition of the importance of populations both to and within law. Second is the population perspective's normative stance toward population health. Following public health's population perspective, population-based legal analysis views the promotion of public health as a positive good. But it goes beyond public health in postulating that the promotion of public health is not simply a norm, but also a legal norm that should be embraced by and incorporated into the legal system. Third, population-based legal analysis adopts the methodologies of public health. This does not simply mean that consideration is given to empirical evidence; courts have been

doing that for a long, long time. It means instead that empirical and probabilistic reasoning joins analogical and deductive reasoning and other standard methods of legal interpretation and decision making as among those
ways that lawyers and the law come to know what is. In other words,
population-based legal analysis demands that lawyers and judges think
empirically and probabilistically.

These three key attributes of population-based legal analysis are com-
plemented by several additional features, including an emphasis on social
determinants, a recognition of the interdependency of health and the
human condition, and an appreciation of the complementary and reciprocal relationship between individuals and populations, government power
and individual rights. These factors will become more apparent in the following sections, which describe and defend the core attributes of population-based legal analysis and distinguish it from conventional approaches
to legal decision making. Subsequent sections further demonstrate the distinctions between population-based legal analysis and contemporary
American jurisprudence by using it to critique and examine one case concerning the regulation of the food supply, *Supreme Beef Processors, Inc. v.
United States Department of Agriculture*.[4] *Supreme Beef* was chosen not
because it was exceptional, and not to probe the issue of food safety, but
because it illustrates how courts today routinely fail to consider the public
health implications of their decisions as well as how a population
approach would change that analysis.

Populations in Law

A defining attribute of population-based legal analysis is its emphasis on
populations, both as subjects and objects of the law. From the population
perspective, what matters most is the impact of a particular factor or agent
(be it salmonella, a toxin, or even a legal policy) on a definable group (an
exposed population) and the way that the environment and dynamics of
the group shape the agent's interaction with the group's constituent
members.

Influenced by the teachings of epidemiology, the population perspective understands that the characteristics and environments of groups or
populations help determine health outcomes both for populations and

their individual members. Thus, to give an easy example, if one individual in a population of ten has influenza and nine do not, the risk that influenza will infect other members of the population is very different if the group exists within a small classroom than if it is spread over a wide terrain. In other words, the environment of the population affects the risks experienced by its members. Likewise, a disease such as measles is far more apt to spread to unvaccinated individuals if 20 percent of the individuals within the group are vaccinated than if 90 percent are (in which case there would be so-called herd immunity).[5] The characteristics of a group and the environment to which it is exposed affect what happens to its members.

The population perspective, however, does not simply assume that a singular entity known as the population, or the public, exists. As discussed in chapter 1, the population perspective recognizes the multiplicity and contingency of populations and understands that care must be taken in defining populations. For law, this points to the fact that a particular legal rule or policy that may appear to have a positive impact on one population may have a very different impact on another. Moreover, it cautions against simplistic assumptions that any particular law or policy benefits the public as if there were a singular public.

Although U.S. law does not totally ignore populations, its dominant perspective is markedly individualistic. As many commentators have noted, American law generally accepts the ontological individualism of political liberalism, which views individuals as autonomous agents with distinct and subjective preferences. As Heidi Feldman explains, this methodological individualism does not deny the fact that social institutions may influence individuals, but it does insist that "social entities are fundamentally the creatures of individual agents and not the other way around."[6]

From the liberal perspective, individuals matter most and the law exists to safeguard their liberties.[7] For the most part, liberty is viewed as the absence of interference by others, especially the state.[8] Legal rights serve to preserve some legally recognized individual liberties. In the words of Ronald Dworkin, rights serve as trumps against the interference of individuals by others.[9] In the liberal world view, law also validates voluntary transactions between individuals and resolves disputes between them. In effect, law oversees the exercise of individual actions and serves as the guardian of individual liberty.

Of course, as discussed in chapter 1, not all strands of liberalism ignore the importance of populations. Utilitarianism prioritizes general utility; welfare economics seeks to ensure economic efficiency, which presumably maximizes overall wealth.[10] The welfare economics approach has influenced the law and economics movement that has advocated, relatively successfully, for reliance on cost-benefit analysis in regulatory decision making and administrative law.[11] Yet, though law and economics seeks to maximize general wealth rather than an individual's interest, it shares liberalism's "methodological individualism."[12] Most important, law and economics and indeed much of American law accept that individual preferences and circumstances are largely determined subjectively. In addition, law and economics tends to view state action, especially state regulation of the market, as an interference with individual liberties.

Exceptions to individualism do, of course, exist in American law. Thus corporate law prioritizes the agency of groups (e.g., shareholders). It is also sensitive to the interaction of individuals within groups.[13] Thus, for example, corporate law deals with the duties of directors and officers. On the other hand, by establishing corporations as juridical persons, corporate law can also mask the fact that corporations are entities created by and acting on behalf of groups of people. Corporate law thus helps to transform populations into imaginary and artificial individuals.

In contrast, family law appears to adhere more firmly to preliberal, nonatomistic assumptions.[14] Family law focuses not only on individuals but as well on relationships, such as those between parent and child or husband and wife. Moreover, in contrast to corporate law, these relationships are not always voluntary; individuals cannot fully choose either the fact or the nature of some of these relationships (particularly the parent-child relationship). The law thus recognizes the centrality of relationships that exist apart from individual choice. Nevertheless, relatively recent innovations in family law, such as palimony and contractual agreements for the disposition of frozen embryos, suggest that family law may also be adopting a more individualistic perspective.[15]

Constitutional law offers a further example of the law's treatment of populations. Although American constitutional law is probably most well known for its protection of individual rights, it is also concerned with the structure and organization of government, subjects that necessarily implicate the political question of how to organize groups and arrange power between them.[16] Moreover, all individual rights protected by the Constitution are significantly limited by what most courts perceive to be the interests of the state or the majority. But, as discussed more fully in subsequent chapters,[17] both jurists and theorists tend to speak about the majority as if it were a single, natural entity, a super-individual. A similar treatment is often given to minority populations. In effect, constitutional law anthropomorphizes populations.

In contrast, the population approach recognizes that populations are complex and changing. It also notes that both the risks individuals face and the preferences they form are affected by their environments. Hence though granting that individuals are entitled to respect, indeed to grant them respect, population-based legal analysis rejects an unrealistic atomism. Instead, it insists that the law view people as they are, as members of multiple, overlapping, and contingent populations that face different environments. By recalling this critical insight and incorporating it into the fabric of legal analysis, population-based legal analysis highlights questions that are often ignored in the law and views the relationship of individuals to their society and government in a more complex and nuanced way than is usual in contemporary legal discourse.

POPULATION HEALTH AS A LEGAL NORM

The second key component of population-based legal analysis is the value given to public health. Borrowing from the population perspective, population-based legal analysis treats the promotion of public health as an important norm, but it goes further and asserts that this good is both a rationale for law and a chief value of law. Hence it is a value that judges and lawyers should apply when they interpret legal texts and authority. Or, all other things being equal, legal decision makers should consider the promotion of population health as a relevant factor in their analysis.

Undoubtedly, many will object to this assertion, arguing that it injects contested normative or political questions into legal analysis, thereby straying from the supposed neutrality of law.[18] To many theorists, the very value and merit of law is its separation from contested questions of politics, policy, and morals and its reliance on its own norms and procedures, a complex phenomenon loosely encompassed by the idea of the rule of law.[19] To some theorists, law loses its law-like quality—indeed it ceases to be law—if it becomes excessively particularistic or consequentialist.[20] Thus postwar legal process thinkers emphasized the need for neutrality, objectivity, and a relatively thick separation between law and politics.[21] Echoing this perspective, contemporary neoformalists, such as Supreme Court Justice Antonin Scalia, insist that judges abstain from relying on extralegal or extratextual sources, such as policies or widely held social norms.[22] More broadly, many legal theorists continue to yearn for a sharp separation of law from politics.[23]

Nevertheless, as the legal realists showed long ago, law cannot be fully separated from either policy or social norms. Law is inherently a social and political institution. It relies on and draws from the norms and understandings of the society in which it operates.[24] Or, as Joseph Singer describes the legal realist position, "law and legal reasoning are part of the way we create our form of social life."[25]

For our purposes, however, the questions whether lawmakers can or should look outside of law to decide legal questions and whether law can or ought to be separated from politics are somewhat beside the point because population-based legal analysis does not treat the promotion of population health as an extralegal norm. Rather, recognizing that it is a fundamental human good, and that societies establish law in part to achieve and preserve that good, population-based legal analysis asserts that the promotion of population health is a legal norm that can be appropriately used by courts operating within the rule of law. In effect, population-based legal analysis treats the promotion of population health as akin to other widely recognized legal values such as fidelity to precedent or objectivity of the decision maker.[26] It is thus recognized as among those norms that courts must consider and apply in appropriate circumstances. This does not mean that it is considered the only or most privileged legal norm, only that it is among those that are and ought to be woven into the fabric of legal culture and legal decision making.

Interestingly, this view is not as foreign to law as it first appears. As discussed in chapter 2, before the New Deal, courts in the United States frequently relied, either explicitly or implicitly, on the common law maxim *salus populi suprema lex*,[27] evidencing their belief that the furtherance of public health, safety, and the common good was not only an appropriate

goal of law, it was the highest law, and thus at times outcome determinative. Moreover, public health issues and claims were central to numerous
fields of law. Indeed, in many ways, before the New Deal, judges viewed
population health as a legal norm. Hence, population-based legal analysis
seeks not to establish a new legal norm but to restore a quite ancient one.

PUBLIC HEALTH METHODS

The third key component of population-based legal analysis is the incorporation of the empirical and probabilistic reasoning of public health
into the law. This follows from population-based legal analysis' assertion
that promoting population health is a goal of law. If it is a legal goal,
then legal decision makers must understand the population health
impact and context of the issues before them and the decisions they render. This requires that they have both a familiarity with epidemiology
and medicine and a willingness to engage in empirical and probabilistic
reasoning.[28]

Since the development of legal realism, legal scholars, jurists, and commentators have bemoaned the neglect or even misuse of empirical and
statistical methodologies in American law.[29] Despite the constant chorus
and the increasing appearance of empirically based claims in complex litigation, a consensus remains that American law continues to depend on
nonempirical, deductive methodologies. Not only are lawyers poorly
equipped to assess or use complex scientific evidence, the findings of such
evidence are often ignored in determining the disposition of legal issues,
especially at the appellate level.[30] Instead, traditional, nonempirical methodologies, including analogical reasoning, textual interpretation, and
deduction from principles remain at the core of how judges and lawyers
approach legal problems.[31] Indeed, empirical reasoning is itself often deni-
grated, treated as if it were in contradiction to legal reasoning.

Population-based legal analysis rejects that assessment. It treats empirical and probabilistic reasoning, and not just epidemiological and scientific
evidence, as vital components of legal discourse and as useful comple-
ments and alternatives to more traditional forms of legal reasoning. As a
result, population-based legal analysis insists that legal decisions need to

be attuned to the relevant factual context and informed, to the extent possible, by the available empirical information. Likewise, though we may adhere to certain broad norms and principles, the specific meaning and content of legal doctrine and decisions must always be open to debate as our environment and knowledge about it changes. Finally, legal analysis must embrace probabilities. It must emphasize that both risks and benefits are generally matters of degree. And the law must accept that few things in life are either absolute or definite. By adopting this perspective, law can become more open to the complexity of human life and the nuances that populations face in their interactions with their environment. The remainder of this chapter illustrates the use of population-based legal analysis in the context of a single case and a simple, but important, population health threat.

THE PROBLEM OF FOOD SAFETY

In February 2008, the U.S. Department of Agriculture (USDA) announced the largest recall of beef in the nation's history. Nearly one hundred and fifty million pounds of beef from Hallmark Meat Packing Company of California were recalled after the Humane Society of America released a videotape showing Hallmark workers using electric shocks and water sprays to prod downer cows to slaughter.[32] Because downer cows may be infected with the abnormal proteins known as prions, which are thought to cause bovine spongiform encephalopathy (BSE, or mad cow disease), the USDA requires separate inspection of all downer cows before they enter the food supply.[33] Hallmark, however, apparently failed to comply with these procedures. By the time of the recall, more than one-third of the 143 million pounds of beef at issue had already been used in the school lunch program and more than ninety-three million pounds had been sold to food wholesalers.[34] But because BSE takes years to develop, it will be a long time before we know whether anyone has become infected by eating Hallmark beef.

We do know, however, that many in recent years have died and many more have become sick due to tainted food. For example, in the spring and summer of 2008, more than 1,440 people in forty-three states became ill from a salmonella outbreak that was later attributed largely to peppers imported from Mexico.[35] In 2006, three people died and 200 people became ill after eating spinach contaminated with E. coli 0157:H7 bacteria.[36] These outbreaks are not unusual. According to the CDC, approximately five thousand Americans die each year from a food-borne illness, eighteen hundred of which are caused by pathogens. Approximately 325,000 Americans are hospitalized and seventy-six million become ill.[37] The continuing threat of food-borne disease may seem surprising. In the late nineteenth and early twentieth centuries, laws were passed requiring milk to be pasteurized and slaughterhouses to be inspected (the second was undertaken in response to the uproar that followed the publication of Upton Sinclair's *The Jungle* in 1906).[38] As a result, the incidence of food-borne disease declined dramatically.[39] In recent years, however, the increased centralization of the food supply plus the emergence of new food-borne illnesses, such as BSE and E. coli 0157:H7, have created new challenges.[40]

In 2007, the GAO added food safety to its list of critically flawed federal programs, lambasting the "fragmented federal food safety system" for "inconsistent oversight, ineffective coordination, and the inefficient use of resources."[41] Critics cite numerous reasons for the problems, including the influence of lobbyists, the failure of Congress to modernize the federal regulatory structure, and reduced budgets at the key regulatory agencies.[42] The federal courts are implicated as well, having made it difficult for regulatory agencies to modernize their approach to food-safety regulation in response to new threats.[43] The *Supreme Beef* case exemplifies the difficulties that food safety regulations have faced in the federal courts.

THE *SUPREME BEEF* CASE

In the 1990s, after several well-publicized outbreaks of E. coli, the Food Safety and Inspection Services (FSIS) within the USDA attempted to modernize its approach to meat inspection.[44] Under the so-called Hazard Analysis and Critical Control Point regulations (HACCP), all meat plants were required to develop and implement their own pathogen control plans for ensuring the safety of their meat. Once a plan was in place, FSIS would conduct tests to determine the levels of different bacteria. Among the bacteria to be tested for was salmonella,[45] a widely occurring pathogen less lethal than E. coli 0157:H7, but which is nevertheless estimated to cause over one million cases of illness a year and more than $1 billion a year in medical costs and lost wages.[46] According to the FSIS, salmonella testing was useful not only to prevent salmonella infection, but also because salmonella can serve as an indicator of unsanitary conditions conducive to more harmful bacteria, such as E. coli.[47] Under USDA regulations, if a plant failed to meet the salmonella performance standards three times in a row, FSIS would withdraw its inspectors from the plant, thereby depriving the plant's products of the requisite USDA certification.[48]

In 1998, Supreme Beef Processors, one of the chief suppliers to the federal school lunch program, failed three times to meet its performance standards for salmonella.[49] After USDA notified Supreme Beef that it would withdraw the inspectors, Supreme Beef sued the agency in federal district court, claiming that the agency lacked authority to issue the salmonella regulations. Both the federal district court and the United States Court of Appeals for the Fifth Circuit agreed, striking down the challenged regulations.[50]

Writing for the Fifth Circuit, Judge Patrick Higginbotham analyzed the case in a manner that was neither exceptional nor surprising. As is typical in an administrative law case, the court reviewed a private party's claim that an agency exceeded its authority and violated its rights. The interests of those who would presumably benefit from the regulation were not, strictly speaking, before the court (or, as administrative law doctrine would put it, other populations did not have standing before the court). The court, however, did permit the National Meat Association, an industry trade group, to intervene, thereby preventing the case from becoming moot because Supreme Beef had gone bankrupt and stopped processing beef.[51]

In considering Supreme Beef's claims, the Fifth Circuit began as courts usually do, by stating the facts. Tellingly, the court's statement of facts did not include a discussion of the problem of food borne illness. Nor did the court provide any account of the E. coli outbreaks that had prompted the promulgation of the HACCP regulations. Instead, after presenting the statutory basis for the agency's regulatory authority, the court reviewed the history of USDA's encounters with Supreme Beef.[52]

The court then turned to its legal analysis and focused on whether the agency had exceeded its authority. The court began by quoting the oft-cited *Chevron U.S.A., Inc. v. Natural Resources Defense Council, Inc.* for the proposition that a court reviewing the validity of an administrative regulation should first "look to the plain language of the statute and determine whether the agency construction conflicts with the text."[53] In *Supreme Beef*, the relevant statute was the Federal Meat Inspection Act, which dates from 1907 (and the fallout from *The Jungle*) and provides the USDA with authority to withhold approval of adulterated meat.[54] Critically, the statute defines "adulterated meat" as meat that has been "prepared, packed or held under insanitary (sic) conditions where it may have become contaminated with filth, or whereby it may have been rendered injurious to health."[55]

As the court understood the case, the key question was whether meat with salmonella could be considered adulterated within the meaning of the statute. If it could not be, according to the court, the USDA lacked the authority to take action against plants with high levels of salmonella in their meat, despite the risks the salmonella posed. Two principle reasons drove this decision. First, the court found that because salmonella exists in raw meat before processing, meat is not contaminated with or rendered injurious simply because it contains salmonella.[56] In effect, salmonella was not an adulterant because meat became infected before rather than during processing. Second, the court reasoned that though some pathogens are so dangerous they are considered per se adulterants regardless of when they contaminate the meat, USDA did not consider salmonella to be in that category.[57] This is because meat with high levels of salmonella can be made safe to eat by adequate cooking, or, in the words of the statute, the "article does not ordinarily render it injurious to health."[58] Thus, the court concluded, FSIS had no statutory authority to regulate salmonella levels.[59] That FSIS asserted that salmonella might serve as a useful proxy for determining the levels of other even more dangerous contaminants did not change the result.[60] Nor did the fact that according to the CDC, more than a million Americans became sick each year from salmonella.[61] As we shall see, a population-based analysis may not have changed the result, but it would certainly have altered the way the court looked at the issue.

Treating Population Health as a Legal Norm

Today, courts are often seen as the protectors of individual rights, a mission they strive to fulfill by operating with impartiality and treating like cases alike. As a result, courts in administrative law cases such as *Supreme Beef* generally stand ready to hear individual claims and to ascertain whether a particular policy, such as the HACCP regulations, exceed an administrative agency's authority. Given this mindset, courts such as the Fifth Circuit in *Supreme Beef* often err on the side of protecting individual interests rather than the health of the nonregulated population. Or, as Goldsmith and colleagues have observed, the American legal system is "predisposed to protect against Type 1 (false positive) errors" rather than Type II (false negative) errors.[62]

A court applying a population approach would reject that predisposition. Coming to the question with the appreciation that promoting population health is an appropriate legal norm, the court would be inclined to read any ambiguity or silence in the statute or precedent in such a way to realize the statute's explicit purpose of protecting "the health and welfare of consumers."[63] In so doing, the court would recognize that despite the Fifth Circuit's claim to have relied simply on the "plain language" of the statute, the Federal Meat Inspection Act was not as clear as the court proclaimed.[64]

For example, the court rejected the argument that the statute permitted the USDA to set levels for salmonella based on the theory that the salmonella may have been in the beef when the beef entered the plant. As the court explained, the USDA could not be sure that infected meat had in fact been "rendered" injurious to health within the plant.[65] In effect, the court read the Federal Meat Inspection Act as prohibiting the government from requiring that beef be tested unless the tests could ascertain that a particular sample of beef had actually been contaminated within the plant.

Yet there is nothing in the statute that explicitly precludes FSIS from presuming that, when high levels of bacteria exist in the end product of a processing plant, some previously uninfected beef is likely to have become contaminated during the grinding and mixing process. Indeed, as the Fifth Circuit acknowledged, the Second Circuit had previously permitted the FDA, using its authority over "insanitary conditions," to regulate botulism levels without regard to whether the botulism entered the food supply before or during processing.[66] A similar conclusion could have been reached regarding the Federal Meat Inspection Act, even using a plain language approach to statutory interpretation. In effect, a court that adopted a population approach could and would have read the statute as more broadly supportive of population health protection than the Fifth Circuit did, even while remaining faithful to both the statute's text and Supreme Court precedent (such as *Chevron*).

The recognition of population health as a legal norm in *Supreme Beef* does not mean that the USDA regulation would have been upheld. The recognition does not imply that public health should always trump or override other norms.[67] To say, for example, that protecting a population of children from food poisoning is a positive legal value that the legal system should seek to promote does not mean that courts should ignore other values, such as religious liberty or individual bodily integrity. The prevention of food poisoning would not justify stoning typhoid Mary or imposing a surveillance system that required random strip searches of all food handlers.

Likewise, the recognition of public health as a norm does not mean that fidelity to authority, precedent, or text should be forsaken. For example, if the Supreme Court had previously ruled that the USDA did not have the authority it claimed to possess in *Supreme Beef*, the Fifth Circuit would have been compelled to invalidate the regulation, regardless of the public health consequences, because another critical legal norm—fidelity to binding authority—would have come into play. So, too, if the Federal Meat Inspection Act had unambiguously constrained the agency's action, perhaps by stating that adulteration consists only of the intentional inclusion of a foreign substance in meat, the court would have likewise remained compelled to find that the agency lacked the power to issue the regulations at issue.

Most important, the recognition of a public health norm does not mean that courts should blindly defer to all regulatory actions that public officials or agencies claim will promote a population's health. After all, not all regulations that purport to promote public health do so. Indeed, history is replete with examples of pernicious laws, such as those in the early decades of the twentieth century permitting the mandatory sterilization of so-called mentally deficient young women, that were defended in the name of public health but were ill designed to do so.[68] If judges adopt a population perspective and grant population health greater weight than they do today, government officials might be even more apt than they are now to defend ill-advised laws that do not promote the health of populations as efforts aimed at doing precisely that. If so, courts will need to be even more sensitive than they are today at sorting those laws that may promote the health of populations from those that are not likely to do so. Treating public health as a canon means treating protection of population health as an important legal goal. That requires a careful consideration of public health claims, not mere acquiescence to those claims.

Ultimately, treating public health as among the ethical guideposts for lawmakers would mean that public health would be one goal that a lawmaker (judge, legislator, or regulator) would seek to promote. An ethical and conscientious lawmaker would have to consider how that could be done while adhering to other important ethical imperatives and balancing a multitude of risks and costs. The task would not be easy. It would also require both sensitivity to the role of populations and familiarity with public health's methodologies and modes of reasoning. But, if we understand that protecting public health is critical to maintaining an ethical society, then it is no less important a task than many of the others that judges struggle with day in and day out.

Recognizing the Role of Populations

Population-based legal analysis puts populations at the center of legal analysis. This approach contrasts sharply with that used by the Fifth Circuit in *Supreme Beef* and in most administrative law cases today. Many of the iconic statutes and doctrines in administrative law, from the 1946 Administrative Procedures Act to the doctrines of standing and reviewability, presuppose the centrality of individuals over groups.[69] For example, under the standing doctrine, an individual consumer could not challenge the adequacy of USDA's regulation without demonstrating a personal injury that was "distinct and palpable."[70] A generalized grievance based merely on the possibility of exposure to salmonella-infected beef would not be sufficient to establish standing to bring a claim.[71] As a result, mere membership in the population of children who eat school lunches, and might thus be at higher risk for becoming ill after having eaten a Supreme Beef burger, would likely not be enough to obtain judicial review.

The individualistic stance of American administrative law does not mean, of course, that the law is wholly uninterested in populations. The

Supreme Court has recently reaffirmed, for example, that states have standing to protect their quasi-sovereign interests and challenge the refusal of the U.S. Environmental Protection Agency's (EPA) to regulate greenhouse gases.[72] Without saying so explicitly, this decision effectively enables a state, by citing its own territorial and procedural interests, to act as representative of its populations and aggregate their own discrete but difficult to ascertain injuries due to climate change into concrete harms that satisfy Article III's requirement that a claimant in federal court have an injury-in-fact. More broadly, standing law recognizes so-called associational standing, which permits a group or association to bring a claim on behalf of its members. Yet, though this doctrine would appear to recognize the importance and agency of groups such as the National Meat Association, on closer inspection, it also has a distinctly individualist bias, in that associations have standing only if and when an individual member would have it.[73] The law thus recognizes a group or association as the sum of its individuals, but fails to consider how the fact of association itself may alter the needs and conditions of members.

In contrast, when the multiplicity and contingency of populations is fully embraced, the analysis of a case such as *Supreme Beef* can differ dramatically. The Fifth Circuit considered that case, for example, as is typically done, as if only two parties were before it: *Supreme Beef* and the USDA.[74] Although the court undoubtedly understood that the USDA was a governmental entity that theoretically represented or served a broader population, the court did not give much attention to the interests of some of the groups, such as school children, who might have been most significantly affected by the invalidation of the regulations. Had the court adopted a population perspective and considered the case's impact on different groups, especially those vulnerable to the dangers of food poisoning, it might have been less inclined to read the statute narrowly to protect the interests of just one entity, Supreme Beef.

The court's construction of the Federal Meat Inspection Act also demonstrates additional distinctions between a legal analysis premised on individualism and a population-based perspective. According to the court and even the USDA, salmonella could not be treated as a per se adulterant, in part because consumers can reduce the risk of disease by properly cooking infected meat.[75] This assertion implicitly locates "injuriousness" or responsibility for it with individuals who fail to adequately cook their meat.

A population perspective, in contrast, would not begin by assuming that injuriousness was an individual matter. Instead, it would locate the etiology of food-borne disease in factors common to particular populations. Thus a population perspective might note (if there were facts to support the proposition) that children who ate lunch in the federal school lunch program were at particularly high risk for salmonella. If that were the case, the population perspective might focus on a shared characteristic of that population (eating in the school lunch program) and locate injuriousness with it, rather than with the children who became ill. Indeed, because the population perspective does not insist, as liberal individualism does, that agency must generally lie primarily within individuals, the population perspective would question whether individuals within the population of school lunch eaters were in any position to significantly reduce their risk of exposure to salmonella. Moreover, the population perspective would question both the efficacy and appropriateness of locating primary responsibility on individuals rather than on meat producers or the government. In effect, the population perspective would question whether the absence of regulation would affect the liberty of school children who might wish to eat untainted meat and remain healthy but, in the absence of adequate regulatory oversight of the meat supply, cannot do so.

The Fifth Circuit in *Supreme Beef* also concluded that salmonella was not an adulterant because it was a naturally occurring bacterium in beef before processing.[76] That conclusion, however, rested on the assumption that high levels of salmonella in beef is a given, an inevitable, naturally occurring phenomenon. A population-based approach, in contrast, would have questioned that presupposition and asked whether the structure and organization of the industry and the government's oversight of it increased cattle's exposure to bacteria.[77] Comparing contamination rates in different environments and looking at the entire context in which meat is brought to market might bring the court's overly simple individualistic assumptions about the inevitability of salmonella poisoning into question. Had the court asked questions such as whether consumers of meat processed in plants that used only free-range cattle have the same rates of salmonella as consumers of Supreme Beef products, the court's conclusion that beef is not rendered injurious in processing plants might have proved problematic.

The population perspective would thus change the nature of the legal analysis, shifting the focus from one that is almost exclusively on atomistic

individuals to one that considers the interests, influence, and environments of groups. This perspective would not necessarily have changed the
outcome in *Supreme Beef*, though it likely would have, but it would have
made it more difficult for the court to reject USDA's regulations.

Applying Public Health Methodologies

The disregard of empirical reasoning in legal analysis is starkly evident in
both the opinion of the court and the arguments of the lawyers in *Supreme
Beef*. For example, in determining what it means for meat to be adulterated, the court relied overwhelmingly on a plain language methodology
that focused on a narrow, parsimonious interpretation of the word *rendered*. This approach, however logical from a linguistic perspective, failed
to consider multiple empirical questions that could have shed a different
light on the matter. The court did not ask, for example, whether the meat
from a plant with inadequate infection-control procedures was in fact
more likely to have higher levels of salmonella than meat from a plant with
more rigorous infection control procedures. If so, one might conclude that
meat in a plant without the procedures was indeed rendered injurious to
health.

Likewise, the critical assumption that salmonella was not a per se adulterant, a proposition supported by case law[78] and not challenged by the
USDA, appears to have been based more on deduction and reliance on
precedent than on an empirical analysis of the dangers that salmonella
posed to different populations. As a result, the court never inquired as to
the extent to which some populations were exposed to inadequately
cooked meat. Indeed, from the analysis provided by the court, it is not
clear that such evidence, had the USDA presented any, would have been
found relevant to the determination of whether salmonella was a per se
adulterant.

To be sure, the increased reliance on empirical reasoning and evidence
called for by population-based legal analysis presents its own risks. In
particular, a decision to place greater weight on epidemiological facts
could result in overly high, if not insurmountable, evidentiary burdens on
those who seek to promote population health. For example, as chapter 9
will more fully address, an increased reliance on epidemiological evidence

in tort law, coupled with the Supreme Court's demand that courts review the reliability of epidemiological evidence, has made it increasingly difficult for plaintiffs to prevail in toxic tort cases.[79] In effect, in tort law the demand for epidemiological evidence and a concern for the quality of that evidence have been turned upside down to make it more rather than less difficult for plaintiffs to prevail on health-related claims.

A similar phenomenon may be at work in some aspects of federal administrative law. The Information Quality Act (IQA) required the Office of Management and Budget to issue guidelines to ensure "the quality, objectivity, utility and integrity of information disseminated by Federal agencies."[80] Although the act on its face seemed—in taking epidemiological evidence seriously—to embody a population perspective, critics contend that the IQA process has in fact given regulated industries a forum for contesting and chilling regulatory decisions adverse to their interests.[81] If so, the demand for reliable empirical information has been used to create a barrier against interventions designed to protect public health and safety.

Both the IQA and the fate of epidemiological evidence in tort law offer a cautionary tale about the use of empirical evidence in population-based legal analysis. In the real world, epidemiological evidence is often unavailable and is almost always incomplete. Sometimes evidence is lacking because too few resources are devoted to studying the issue. In other instances, there has been too little time to conduct a careful analysis of a newly emerging problem, such as a new pathogen. In some cases, ethical prohibitions make it difficult to study a particular issue. Moreover, a single or even several studies rarely provide clear and conclusive answers to the empirical questions that can and should be asked about the impact of an agent or activity on multiple populations.[82] Scientific knowledge accrues incrementally; study results are always subject to further research and analysis. In addition, uncertainty and the possibility of new and contradictory findings remain ubiquitous.[83] As a result, the demand that health interventions be based on clear and reliable empirical support can easily result in neglecting problems and forestalling potentially effective interventions.

Because of these difficulties, many advocates for population health protection have embraced the so-called precautionary principle, especially in its weak form.[84] Although many definitions exist, the precautionary principle can be defined as holding that if there is reason to believe that an activity or agent may harm human health or the environment, protective measures should be taken, even in the absence of conclusive scientific evidence pertaining to the causal responsibility of the agent or activity.[85] Under this approach, the USDA, in a case such as *Supreme Beef,* might be justified in regulating salmonella levels in beef, even in the absence of any conclusive studies demonstrating the dangers of salmonella in uncooked meat.

As Joel Tichner has noted, there is a long history of reliance on the precautionary principle in public health.[86] Many of the greatest public health achievements of all time—including John Snow's decision to remove the handle on the Broad Street pump, as well as the decisions of countless municipalities in the nineteenth century to provide clean drinking water—were undertaken without conclusive reliable empirical support. Indeed, historically, legal efforts to protect populations from epidemics and other threats have seldom been supported with the rigorous empirical support that contemporary regulatory theory demands. Public health, after all, is an activist and interventionist discipline that advocates protecting the health of populations even when all the evidence is not in. As the eminent epidemiologist Sir Austin Bradford Hill observed, public health cannot "ignore the knowledge we already have, or . . . postpone the action that it appears to demand at a given time."[87] A population-based approach to the law, therefore, cannot impose unattainable demands for epidemiological evidence without undermining its own norms.

On the other hand, a population-based approach would not adopt an overly strong version of the precautionary principle and disregard the importance of empirical evidence and, more significant, empirical reasoning. Empirical studies in epidemiology and other related disciplines provide the basis for our understanding of the determinants of human health as well as the efficacy and impact of different interventions. Moreover, empirical reasoning, even when undertaken without the benefit of formal analyses and studies, provides a model for an approach to the law that is sensitive to how laws relate to and affect the environment. Empiricism also provides the basis for an appreciation of the contingent and changing nature of legal knowledge. It also cautions us against relying on a simplistic application of the precautionary principle that is insensitive to the need for and limits of empirical evidence as well as the relative nature of risk.[88]

A population-based approach to law must therefore adopt an empirical spirit that is humble about the capacity of empiricism, recognizing both the importance and virtues of an empirical stance, at the same time noting the limits of scientific knowledge and the dangers of imposing unrealistic or overly rigid demands for specific types of evidence.[89] Such an approach would be consistent with a so-called weak form of the precautionary principle.[90] It would accept the value of protecting populations from likely threats even in the absence of conclusive evidence but, in contrast to a strong form of the precautionary principle, would not require prohibition of all actions and activities in the absence of rigorous evidence as to their safety. A weak precautionary principle lacks the bias against new technologies and interventions that arises from very strong forms of the precautionary principle.[91]

Thus, in a case such as *Supreme Beef*, a population-based approach would not be prejudiced against the new and novel techniques that the USDA introduced in its regulations. Rather, it would focus on what is known about the health risks of salmonella to different populations as well as what is known about the efficacy of the type of testing programs that the USDA sought to impose. Most important, though this approach would not impose unrealistic and unattainable demands for empirical evidence, it would continue to value empirical evidence and insist that empirical questioning must be part of any legal analysis. As a result, a population-based legal analysis would always remain open to empirical evidence and falsification; the outcomes suggested in one period may not survive in another.

In incorporating the methodologies of epidemiology, population-based legal analysis would also differ from that utilized in *Supreme Beef* by employing probabilistic reasoning. Applying a hundred-year-old statute that understandably lacked attention to probabilities, the *Supreme Beef* court conceptualized the issue before it as either black or white. Either salmonella was or was not an adulterant; either it was or was not per se injurious to health. To the court, salmonella's presence in cattle outside meat processing plants meant that the pathogen was not an adulterant contaminating meat in the plants. The increase, if any, of the probability of infection that might occur depending on how meat was processed was simply beside the point. If the risk of bacteria outside the plant was more than zero, the court assumed that the meat was not rendered injurious within the plant. Likewise, given that the risk of human disease could be reduced to near zero by proper cooking, the court assumed that meat could not be considered per se injurious. In both instances, the court failed to consider that both processing and cooking simply altered the probabilities of infection, most likely differently, for different populations. The critical question—what increases or decreases of risk for different populations should be legally sufficient to justify or invalidate the USDA's regulations—was never considered.

An empirical and probabilistic approach would have eschewed deduction, parsimonious textual interpretation, and the court's absolutist position and recognized that risks are relative and predictions can be only probabilistic. From this perspective, the specific attributes of the USDA's regulation and how it might or not affect different populations' risk of contracting a food-borne disease would have been highly relevant. The question thus would have been whether the USDA could enforce this particular regulation rather than whether it has jurisdiction over bacteria that entered the food supply before it got to the processing plant's door. The result might have been an analysis less crystalline but ultimately more illuminating because it would have recognized that the issue was not simply about the burdens placed on processors, or the scope of the USDA's jurisdiction, but whether a very particular exercise of regulatory authority could in fact further the agency's mandate to protect populations from meat contaminants that are injurious to health.

Unfortunately, in *Supreme Beef,* as so often in American law, the most critical questions, about the probable risk to the health of different populations and the probable efficacy of the proposed intervention to reduce those risks, were never asked. As a result, meat processors were given a significant victory in their battle against regulation. More broadly, cases such as *Supreme Beef* help to perpetuate a regulatory climate that is hesitant about interventions and relies all too heavily on the proposition that individuals can reduce their own risks. Sometimes individualistic, laissez faire works. Often it does not.

NOTES

1. Numerous books, articles, and symposia have appeared in recent years in the field of public health law. *See* LAWRENCE O. GOSTIN, PUBLIC HEALTH LAW:

Power, Duty, Restraint (2d. ed. 2008); Law in Public Health Practice (Richard A. Goodman et al. eds., 2d ed. 2007).

2. The indeterminacy of at least some legal rules and the fallacy of formalist approaches to law have long been demonstrated by legal realists and their progeny. For a discussion of this literature, see Brian Leiter, *American Legal Realism*, 3–5 (Univ. Tex. Sch. of Law Pub. Law & Legal Theory Research Paper No. 042, 2002), http://ssrn.com/abstract_id = 339562 (last visited Mar. 26, 2008). In noting that legal rules can be indeterminate, I am not adopting a strong version of rule skepticism. I am merely claiming that traditional methods of legal reasoning are at times as incapable of providing certain and enduring answers as is population-based legal analysis.

3. *See* Gerald B. Wetlaufer, *Systems of Belief in Modern American Law: A View from Century's End*, 49 Am. U. L. Rev. 1, 6 (1999).

4. 275 F.3d 432 (5th Cir. 2001).

5. Roy M. Anderson & Robert M. May, *Vaccination and Herd Immunity to Infectious Diseases*, 318 Nature 323, 323 (November 1985).

6. Heidi Li Feldman, *Science, Reason & Tort Law*, in 1 Law and Science 35, 42 (Helene Reece ed., 1998).

7. Samuel Freeman, *Illiberal Libertarians: Why Libertarianism Is Not a Liberal View*, 30 Phil. & Pub. Affairs 105, 105–51(2001).

8. Isaiah Berlin, *Two Concepts of Liberty*, in Liberalism and Its Critics 28 (Michael Sandel ed., 1984).

9. Ronald Dworkin, Taking Rights Seriously xi (1977).

10. *See* chapter 1, *supra*.

11. Richard A. Posner, Economic Analysis of Law 637–45 (6th ed. 2003).

12. Feldman, *supra* note 6, at 40.

13. O'Kelley & Thompson, Corporations and Other Business Associations 1–15, 235–41 (5th ed. 2006).

14. Maggie Gallagher, *Rites, Rights, and Social Institutions: Why and How Should the Law Support Marriage?*, 18 Notre Dame J. L. Ethics & Pub. Pol'y 225, 225–41 (2004).

15. Howard Fink & June Carbone, *Between Private Ordering and Public Fiat: A New Paradigm for Family Law Decision-Making*, 5 J.L. & Fam. Stud. 1, 18–69 (2003).

16. *See* The Federalist No. 10, at 77–84 (James Madison) (Clinton Rossiter ed., 1961).

17. *See* chapters 4–7, *supra*.

18. *E.g.*, Herbert Weschler, *Toward Neutral Principles of Constitutional Law*, 73 Harv. L. Rev. 1, 14–20 (1959) (arguing that courts in constitutional cases must base their decision on neutral principles, not political justifications).

19. For a definition of the rule of law as rule by law and a discussion of various views about the concept, see Frank Lovett, *A Positivist Account of the Rule of Law*, 27 L. & Soc. Inquiry 41, 59–66 (2002).

20. Brian Z. Tamanaha, *The Perils of Pervasive Legal Instrumentalism* 63–67 (St. John's Univ. Sch. of Law Legal Research Paper Series Paper No. 05–011, 2005), http://ssrn.com/abstract = 725582 (last visited Oct. 10, 2008).

21. *See* Wetlaufer, *supra* note 3, at 21–34.

22. ANTONIN SCALIA, A MATTER OF INTERPRETATION: FEDERAL COURTS AND THE LAW 16–17 (Amy Guttman, ed., 1997).

23. *See* Tamanaha, *supra* note 20, at 63–67. Likewise, some positivists reject the incorporation of empiricism into the law for precisely this reason. *See* Wetlaufer, *supra* note 3, at 44–46 (citing theorists).

24. Legal positivists also see social facts as providing the foundation for a legal system and law. *See* Michael Steven Green, *Legal Realism as Theory of Law*, 46 WM. & MARY L. REV. 1915, 1940 (2005) (discussing H. L. A. Hart). Legal realists and their many heirs share this perception of law as rooted in social reality. *See, e.g.*, Lon L. Fuller, *Positivism and Fidelity to Law—A Reply to Professor Hart*, 71 HARV. L. REV. 630, 630–34 (1958).

25. Joseph William Singer, *Review Essay: Legal Realism Now*, 76 CAL. L. REV. 467, 474 (1988) (reviewing LAURA KALMAN, LEGAL REALISM AT YALE 1927–1960).

26. I am indebted to my colleague Richard Daynard for articulating the idea that public health can be viewed as a legal canon. Richard A. Daynard, *Regulating Tobacco: The Need for a Public Health Judicial Decision-Making Canon*, 30 J. L. MED. & ETHICS 281, 281 (2002).

27. *See* chapter 2, *supra*.

28. *See* chapter 1, *supra*.

29. DAVID L. FAIGMAN, LEGAL ALCHEMY: THE USE AND MISUSE OF SCIENCE IN THE LAW *passim* (1999).

30. Daubert v. Merrell Dow Pharmaceuticals, 509 U.S. 579, 600 (1993) (Rehnquist, C. J., concurring in part and dissenting in part).

31. Daniel W. Shuman, *Expertise in Law, Medicine and Health Care*, 26 J. HEALTH POL. POL'Y & L. 267, 267–90 (2001).

32. David Brown, *USDA Orders Largest Meat Recall in U.S. History*, WASH. POST, Feb. 18, 2008, at A-01.

33. *Statement by Secretary of Agriculture Ed Schafer Regarding Hallmark/ Westland Meat Packing Company Two Year Product Recall*, Feb. 17, 2008, http:// usda.gov/wps/portal/!ut/p/_s.7_0_A/7_0_1OB/?contentidonly = true&contentid = 2008/02/0046.xml (last visited Jan. 16, 2009).

34. Andrew Marlin, *Some Tainted Meat Used in School Lunches, U.S. Says*, N.Y. TIMES, Feb. 22, 2008, at C-3.

35. Centers for Disease Control and Prevention, *Investigation of Outbreak of Infections Caused by* Salmonella Saintpaul (Aug. 25, 2008), http://www.cdc.gov/ Salmonella/Saintpaul (last visited Oct. 26, 2008).

36. Eric Schlosser, *Has Politics Contaminated the Food Supply?*, N.Y. TIMES, Dec. 11, 2006, at A-27.

37. Division of Bacterial and Mycotic Diseases, Centers for Disease Control and Prevention, *Disease Information: Foodborne Illness* (Oct. 25, 2005), http://www .cdc.gov/ncidod/dbmd/diseaseinfo/foodborneinfections_g.htm.

38. Robert V. Tauxe & Emilio J. Esteban, *Advances in Food Safety to Prevent Foodborne Diseases in the United States*, *in* SILENT VICTORIES: THE HISTORY AND PRACTICE

OF PUBLIC HEALTH IN TWENTIETH CENTURY AMERICA 18, 22–29 (John W. Ward & Christian Warren eds., 2007).

39. *Id.*

40. *Id.* For a discussion on the changing shape of the American food industry, see ERIC SCHLOSSER, FAST FOOD NATION: THE DARK SIDE OF THE ALL-AMERICAN MEAL 193–222 (2001).

41. U.S. Government Accountability Office, *High Risk Series: An Update*, GAO 07–310 (January 2007), at 69.

42. Andrew Martin, *Stronger Rules and More Oversight for Produce Likely after Outbreaks of E. coli*, N.Y. TIMES, Dec. 11, 2006, at A-1; Schlosser, *supra* note 36, at A-27.

43. *See, e.g.*, Blake B. Johnson, *The Supreme Beef Case: An Opportunity to Rethink Federal Food Safety Regulation*, 16 LOY. CONSUMER L. REV. 159, 171–74 (2004).

44. Tauxe & Esteban, *supra* note 38, at 31–32.

45. Food Safety and Inspection Service, U.S. Department of Agriculture, *Pathogen Reduction; Hazard Analysis and Critical Control Point (HACCP) Systems: Final Rule*, 61 FED. REG. 38805 (July 25, 1996), http://www.fsis.usda.gov/OA/fr/rule1.pdf (last visited Feb. 6, 2007).

46. Tauxe & Esteban, *supra* note 38, at 33 (giving numbers of cases of salmonella illness in the United States in 1997); Andrew C. Voetsch et al., *FoodNet Estimate of the Burden of Illness Caused by Nontyphoidal* Salmonella *Infections in the United States*, 2004 CLINICAL INFECTIOUS DISEASE, Supp., S127, S127 (2004).

47. Food Safety and Inspection Service, *supra* note 45, at 38835.

48. 9 C.F.R. 310.25(b)(3)(iii)(2007).

49. David Jackson and Geoff Dougherty, *Meat from Troubled Plants Sold to U.S. Lunch Program*, Chicago Tribune, Dec. 9, 2001, at C-17.

50. Supreme Beef Processors, Inc. v. U.S. Dep't of Agric., 275 F.3d 432 (5th Cir. 2001) (affirming Supreme Beef Processors, Inc. v. U.S. Dept. of Agric., 113 F. Supp. 2d 1048 (N.D. Tex. 2000)).

51. *Id.* at 435.

52. *Id.* at 434–36.

53. *Id.* at 438 (*citing* Chevron U.S.A., Inc. v. Natural Res. Def. Council, Inc., 467 U.S. 837 (1984)).

54. 21 U.S.C. § 608 (2000).

55. 275 F.3d at 434 (citing 21 U.S.C. § 601 (m)(4)).

56. *Id.* at 438–39.

57. *Id.* at 439; 21 U.S.C. § 601 (m)(1).

58. 21 U.S.C. § 601 (m)(1).

59. 275 F.3d at 441–42.

60. *Id.* at 439.

61. Division of Bacterial and Mycotic Diseases, Centers for Disease Control and Prevention, *Salmonellosis* (May 21, 2008), http://www.cdc.gov/nczved/dfbmd/disease_listing/salmonellosis_gi.html (last visited Oct. 10, 2008).

62. Peter Goldsmith, Nesve Turan, & Hamish Gow, *Food Safety in the Meat Industry: A Regulatory Quagmire*, at 8, http://www.ifama.org/tamu/iama/conferences/2003Conference/papers/goldsmith.pdf (last visited Oct. 26, 2008).

63. 21 U.S.C. § 602 (2000). The argument in the text is compatible with an intentionalist approach to statutory interpretation. *See* Wendy E. Parmet, *Plain Meaning and Mitigating Measures: Judicial Interpretations of the Meaning of Disability*, 21 BERKELEY J. EMP. & LAB. L. 53, 67 (2000).

64. 275 F.3d at 442.

65. *Id.* at 439–40.

66. *Id.* (distinguishing United States v. Nova Scotia Food Prods. Corp., 568 F.2d 240 (2d Cir. 1977)).

67. Daynard, *supra* note 26, at 81 (2002).

68. *E.g.*, Buck v. Bell, 274 U.S. 200 (1927).

69. 5 U.S.C. §§ 551–559 (2008).

70. Allen v. Wright, 468 U.S. 737, 752 (1984).

71. Lujan v. Defenders of Wildlife, 504 U.S. 555, 575 (1992).

72. Massachusetts v. EPA, 549 U.S. 497, 127 S.Ct. 1438 (2007). The Court did not stress the state's right to represent the claims of its affected populations, but focused instead on the semisovereign interests of the state qua state.

73. *See* United Food and Commercial Workers Union Local 751 v. Brown Group, Inc., 517 U.S. 544, 554–57 (1996).

74. *See* 275 F.3d at 432.

75. *Id.* at 439 (citing American Pub. Health Ass'n v. Butz, 511 F.2d 331, 334 (D.C. Cir. 1974)).

76. *Id.* at 439–40.

77. *See* SCHLOSSER, *supra* note 40, at 194–204.

78. American Pub. Health Ass'n v. Butz, 511 F.2d at 334.

79. *See* Daubert v. Merrell Dow Pharms., Inc., 509 U.S. 579 (1993); *see* chapter 9, *infra.*

80. Pub. L. 106–554 § 515(a), 114 Stat. 2763A-153–154 (Dec. 21, 2000) (published at 44 U.S.C. § 3516, note).

81. OMB Watch, *The Reality of Data Quality Act's First Year: A Correction of OMB's Report to Congress* (July 2004), http://www.ombwatch.org/info/data qualityreport.pdf (last visited Oct. 10, 2008).

82. Sheldon Krimsky, *The Weight of Scientific Evidence in Policy & Law*, 95 AM. J. PUB. HEALTH Supp. 1, 129, 129 (2005).

83. Andy Stirling & David Gee, *Science, Precaution, and Practice*, 117 PUB. HEALTH REP. 521, 524–26 (2002).

84. Joel A. Tichner, *Guest Editorial—Precaution and Preventive Public Health Policy*, 117 PUB. HEALTH REP. 493 (2002). *See also* David Rosner & Gerald Markowitz, *Industry Challenges to the Principle of Prevention in Public Health: The Precautionary Principle in Historical Perspective*, 117 PUB. HEALTH REP. 501, 509–10 (2002). For a discussion of different forms of the precautionary principle and a critique of its "harder"

forms, see Cass R. Sunstein, *Meador Lecture Series 2004–2005: Risk and the Law: Precautions against What? The Availability Heuristic and Cross-Cultural Risk Perception*, 57 ALA. L. REV. 75, 80–87 (2005).

85. Tichner, *supra* note 84, at 493.

86. *Id.*

87. *Id.* (quoting Austin Bradford Hill, *The Environment and Disease: Association or Causation*, 58 PROCEEDINGS ROYAL SOC. MED. 295, 295–300 (1965)).

88. Stirling & Gee, *supra* note 83, at 521–31.

89. *See id.* at 117 (discussing the importance of humility).

90. For a discussion of the different forms of the precautionary principle, see Sunstein, *supra* note 84, at 78–79.

91. Cass R. Sunstein, *Preferences and Rational Choice: New Perspectives and Legal Implications: Beyond the Precautionary Principle*, 151 U. PA. L. REV. 1003, 1036–38 (2003).

CHAPTER 4

Population Health and Federalism: Whose Job Is It?

It is one of the happy incidents of the federal system that a single courageous state may, if its citizens choose, serve as a laboratory; and try novel social and economic experiments without risk to the rest of the country.

—*New State Ice Co. v. Liebmann*, 285 U.S. 262, 311 (1932)
(Brandeis, J., dissenting)

W HAT DO INFECTIOUS EPIDEMICS, hurricanes, cigarettes, and handguns have in common? First, each can harm the health and well-being of multiple populations. Second, the source of each of these threats extends beyond the boundaries of any single locality or state, yet each of these public health threats affects different regions differently. Third, optimal interventions for each of these threats would include local, statewide, national, and perhaps international components. Yet, in the United States, efforts to protect diverse populations from each of these dangers are hampered by uncertainty and confusion as to whether the job belongs primarily to the federal government or to the states.

Sometimes, as evident in the bungled response to Hurricane Katrina in 2005, poor communication and coordination between federal and state officials is the cause of the problem.[1] Sometimes, as was also true when Katrina struck, public health protection is jeopardized by constitutional doctrines that raise doubts as to the authority of each level of government to act.[2] Not surprisingly, private interests threatened by public health regulations have become adept at playing the federalism game, challenging state regulations for intruding on the federal government's jurisdiction while questioning federal regulations as violating states' rights. Although such inconsistency may be expected from regulated interests, it is more problematic when it appears in judicially created doctrines.

The uncertainty caused by federalism is not new. In the early years of the Constitution it was generally assumed that the states, acting through their so-called police powers, were the legal entities authorized to protect public health. Indeed, courts in the nineteenth century often asserted that if the matter at hand was a public health regulation, it clearly belonged to the states.[3] Nevertheless, the federal government became involved with public health quite early on. For example, in 1796, Congress authorized the federal government to impose maritime quarantines.[4] Very shortly thereafter, Congress enacted a law to support the distribution of the newly discovered smallpox vaccination.[5] Ever since, both the states and the federal government have undertaken an active, if inconsistent, role in protecting population health.

What is new today is the degree to which uncertainties over federalism threaten to disable both the states and the federal government from undertaking public health measures. Also new is the lack of weight given to the population health issues at hand when courts decide the boundaries of federalism. In effect, the formalities of federalism, rife with their own complexities, now threaten to overshadow the ability of any government to effectively protect the health of its populations. These formalities may also undermine the fundamental principles federalism was meant to serve. A population-based perspective that recalls that protection of population health is a vital goal of governments and law as well as the centrality of populations to legal analysis holds the potential for improving public health protection and revitalizing the law of federalism.

THE ROLE OF THE POLICE POWER

Federalism, it has been said, is the great genius of American constitutionalism. By splitting the "atom of sovereignty," the framers of the Constitution created a governmental structure in which power is shared, diffused, and checked.[6] As a result, multiple jurisdictions are available to address pressing public problems and protect individual and minority interests. Both the empowering and the limiting aspects of federalism are relevant to protecting population health.

Traditionally, public health protection was assumed to fall within the province of the states.[7] This is because under the structure established by the framers and enshrined in the Constitution, the federal government is a government of limited, albeit impressive, authority. It can only exercise those powers granted to it by the Constitution, including the powers enumerated in Article I, Section I granting Congress the power to "regulate Commerce with foreign Nations, and among the several States and with the Indian Tribes," to "lay and collect Taxes, Duties, Imposts and Excises, to pay the debts and provide for the common Defense and general Welfare of the United States," and to make all laws "which shall be necessary and proper for carrying into Execution the foregoing Powers."

Although the Constitution's preamble states that the document was executed to promote the general "welfare," the Constitution does not explicitly give the federal government any authority to protect public health or to regulate in order to further the general good. This point is sometimes noted in connection with the Tenth Amendment, which expresses the "truism" that "the powers not delegated to the United States by the Constitution, nor prohibited by it to the States, are reserved to the States respectively, or to the people."[8]

Thus the Constitution reserves to the states the authority not given to the federal government. Under traditional constitutional theory, this authority includes the power to protect the public's health and welfare. This point was expressed famously by Chief Justice Marshall in 1824, when he stated that "inspection laws, quarantine laws, [and] health laws of every description" are among the mass of powers that continued to reside with the states after the Constitution's ratification.[9]

As discussed in chapter 2, these diffused and difficult to define powers are known as the police powers, a term that derives from the ancient Greek *polis* for political community. Throughout the nineteenth century, the police powers were often identified by courts with the protection of public health and safety as well as morals. In numerous cases courts relied on a simplistic equation between public health and the police powers to decide the constitutionality of a state law that was charged with exceeding the state's jurisdiction. For example, when Chief Justice Marshall upheld a state law authorizing the erection of a dam on a stream used for interstate commerce, he noted that the dam would improve the health of the inhabitants of the stream's banks.[10] Likewise several decades later, the Supreme Court upheld an inspection fee imposed on vessels arriving at the port of New Orleans on the theory that the state could take measures to protect the city from the importation of deadly diseases.[11]

This simple identification of public health with the states' police powers was always riddled with exceptions and subject to potential problems. Most notable was the overlapping and increasingly important scope of federal authority. Although the Constitution does not grant the federal government any public health powers per se, it quickly became accepted that those powers that Article I grants to the federal government are "plenary" and can be used to achieve public health goals.[12] The earliest example of this may have been the 1796 act authorizing the establishment of maritime quarantines.[13] This law, which was enacted after vigorous congressional debates over the scope of federal authority, demonstrates vividly how Congress could use its Article I commerce powers to tackle a public health problem. The 1965 amendments to the Social Security Act, which created the Medicaid and Medicare programs and provided health insurance to millions, provide more modern and far-reaching examples of Congress's use of one of its enumerated powers (to tax and spend) to achieve a goal that might traditionally have been thought of as within the states' police powers.[14]

The 1796 quarantine act illustrates another conceptual obstacle for any effort to divide the world of legal powers along neat federal or state lines. Although maritime quarantines are core public health laws in that they are instituted to prevent diseases from being imported, they are also often motivated by concerns about the impact of disease on commerce and tariff revenue. Similarly, many if not most laws that an observer might reflexively call a public health law result from mixed motivations. Laws also tend to have myriad effects. Thus the placement of commercial laws on one side of the federalism divide and public health laws on the other side is not quite as simple, or sensible, a task as it may at first appear.

Nevertheless, for many decades, the inherent difficulty of determining whether a law was or was not about public health did not present a significant impediment to either federal or state efforts to enact public health regulations. From the New Deal until the 1990s, the Supreme Court adopted a highly deferential stance toward both state and federal laws that either appeared to protect public health or purported to do so. Recognizing the problematic nature of drawing fine lines between Congress's power under Article I and the states' police powers, and concluding that the allocation of power and responsibility could be best dealt with by the political process, the Supreme Court settled on a doctrinal approach that essentially provided no federalism-based limitations on congressional action.[15] As a result, the federal government was able to establish a broad range of regulations and programs that aimed either directly or indirectly at public health. The enactment of the Occupational Safety and Health Act,[16] the National Childhood Vaccine Program,[17] and the Food Drug and Cosmetic Act,[18] all gave lie to the traditional view that the protection of population health generally belongs to the states as opposed to the federal government.

Yet, states continued to be key players in population health protection. Even as the federal government's involvement in the area grew, with the apparent blessing of the New Deal and post-New Deal Supreme Courts, state and local governments continued to provide the bulk of direct, core public health activities (such as surveillance, restaurant inspection, and medical licensing).[19] In addition, although some state public health activities were found to be unconstitutional under federalism-based theories designed to protect interstate commerce, such holdings were relatively few until the mid-1980s. Until then, the ability of both the state and federal governments to protect public health was rarely limited by questions of federalism. Today questions abound.

LIMITS ON STATE ACTION—THE DORMANT COMMERCE CLAUSE

Since the mid-1980s, decisions rendered under both the so-called negative or dormant commerce clause as well as the doctrine of preemption have increasingly challenged the states' ability to protect population health. Although each doctrine is distinct, both demonstrate the dangers that judicial enforcement of federalism can present for population health.

Consider first the evolution of the dormant commerce clause doctrine. The doctrine itself dates back to the early days of the nineteenth century, when the Constitution's grant to Congress of authority to regulate commerce was understood as depriving states of the same power.[20] Under this exclusive powers approach, jurists assumed that because the Constitution vested the power to regulate interstate commerce with the Congress, it effectively took any such powers away from the states. Thus state regulations of interstate commerce were deemed to be unconstitutional, even though there is no language in the Constitution to that effect. (Hence, the negative commerce clause.) On the other hand, because courts deemed the protection of public health to be solidly within the core of the states' police powers, a state regulation would be held constitutional and not an impermissible regulation of interstate commerce if the law were viewed as a public health law. As a result, the characterization of a law as a public health law was extremely important to the determination of the law's constitutionality. In that sense, the early dormant commerce clause doctrine recognized the importance of public health to legal decision making.

By the mid-nineteenth century, however, the exclusive powers approach came under pressure. Courts recognized that some state regulation of interstate commerce was desirable or at least inevitable.[21] Moreover, courts perceived that states might use putative public health measures as a pretext for interfering with interstate commerce.[22] As a result, alternative rationales were offered to justify federalism boundaries under the dormant commerce clause.

One highly influential rationale explained the dormant commerce clause doctrine as embodying the Constitution's disdain for discrimination and favoritism between the states.[23] Seeking to protect commerce from the evils of state protectionism and balkanization, this theory found state laws that appeared either facially or by their impact to discriminate against out-of-state economic interests as unconstitutional. In other words, state laws that were viewed as protectionist were found to violate the Constitution.

Initially this approach did not present a major hurdle for state public health laws. Although state laws that purported to protect public health were occasionally found unconstitutional because of their discriminatory nature or the whiff of protectionism that surrounded them, courts generally maintained a relatively deferential stance toward laws enacted in the name of public health.[24] For example, although striking down a municipal ordinance that required milk to be pasteurized within five miles of the city as protectionist, the Supreme Court reminded lower courts that a state has an "unquestioned power to protect the health and safety of its people."[25] A few years later, in upholding an injunction against a newspaper publishing advertisements for optometrists, the Supreme Court cautioned that "the Constitution when conferring upon Congress the regulation of commerce . . . never intended to cut the States off from legislating on all subjects relating to the health, life, and safety of their citizens, though the legislation might indirectly affect the commerce of the country."[26]

This deference to the states' police power eroded after the Supreme Court settled on a two-tiered analysis for determining whether state laws, including those that purport to protect health or safety, violate the dormant commerce clause. Today, courts treat as per se unconstitutional those state laws that "directly regulate[] or discriminate[] against interstate commerce."[27] On the other hand, state laws that have a less direct or only an incidental impact upon commerce fall into the second tier and are usually subject to the so-called *Pike* balancing test that asks whether the state law is legitimate and whether the burdens it places on commerce outweigh its local benefits.[28] Although the first tier of the analysis would seem to create the greater obstacle for legal interventions designed to protect public health, in fact, both tiers may pose problems for legal measures aimed at protecting population health.

The first and perhaps seminal case applying the first tier was *City of Philadelphia v. New Jersey*,[29] in which the Supreme Court considered a challenge to a New Jersey law that prohibited the importation of most "solid or liquid waste which originated or was collected outside the territorial limits of the State."[30] In an opinion by Justice Stewart, the Supreme Court found the statute unconstitutional, stating that "where simple economic protectionism is effected by state legislation, a virtually *per se* rule of invalidity has been erected."[31] Moreover, the Court continued, the question of whether the statute was intended to address an environmental problem was not relevant to the statute's constitutionality. As long as the state used discriminatory means, the statute was effectively assured of being found unconstitutional, even if the statute addressed a legitimate or pressing problem, such as solid waste disposal.

In announcing this per se rule, Justice Stewart had to discuss quarantine laws that had long been considered constitutional. Overlooking the fact that quarantines also applied to persons as well as to goods, Justice Stewart described the quarantine exception to the dormant commerce clause as a very narrow one that applies only when laws ban the importation of noxious articles that pose an immediate hazard to the state that institutes the quarantine. Justice Stewart noted that "there has been no claim here that the very movement of waste into or through New Jersey endangers health, or that waste must be disposed of as soon and as close to its point of generation as possible."[32]

Responding in dissent, Justice Rehnquist stressed the severity of the environmental and health problems posed by solid waste and argued that the majority failed to give the state adequate leeway to address those dangers.[33] Yet in emphasizing the state's very real interests in protecting its population, and in noting the historic breadth of the quarantine power, the justice failed to consider the burdens that New Jersey was potentially imposing on other states' efforts to protect their own populations. Thus neither the majority nor the dissent recognized that *Philadelphia* presented a key question for public health federalism: which level of government— state or federal—is best suited to protect the health of multiple populations?

Had the justices asked that question, they might well have concluded that in the case at hand, a federal solution was preferable. But that would only have led them to another also critical question: in the absence of an effective federal response, how much leeway should be given to state efforts to address problems that could theoretically be better addressed at the federal level? As will be discussed, a population-based approach will tend to err in upholding such state laws, at least against federalism-based attacks, not only because they may at times improve the health of populations but also because they can provide data for understanding how population health issues should and should not be addressed.[34] In *Philadelphia*, however, neither the majority nor dissent asked such questions. Instead, the majority offered a formulaic per se test and the dissent nostalgically preached the virtues of the letting states solve their own problems.

Despite the Court's failure to consider the population health issues immanent to the case, the per se test adopted in *Philadelphia* did not itself represent a major blow to many contemporary public health laws. Since the development of techniques other than quarantine to prevent the spread of most epidemics, few public health problems require legal interventions as overtly discriminatory against interstate commerce as was the New Jersey solid waste law.

Nevertheless, the Court's approach in *Philadelphia* presaged a significant hurdle for public health protection as well as a major departure from a population perspective. The difficulty lies in part from the Court's expansive interpretation of protectionism in subsequent cases. For example, in *C. & A. Carbone, Inc. v. Town of Clarkstown*,[35] the Supreme Court applied the *Philadelphia* approach to a municipal ordinance that required all solid waste within the town to be deposited at a local waste transfer station. In contrast to the statute at issue in *Philadelphia*, this ordinance did not bar the importation of any goods, it simply required a particular procedure to occur before the disposal of any local waste. Moreover, as Justice Souter astutely noted in his dissent, the ordinance served to help finance the local transfer station by guaranteeing it a steady supply of waste to process.[36] And, of course, by helping finance the station, the ordinance helped ensure the sanitary disposal of the waste. Thus the ordinance could be viewed as a sanitary law, among the most well-accepted exercises of the police power. The *Carbone* majority, however, applied *Philadelphia* and viewed the ordinance as discriminatory against out-of-state interests because it required local producers of waste to use or pay for the local transfer station. So understood, the law was seen as protectionist and hence per se unconstitutional. In effect, the majority found that the ordinance's efficacy in addressing the waste disposal problem was not germane to the constitutional question.

More recently, the Supreme Court has appeared to reverse course and grant public health protection somewhat greater weight in dormant commerce clause cases. In *United Haulers Association, Inc. v. Oneida-Herkimer Solid Waste Management Authority*, the Supreme Court upheld a "flow control" ordinance quite similar to the one struck down in *Carbone*, with one exception.[37] According to the majority opinion, authored by Chief Justice Roberts, the flow ordinance in *United Haulers Association* favored a public, rather than a privately owned, waste transfer station.[38] The Court found that distinction critical because "unlike [a] private enterprise, government is vested with the responsibility of protecting the health, safety, and welfare of its citizens."[39]

Rhetorically, the Court's opinion in *United Haulers Association* appears to adopt a population perspective by recognizing the importance of using law affirmatively to protect the health of populations. Indeed, the Court even suggests that government has such a duty. The opinion also appears to appreciate that states and local governments were traditionally responsible for overseeing the safe disposal of waste.[40]

Nevertheless, the impact of *United Haulers Association* on the first tier of the Supreme Court's dormant commerce clause jurisprudence remains unclear. Although the distinction between a publicly controlled and privately controlled waste transfer station is not trivial from the perspective of an approach to law that emphasizes the government's affirmative role in promoting health, it is nevertheless relatively narrow and does not provide any cushion for state laws that regulate the private sector. Hence, the interests of commerce by the private sector continue to trump population health, at least when regulations can be said to discriminate against interstate commerce. Moreover, the Court's opinion in *United Haulers Association* adheres to a rigid formalism that privileges the nominal distinction between public and private entities, without paying any attention to whether the regulation at issue does in fact benefit—or is even designed to benefit—the health of populations. Indeed, the opinion is remarkable for its blindness to the empirical world.

The preference in contemporary dormant commerce clause doctrine for formalism and the concomitant neglect of empirical considerations is also evident in a series of cases that relate to what is known as extraterritoriality. Since 1982, the Supreme Court has expressed concern about state laws that have an extraterritorial effect and impose legal obligations on out-of-state activities.[41] According to the Court, by regulating out-of-state activities these laws inappropriately and almost always unconstitutionally burden interstate commerce because they subject economic entities to multiple and potentially inconsistent regulations.[42]

As a result, lower courts have treated extraterritorial laws as falling within the first tier and have applied a per se rule, thereby invalidating state laws that seek to regulate the distribution of harmful material by the Internet (including child pornography and cigarettes).[43] Strikingly, these cases give little or no weight to the population health impact of their decisions. Nor do the cases consider the possibility that different populations experience public health problems differently and therefore may, at times, benefit from a local or state regulation. Finally and most problematically from a population health perspective, these cases often fail to appreciate, never mind incorporate, public health methodologies. In demanding a singular approach to complex problems and by preventing states from developing new and varied solutions, these cases threaten to thwart society's ability to test and analyze different approaches to public health problems. In effect, the cases fail to understand that empirical verification requires the existence of populations facing different conditions and the testing of different solutions. Or, to put it most simply, the courts fail to grasp that we cannot know whether a particular approach to a public health problem, be it cigarette smoking or drunk driving, works unless we can compare its impact to that of different approaches in relatively similar populations. By shutting down the "laboratories of democracy," courts undermine everyone's ability to make informed judgments about the efficacy of regulations.

Theoretically, empirical evidence about the health impact of a regulation should play a greater role when courts review regulations in the second tier; in other words, when courts review laws that are not thought to be protectionist or do not impose direct regulations on interstate commerce. According to settled doctrine, these laws are subject to the *Pike* test and are upheld as long as the burdens placed on interstate commerce do not clearly exceed the local benefits obtained by the laws.[44] According to the Supreme Court, in undertaking this test courts should respect a state's goals.[45]

Often courts do appear to value a state's attempt to protect population health. After rejecting the application of the per se rule to public entities in *United Haulers Association*, for example, the Supreme Court upheld the flow control ordinance under the *Pike* test. According to the Court, the ordinance passed the test because any "incidental" impact on interstate commerce would not exceed the ordinance's public benefits, which were said to include helping finance waste disposal and encouraging recycling and the proper disposal of hazardous materials.[46] In reaching this conclusion, the Court asserted that it would not rigorously review state police power actions.

At times, however, the Court has appeared to do just that. For example, in *Kassel v. Consolidated Freightways Corp.*, the Court struck down an Iowa law that limited the length of "doubles," or twin trucks, to sixty feet.[47] Although the state claimed that the law was designed to prevent highway accidents, the Supreme Court, in a plurality opinion by Justice Powell, concluded that the state had not proven that the statute would in fact benefit

safety. In undertaking this review, Justice Powell granted little or no deference to the state's claim that the regulation would protect public health.
Instead, his analysis suggested that as long as the safety claim could not
be proven, the burdens placed on interstate commerce, which were far
easier to observe, would be decisive. In effect, as under the first tier of
analysis, Justice Powell prioritized free trade over population health without providing any rationale of why he was doing so and without offering
any methodology for balancing, as the *Pike* test purports to do, a regulation's health effects against its impact on commerce. Indeed, the Court's
inability to explain how to conduct such a balancing test in any rigorous
or even understandable fashion has led justices with such divergent views
as Justices Brennan and Scalia to condemn the test.[48]

The *Kassel* plurality's approach to analyzing state laws that are not obviously protectionist or extraterritorial in their reach can have devastating
consequences for efforts to use the law to promote public health. For example, in *Consolidated Cigar Corp. v. Reilly*, a Massachusetts law that required
warning labels on cigar packages was found unconstitutional by the Court
of Appeals for the First Circuit under the *Pike* test.[49] The court never
explained why the burdens on interstate commerce that resulted from the
labeling requirement outweighed the health benefits the state sought to
achieve under the regulation. Indeed, the opinion is striking for its lack of
rigorous analysis.

Unless the reluctance of the Court in *United Haulers Association* to rigorously review police power actions is applied more broadly, and consistently, the *Pike* test may continue to inhibit efforts by states to use their law
to protect the health of populations. As the economy becomes more complex and interrelated, local state laws inevitably pose a greater burden on
interstate commerce. Consider, for example, state laws that require physicians to be licensed. These laws have been considered an appropriate exercise of the states' police power for well over a hundred years.[50] Decades
ago, they had no obvious or discernable effect upon interstate commerce
because it was difficult, if not impossible, to envision how a physician
could practice medicine across state lines. By the late twentieth century,
the development of telemedicine suggested that these very traditional laws
could indeed pose problems for interstate interests. By the dawn of the
twenty-first century and the rise of the Internet, laws that block the practice
of medicine over the Internet may seem to stand in the way of commerce.

At the same time, public health studies are increasingly demonstrating the national, indeed global, nature of many public health problems. From cigarettes to avian influenza, motor vehicle injuries to HIV, it is no longer plausible to believe that public health protection can succeed if it is limited to interventions that do not touch on out-of-state interests. Nor can broad social determinants of health be effectively addressed without affecting commerce beyond the state's borders. Thus, the protection of population health increasingly requires efforts that cross state lines and affect out-of-state interests. Unfortunately, the current, formalistic doctrine, which is uninformed by the concerns, perspectives, and methodologies of public health, does not provide a solution. As a result, despite the traditional identification of the police powers with public health and the Supreme Court's frequent paeans to states' rights, the contemporary dormant commerce clause doctrine creates a formidable and inconsistent barrier to using law to protect the health of populations.

FEDERAL AUTHORITY TO PROTECT PUBLIC HEALTH

The increasing difficulty that states face in attempting to regulate on behalf of public health and the increasing interstate nature of health problems argue for expanding the federal government's role in protecting population health. The federal government, after all, has more resources than the states to deal with public health threats. Moreover, only the federal government can enact regulations that explicitly extend across state lines and address interstate (as well as international) threats. Indeed, in contrast to the states, the federal government is not limited by the Court's dormant commerce clause doctrine. Rather, it is directly empowered by the Constitution to enact laws that regulate interstate commerce, even if such laws restrain or burden interstate commerce. Hence, to the extent that public health regulations implicate interstate commerce, as they increasingly do, it appears sensible to assume that the federal government should assume primary responsibility for public health protection at least within the United States.[51]

To a large extent, that has already happened. Throughout the twentieth century the federal government's involvement in matters relating to public health expanded greatly.[52] The process began in 1906 with the enactment of the Food and Drug Act,[53] and accelerated during the New Deal as the federal government became more involved in numerous aspects of the economy and the Supreme Court adopted an extremely broad interpretation of Congress's authority under both the commerce clause and the tax and spend clause.[54] This not only opened the door for enhanced federal involvement in such core New Deal projects as workers' rights and financial security, matters that indirectly affect the health of broad populations, but also ultimately in more traditional public health activities, such as the regulation of product safety or the quality of air and water, and even to a degree, the practice of medicine.[55] Today, not only does the federal government provide a large share of funding for state public health agencies, it has also come to dominate many core public health activities that once resided solely with the states.[56]

The breadth of federal regulation in areas that were previously left to the states has led to the increasing displacement, or preemption, of state laws. Under the supremacy clause, federal laws trump conflicting state laws.[57] In addition, when Congress acts pursuant to its Article I authority, it may chose to preempt either some or all state laws related to the field.[58] However, statutory language pertaining to preemption is notoriously ambiguous, especially about whether Congress intends to preempt private tort actions.[59] In addition, federal statutes can be found to preempt state action even in the absence of any specific federal statutory language, either because a state regulation conflicts with federal policy or because the federal regulation of the issue is so pervasive as to evidence Congress's attempt to occupy the entire field.[60]

In recent years, industries regulated by states or subject to state tort actions have increasingly relied on preemption as a defense.[61] Moreover, federal agencies, such as the Food and Drug Administration (FDA), have recently taken a new and more expansive view of the preemptive effect of their regulations.[62] Although the Supreme Court has repeatedly asserted a presumption against preemption of state health and safety laws, meaning that preemption should not be found in the absence of clear statutory language mandating it,[63] neither the Supreme Court nor the lower courts have consistently adhered to that approach, resulting in new obstacles for state efforts to protect population health.[64] For example, in 2008 in *Rowe v. New Hampshire Motor Transport Association*, the Supreme Court found that the Federal Aviation Administration Authorization Act of 1994 preempted the state of Maine's efforts to prevent shipping companies from delivering tobacco products to minors.[65] In so doing, the Court refused to find or imply any "public health exception" to the sweep of federal preemption.[66] The same day, the Court also found that the Medical Device Acts Amendments of 1976 preempted state tort actions brought against defective medical devices that had been subject to premarketing approval by the FDA.[67]

A few weeks later an equally divided Court affirmed without opinion a lower court ruling upholding a Michigan law barring drug claims except when the manufacturer has defrauded the FDA.[68] However, Chief Justice Roberts, who has thus far been a strong supporter of preemption, did not participate in that case, leaving it unclear as to how the Court will rule in future cases about the preemption of drug liability claims. Whatever the Court ultimately concludes about the preemptive impact of FDA regulations, it is likely that state efforts to protect population health will continue to face the hurdle of federal preemption. As will be discussed, from a population-based approach this is problematic to the extent that preemption is unaccompanied by effective federal population health interventions, as may be the case with an overly expansive finding of FDA preemption.

The growth of federal involvement in traditional state public health activities, as well as the increasing tendency of regulated industries to assert preemption claims, stands in stark contrast to a series of Supreme Court decisions in the 1990s that appeared to restrict the scope of federal authority under the commerce clause.[69] Although, as we shall see, the Court has recently pulled back from the so-called new federalism approach heralded by these cases, uncertainty continues to cloud federal efforts to protect population health.

Without doubt the key case was *United States v. Lopez*, decided in 1995.[70] As previously noted, since the New Deal courts had read the federal government's authority under the commerce clause broadly to allow Congress to regulate almost anything, from homegrown wheat to racial discrimination.[71] In fact, between 1936 and 1995 the Supreme Court denied every challenge brought under the commerce clause to a federal regulation of private sector activity.

Lopez affirmed such a challenge. The federal statute at issue was the Gun-Free School Zones Act, which made it a federal crime to possess a firearm within a thousand feet of a school.[72] In declaring this statute unconstitutional, Chief Justice Rehnquist, writing for a 5–4 Supreme Court majority, emphasized both the limits on Congress's power under the commerce clause and the Court's role in reviewing congressional oversteps. Perhaps most significantly for population health, the Court stated that when, as in the case before it, Congress attempts to regulate a noncommercial activity by claiming that it affects interstate commerce, the effect must be substantial and the Court must conduct an independent review that does not rely exclusively on the assertions or findings of Congress.[73] Without such stringent oversights, the Court stated, Congress's power under Article I would be transformed into "a general police power of the sort retained by the States."[74] Interestingly, in suggesting that Congress's authority under the commerce clause had to be read narrowly to preserve a domain for the states and their police power, the Court did not consider the narrowing effect that decisions under the dormant commerce clause had on just such authority.

Lopez was followed in 2000 by United States v. Morrison,[75] in which the same 5–4 majority that prevailed in Lopez, found that Violence Against Women Act[76] unconstitutional because Congress was regulating a matter (gender-based violence) that was not commercial in nature and did not substantially affect commerce. Once again, the Court gave little or no deference to Congress's findings of an impact on commerce, essentially ignoring what Justice Souter termed a "mountain of data" showing the effects of violence against women on interstate commerce.[77]

Five years later, however, the Supreme Court, again by a 5–4 vote, appeared to reverse direction. In Gonzales v. Raich, a majority of the Supreme Court held that Congress had the authority to prohibit the possession or use of medical marijuana that was to be used intrastate and in accordance with California law.[78] In distinguishing Lopez Justice Stevens, writing for the majority, emphasized two factors. First, in contrast to the Gun-Free School Zone Act, the federal Controlled Substances Act at issue in Gonzales regulated "quintessentially" economic activity.[79] Moreover, the act created a comprehensive regulatory scheme, which the majority believed needed to be assessed for its overall effect on commerce. This latter point was critical to Justice Scalia, who in a concurring opinion, argued that Controlled Substances Act's application to medical marijuana was constitutional not because the locally grown marijuana affected commerce but because Congress had the power under the "necessary and proper" clause to prohibit the possession and use of intrastate marijuana in order to safeguard a larger regulatory scheme of interstate activity.[80] Justice Scalia emphasized that only when federal regulation of wholly intrastate activities is necessary for the success of a broader, interstate regulatory scheme is it constitutional.

In dissent, Justice O'Connor painted a very different picture. Central to her understanding of the case, was the "role of States as laboratories. The States' core police powers have always included authority to define criminal law and to protect health, safety, and welfare of their citizens."[81] Hence rather than focusing on the totality of the federal statute and how it related to interstate commerce, Justice O'Connor began with the premise that laws relating to health and safety ought generally to belong to the states. She then found that federal laws that intrude on the state's authority should be reviewed stringently to determine whether they had a sufficient nexus to interstate commerce to warrant federal intervention. To look at the federal law as a whole the way the majority did was, according to Justice O'Connor, "tantamount to removing meaningful limits on the Commerce Clause."[82]

Although the majority's holding in *Gonzales* suggests that, at least for now, the Court is unwilling to extend *Lopez* and strike down comprehensive federal statutes (at least when they prohibit socially unacceptable drugs), the deep division of the *Gonzales* Court shows that the lines between federal and state authority remain in flux. Moreover, the majority decision depended on the fifth vote of Justice Scalia, whose approach to the case emphasized the narrowness of the majority's holding. Critically, none of the justices considered the public health implications of the ruling as critical to the outcome. Indeed, to all but Justice Scalia, who focused on the broader regulation at issue, the formalities of federalism were not only dispositive, they were all that mattered.

A similar formalism and disregard for the population health ramifications of federal law is evident in a series of decisions limiting Congress's ability to use the commerce clause to impose obligations upon state governments. In *New York v. United States*, the Supreme Court struck down a federal law requiring states to develop plans for disposing of low level radioactive waste.[83] In the later case of *Printz v. United States*, it struck down a requirement that local law enforcement officials conduct background checks on gun purchasers.[84] In both cases, the Court read the Tenth Amendment as limiting Congress's ability to use the commerce clause to "commandeer" or place affirmative obligations on the states. Vital to each decision was the majority's contention that the Framers envisioned the states to be separate and sovereign entities.

These no-commandeering decisions may have a greater impact on population health than either *Lopez* or *Gonzales*. Precisely because Congress has been sensitive to the traditional role that states have played regarding population health, many federal laws that aim to protect public health follow a cooperative federalism model, setting federal parameters and obligations on states, which are entrusted with actually enforcing the policy at hand. The no-commandeering cases question this federal reliance on the states. Moreover, these decisions may make it difficult for the federal government, which lacks a large, dispersed public health workforce, to work with and through the states to respond rapidly to a public health emergency, such as an influenza pandemic. This point was presciently made by Justice Stevens in his pre-September 11 dissent in *Printz*: "Matters such as the enlistment of air raid wardens, the administration of a military draft, the mass inoculation of children to forestall an epidemic, or perhaps threats from international terrorists, may require a national response before federal personnel can be available to respond."[85]

The federal government's ability to protect population health would be further jeopardized if the federal courts were to constrain the federal government's ability to use its power to tax and spend in order to achieve population health goals. Since the New Deal, the Supreme Court has interpreted Congress's so-called spending power broadly to achieve goals including public health protection that are not themselves enumerated in Article I.[86] In addition, the Court has affirmed that Congress can attach conditions to the money that it gives states.[87] In other words, when it pays the bills, Congress can commandeer states, but only within some limits.

To ensure that Congress does not use its economic clout to purchase away the role of the states, the Supreme Court has articulated some outer limits on Congress's power to attach conditions to grants to states. In *South Dakota v. Dole*, which upheld a federal law requiring states receiving federal highway funds to establish twenty-one as the legal drinking age, Justice Rehnquist identified two key requirements for Congress's use of the spending power to impose conditions on states.[88] First, Congress must be unambiguously state the conditions that states must meet in return for receiving the desired federal funds. Theoretically, this permits states to reject the funds and ignore the federal mandate. Second, conditions placed on a state must be reasonably related to the programs the federal government funds. In other words, Congress can require states to set twenty-one as the drinking age because underage driving leads to highway accidents on federally funded roads. But Congress probably could not use federal highway funds to require states to change the licensing requirements for physicians. For that requirement, Congress would probably have to use some of its health care dollars.

Thus far, the combination of this broad, albeit ambiguous, interpretation of the spending clause and an almost unlimited budget has meant that Congress still enjoys a relatively unfettered ability to spend in the name of public health and establish standards and priorities for states to follow to obtain federal funds. Such diverse federal programs as the Medicaid and bioterrorism prevention programs all follow that model. Countless other programs could be named.

Congress's ability to use its spending powers so broadly, however, is not without critics. In *Dole* itself, Justice O'Connor in dissent expressed a different understanding of the spending clause, one that saw Congress's ability to achieve regulatory goals via that clause as limited to those categories in which Congress otherwise has regulatory power under the Constitution.[89] More recently, the Supreme Court has emphasized that Congress must provide states with clear notice before providing for private enforcement of federally imposed conditions.[90] Moreover, some lower courts, and many critics, have argued with force and passion that the federal spending power needs to be reined in, lest the very concept of state sovereignty be eviscerated. [91] This argument, which is increasingly gaining attention, may well portend the next direction for the new federalism. If so, the federal government's ability to protect the health of populations will face dire threats.[92] Astonishingly, this may occur even as courts circumscribe the ability of states to respond to public health problems.

A POPULATION HEALTH FEDERALISM

The discussion thus far has focused on the problems the Supreme Court's federalism jurisprudence has posed for either state or federal laws that purport to protect public health. Of course, imposing those hurdles is only problematic from a population perspective if the laws thwarted actually promote population health. Undoubtedly, that is not always the case. For example, it seems unlikely that the Gun-Free School Zone Act at issue in *Lopez* had much public health significance given that the problem it addressed was already the subject of relatively similar laws in many states.[93] Likewise, it is questionable whether federal requirements that public schools receiving federal funds use an abstinence-only approach to sex education protect the health of minors.[94]

From the vantage point of population-based legal analysis, however, contemporary federalism jurisprudence is troubling not simply because it erects obstacles to particular federal statutes that purport to protect public health (indeed from a public health perspective such statutes should often be struck down if they use public health as a pretext), but for two other reasons as well. First, current federalism doctrine fails to consider the population health impact of either particular decisions or the doctrine writ large. Second, the doctrine neither values nor incorporates an understanding of the relationship between federalism and populations. In effect, the Court has constructed a highly formal doctrinal apparatus to determine how to allocate authority between multiple and overlapping jurisdictions without noticing that federalism implicates the interaction of different populations and thus can be better understood by adopting a population perspective.

The Court's failure to consider the population health impact of its jurisprudence is both obvious and highly problematic. Whereas a hundred years ago the Court gave great weight to whether a statute could be viewed as a public health statute—leading to the simplistic division of the regulatory world into those matters that fell within the police power and those that did not—the Court today has moved to the opposite extreme, in which the question of whether a regulation relates to population health is often irrelevant. Although the Court still claims that a state's public health goals are relevant to the application of the *Pike* test, they are not consistently treated as such. As noted earlier, federal judges sometimes appear to pay far more attention to a regulation's burdens on commerce than to its potential population health effects. Moreover, courts are apt to discount or disregard empirical evidence relating to a statute's population health impact, while accepting almost at face value claims relating to the burdens a statute imposes on commerce. Thus not only do the federal courts now

frequently ignore public health claims in particular cases, they also sometimes reject, ostensibly as beyond their competence, the empirical and epidemiological evidence that public health can provide in support or
refutation of particular public health statutes. As a result, federalism decisions are rendered with little or no consideration of whether they will
improve or harm population health. Nor do courts give thought to
whether a determination that a particular matter can be addressed by a
different branch of government is empirically sound.

Different rationales can be given for this neglect. One obvious defense
is that population health is a value exogenous to the principles to which
courts must adhere when determining questions of federalism. Or, to put
it another way, public health protection is a matter for the legislatures, not
constitutional courts. When deciding constitutional questions, defenders
of today's doctrinal approach argue, courts must be bound by the text and
history of the Constitution's framing.[95]

A full refutation of this approach to constitutional interpretation is well
beyond the bounds of this discussion. Nevertheless, it is worth recalling
that such text-based arguments should have little weight when the matter
at hand is the dormant commerce clause, which itself lacks any textual
basis. That nontextual doctrine is a part of our constitutional tradition,
both because there are valid reasons for limiting state burdens on interstate commerce and because history has granted it legitimacy. That historic
record, however, does not support the exclusion of public health considerations from analysis in either dormant commerce clause causes or cases
concerning Congress's Article I powers. As noted, the Court's earliest federalism cases relied on a rough and ready identification between the police
power and public health to determine the appropriate boundaries between
federal and state action. The fact that we now can recognize the sloppiness
of that analysis, and have more sophisticated social science and empirical
tools to assess regulations, does not necessitate that we ignore the role
once given to public health. Instead, it provides an opportunity to improve
the quality of the analysis. Thus if courts want to remain faithful to precedent and early understandings of the Constitution, they will not neglect
population health's import to federalism. They will instead give it weight
while utilizing contemporary methodologies.

More important, excluding population health as a value from the
Court's federalism analysis substitutes an empty formalism for a realistic

engagement with the rationales for federalism. In both its dormant commerce clause and its Article I analysis, the Supreme Court has moved toward a seemingly complex but highly formulaic mode of analysis that relies on ready-to-use tests (per se or not per se, commercial or not commercial) and abstract values such as the dignity of the states in lieu of a meaningful discussion as to why the Constitution provides for, and we continue to appreciate, federalism.

In fact, the division of powers between the states and federal governments is not simply the result of historical circumstance (though they are partially that). Nor do doctrines that lack a clear textual basis, such as those applying the so-called dormant commerce clause, deserve our adherence solely on grounds of textual fidelity. Instead, federalism merits respect and continues to resonate in the twenty-first century precisely because it provides an important way of solving various problems of political governance, as evident by the fact that other parts of the world, such as Europe, are working toward their own form of federalism.[96]

Before the U.S. Constitution was adopted, political theory assumed that "a state with more than one independent sovereign power within its boundaries was a violation of the unity of nature; it would be like a monster with more than one head, continually at war with itself."[97] Federalism defied that convention and created a political system with multiple sovereignties. Most obviously, this allowed for multiple centers of powers, complimenting the checks and balances usually identified with the separation of powers. As James Madison noted in the *Federalist Papers*, this division of power provided a "double security" for the people.[98]

In its recent federalism decisions, the Supreme Court has emphasized this power-limiting aspect of federalism. Concurring in *Lopez*, Justice Kennedy pointed to "the theory that two governments accord more liberty than one" to justify the imposition of limits on Congress's reach, stating that federalism's ability to enhance liberty "requires for its realization two distinct and discernable lines of political accountability: one between the citizens and the Federal Government; the second between the citizens and the States."[99] Likewise in *New York v. United States*, Justice O'Connor cited the need for clear lines of political accountability as one rationale for prohibiting Congress from commandeering the states.[100]

There is no doubt that federalism can and does appropriately serve to enhance accountability, thereby safeguarding liberty, but an overly strict interpretation of federalism-based limits on the operation of governments obscures federalism's concurrent capacity to invigorate governments' ability to carry out those functions for which they were constituted. Indeed, the ingenuity of federalism is that it not only provides multiple forums to check power and protect liberty understood as the negative freedom from government restraint, but that it also provides multiple forums to exercise power and promote positive forms of liberty, including those associated with public health protection.

This vision of federalism is most clearly discernable in the Constitution's creation of a federal government that has direct regulatory authority and is not reliant on the states. Indeed, this critical aspect, which Justice O'Connor cited in *New York v. United States*, was actually defended in the *Federalist Papers* as a way to prevent the federal government from being as weak as it was under the Articles of Confederation.[101] As John Jay asserted in the *Federalist Papers,* such a weak government could not carry out those very functions for which governments are formed, such as protecting the safety of the people.[102]

American federalism was thus designed in large measure to establish a strong but limited national government that had the capacity to deal with threats that were beyond the ability of individual states to carry out. In the age of the Framers, foreign armies posed the most obvious threats. But by the 1790s, when Congress was debating the enactment of a national quarantine law, it had already become clear that health threats could also require a national response. Today, when pandemics can travel around the world in a matter of hours, the need for federal intervention in the prevention of infectious diseases is as evident as is the need for federal protection against foreign enemies. More broadly, as we have come to understand the role that interstate and international commerce play in creating the social determinants of health, the need for a federal response is even clearer. Our federalism permits an adequate federal response by giving Congress plenary powers to deal with matters pertaining to international and interstate commerce and by permitting Congress to use its vast spending powers to work with states as well as private entities to undertake a wide array of public health activities, some of which may require relative uniformity between the states and some of which Congress can and does support while permitting significant variation between the states.

Federalism, however, also helps ensure the well-being of populations by maintaining states as smaller governmental entities with the capacity to safeguard the health of different populations. Although it is a cliché, it remains true that state governments, closer to the people, are often more able to respond quickly and innovatively to particular health problems. This is not simply because the costs of enacting legislation are less at the state level, but also because the very possibility of fifty plus jurisdictions increases the likelihood of novel and innovative interventions. Any one intervention may not be well designed and it may indeed impose unjustifiable costs on the economy or civil liberties. But a state's experience with it can teach us something about the interaction between law and the health problem at hand, because, as Justice Brandeis observed so long ago, states can and do serve as "laboratories," in which different approaches to a problem can be attempted.[103] By creating fifty plus locations for population health interventions, federalism provides multiple opportunities for communities to undertake efforts to address the threats they face and deem problematic. Often, such state efforts provide a model for other states, or the federal government, to follow or refrain from following. In either case, the interventions can increase our understanding about how to safeguard the health of populations and perhaps provide the only opportunity we may have to actually compare, and thereby learn about, the efficacy of different interventions. Moreover, the very fact that state public health laws impose costs on interstate commerce creates political pressure for Congress to respond by devising national solutions.[104]

That one of the rationales for federalism is its ability to enhance the ability of both the states and the federal government to protect public health and safety implies that courts should not ignore the population health impact of federalist decisions. Cases such as *Lopez* that purport to limit Congress's power to preserve the sovereignty of states without considering why state sovereignty matters have the analysis backward. Likewise, decisions that restrict the states' police power without undertaking any consideration of whether the regulation at issue could indeed protect the health of the states' occupants fail to appreciate that the police power is one of the reasons why there are states.

The question remains, however, what it would mean to incorporate public health into a federalism analysis. Most clearly, as has already suggested, it would entail a meaningful consideration of the impact of particular federalism decisions and rules on the health of varying populations, particularly those within and without a state. This would demand a rejection of formalistic and categorical reasoning in favor of an approach far more accepting of empirical evidence. Second, applying a public health perspective to federalism doctrine would require adopting the population perspective that is not only the core of public health but also so vital to federalism. As a result, federalism, the constitutional doctrine most closely associated with the shifting relationships between groups, would begin to take groups or populations seriously.

As discussed, the population perspective postulates that populations matter, in other words, that individuals act differently and are affected when they are in populations. Likewise the perspective emphasizes the interdependency of individuals within a population as well as the fact that populations are not fixed. They are multiple and contingent.

These postulates can enrich federalism. First, they help to clarify why states matter. States matter not only because they are historic remnants nor just because they serve the federalist goal of safeguarding liberty. They also matter because they provide one important way in which to situate and recognize individuals within groups. Once we recall the obvious, that states are made of groups of people, we are reminded of the seemingly self-evident but easily ignored point that different groups have different attributes. They differ with respect to the risks they face, the preferences they form, and the paths they choose. These points should matter when courts determine whether a particular regulation should fall within the province of the states or the federal government.

For example, the populations of different states and even within states vary widely with respect to numerous health issues. Government statistics show that the overall incidence of cancer among men in 2002 varied from over 640 per 100,000 in Rhode Island to only 441.1 per 100,000 in Arizona.[105] On the other hand, in 2002, the death rate from heart disease among women varied from 116.6 to 161.6 per 100,000 in states such as Minnesota and Wyoming to 219.3 to 275.5 per 100,000 in states such as Alabama and Arkansas.[106] Similar population differences can be found between states with respect to a wide variety of health conditions. Careful review of such data can give rise to hypotheses about the different factors that can help explain the different rates of disease between states. A review may suggest, for example, that the population of different states face significantly different exposures to environmental hazards.[107]

On the other hand, for many health issues, the happenstance of state boundaries may have little relevance. Airborne infectious diseases, such as pandemic influenza, can cross state lines with rapid speed, making it foolish to assign to the states the responsibility to respond to such diseases. Perhaps more important, many health issues affect population groups that are not best defined by state residency, but rather by other factors, including socioeconomic status, race or ethnicity, or even occupation. Here, the allocation of responsibility to states may make little sense. The existence of these population differences are and should be treated as relevant to the federalism question. As the Supreme Court appreciated long ago in the now-discarded *Cooley* case, local conditions do exist and often do cry out for local interventions.[108] Appreciating when population factors do and do not correlate with the political divisions we know as states can help federalism analysis to differentiate when it makes sense to allocate authority at a state level and when it does not. Of course, such an undertaking necessarily requires a willingness to forgo formalism and engage with the messy, contingent world of empirical epidemiology.

Likewise, the population perspective reminds us that not only are we all in multiple populations, but that different populations develop different social norms that may or may not be expressed in positive law and that help determine individual risks to disease and mortality. Federalism reflects this understanding by allowing for multiple forums in which citizens may come together as citizens to enact laws to shape and influence their environment.

Under the dormant commerce clause, such a population-based approach might counsel the abandonment of *Philadelphia's* per se test as well as a willingness to review more thoroughly state claims to be enacting on behalf of the police power. Such a review would require courts to dare to face the empirical world of epidemiology and public health. And it might just lead to the invalidation of some state laws that would today survive scrutiny by a judiciary reluctant to immerse itself in a world of inconclusive reports and confusing statistics. But such a review would also reduce the chances that regulations with the potential to protect a population's health will be thrown out simply because of the costs they impose on commerce. In effect, it would create a public health exception to free trade somewhat similar to that which theoretically exists under the World Trade Organization system.[109] It would also signal the important point that the state police power does matter.

At the same time, incorporating a population perspective into the determination of Congress's Article I powers would counsel that courts apply a pragmatic approach. Under this approach, courts would accept the New Deal's perception that there can be no strict division between commerce and public health. Both are inextricably tied to each other. This is not only because matters of commerce affect health and health affects commerce, but also because both are important and essential to the body politic for similar reasons: they are part of what is necessary to enable communities to flourish. Hence Congress's power necessarily implies the power to affect public health.

Yet, under population-based legal analysis, the recognition of the interrelationship between commerce and public health would not dictate adoption of the New Deal Court's laissez faire approach to federal power. To the contrary, population-based legal analysis emphasizes that one of the goals of federalism is to preserve governments' ability to improve the well-being of populations. This suggests that when Congress uses its Article I powers in a way that undermines the ability of states to develop effective, well-targeted interventions, in other words, when Congress degrades the ability of states to protect the health of their populations without offering an equally effective federal tool—for example, by preempting the state's ability to regulate the delivery of tobacco products to minors——courts should be wary.[110] Most obviously, in such situations courts should construe congressional statutes narrowly to preclude excessive preemption of state initiatives. At times, such an approach might lead courts to find that Congress has violated Article I by enacting laws in the name of commerce that in fact cannot be understood as anything other than attempts to address matters that are best left to the police power. Given the deep interconnections between commerce and health, such cases would be rare. They would, however, differ from *Gonzales, Lopez,* and many of the Court's other recent federalism cases because they would depend not upon an abstract regard for federal authority or state sovereignty but rather the ability of a population to achieve particular health objectives.

Notes

1. Select Bipartisan Committee to Investigate the Preparation for and Response to Hurricane Katrina, *A Failure of Initiative, The Final Report of the Select Bipartisan*

Senate Committee to Investigate the Preparation for and Response to Hurricane Katrina, http://katrina.house.gov/full_katrina_report.htm (last visited October 10, 2008).

2. Erin Ryan, *Federalism and the Tug of War Within: Seeking Checks and Balance in the Interjurisdictional Gray Area,* 66 MD. L. REV. 503, 525–27 (2007).

3. *E.g.,* Willson v. Black Bird Creek Marsh Co., 27 U.S. (2 Pet.) 245, 251 (1829).

4. Michael S. Morgenstern, *The Role of the Federal Government in Protecting Citizens from Communicable Diseases,* 47 U. CIN. L. REV. 537, 541–44 (1978).

5. James G. Hodge, Jr. & Lawrence O. Gostin, *School Vaccination Requirements: Historical, Social and Legal Perspectives,* 90 KY. L.J. 831, 844 (2001/2002).

6. Saenz v. Roe, 526 U.S. 489, 504 n. 17 (1999).

7. James G. Hodge, *Implementing Modern Public Health Goals through Government: An Examination of New Federalism and Public Health,* 14 J. CONTEMP. HEALTH L. & POL'Y 93, 94 (1997).

8. U.S. CONST. amend X; United States v. Darby, 312 U.S. 100, 124 (1941).

9. Gibbons v. Ogden, 22 U.S. (9 Wheat. 1) 207 (1824).

10. Willson v. Black Bird Creek Marsh Co., 27 U.S. (2 Pet.) 245 (1829).

11. Morgan's S.S. Co. v. Louisiana Bd. of Health, 118 U.S. 455 (1886).

12. M'Culloch v. Maryland, 17 U.S. (4 Wheat.) 316 (1819).

13. An Act for the Relief of Sick and Disabled Seamen, Ch. 77, 1 State. 605 (1798). For a history of early federal involvement in communicable disease control, see Morgenstern, *supra* note 4, at 541–44.

14. Pub. L. 89–97, 79 Stat. 290 (1965).

15. *E.g.,* United States v. Darby, 312 U.S. 100 (1941).

16. Pub. L. 91–596, 84 Stat. 1590 (1970).

17. Pub. L. 99–660, 100 Stat. 3756 (1986).

18. Ch. 675, 52 Stat. 1042 (June 25, 1938).

19. NATIONAL ACADEMY OF SCIENCES, THE FUTURE OF THE PUBLIC'S HEALTH IN THE 21ST CENTURY 105 (2003).

20. Gibbons v. Ogden, 22 U.S. at 209.

21. *E.g.,* Cooley v. Board of Wardens, 53 U.S. (12 How.) 299, 300 (1851).

22. *E.g.,* Brimmer v. Rebman, 138 U.S. 78, 83 (1891).

23. H.P. Hood & Sons, Inc. v. Du Mond, 336 U.S. 525, 539 (1949).

24. *E.g.,* Dean Milk Co. v. City of Madison, 340 U.S. 349 (1951).

25. *Id.* at 354.

26. Head v. New Mexico Bd. of Exam'rs in Optometry, 374 U.S. 424, 428 (1963).

27. Brown-Forman Distillers Corp. v. New York State Liquor Auth., 476 U.S. 573, 579 (1986).

28. Pike v. Bruce Church, Inc., 397 U.S. 137, 142 (1970).

29. 437 U.S. 617 (1978).

30. *Id.* at 618 (quoting N.J. State. Ann. § 13:17–15 (West Supp. 1978)).

31. *Id.* at 624.

32. *Id.* at 628.

33. *Id.* at 632–633 (Rehnquist, J., dissenting).

34. *See* text accompanying notes 103–04 *infra*.

35. 511 U.S. 383, 390 (1994).

36. *Id.* at 425 (Souter, J., dissenting).

37. 550 U.S. 124, 127 S. Ct. 1786 (2007).

38. 127 S. Ct. at 1794–95. The dissent, in contrast, argued that the facility in *Carbone* was effectively a public entity, even if it was nominally owned by a private party. *Id.* at 1803 (Alito, J., dissenting).

39. *Id.* at 1795.

40. *Id.* at 1796.

41. Edgar v. Mite Corp., 457 U.S. 624 (1982). *See also* Brown-Forman Distillers Corp. v. New York State Liquor Auth., 476 U.S. 573 (1986).

42. Healy v. The Beer Inst., 491 U.S. 324, 336 (1989). The Court may have reined in this doctrine somewhat in Pharmaceutical Research & Mfrs. of Am. v. Walsh, 538 U.S. 644 (2003) (upholding Maine's Medicaid Prescription Drug Program).

43. *E.g.*, Santa Fe Natural Tobacco Co. v. Spitzer, 2001 U.S. Dist. LEXIS 7548 (S.D.N.Y. 2001) *rev'd sub nom* Brown and Williamson Corp. v. Pataki, 320 F.3d 200 (2d Cir. 2003); American Library Ass'n v. Pataki, 969 F. Supp. 160 (S.D.N.Y. 1997).

44. 397 U.S. 137, 142 (1970).

45. Bibb v. Navajo Freight Lines, Inc., 359 U.S. 520, 524 (1959).

46. United Haulers Assoc., Inc. v. Oneida-Herkimer Solid Waste Mgmt. Auth., 127 S.Ct. at 1797.

47. 450 U.S. 662 (1981).

48. CTS Corp. v. Dynamics Corp. of Am., 481 U.S. 69, 95 (1987) (Scalia, J., dissenting in part and concurring in part); 450 U.S. at 678–706 (Brennan J., dissenting).

49. 218 F.3d 30 (1st Cir. 2000), *aff'd in part, rev'd in part sub nom.* Lorillard Tobacco Co. v. Reilly, 533 U.S. 525 (2001).

50. Dent v. West Virginia, 129 U.S. 114 (1889) (upholding medical licensing law against Fourteenth Amendment challenge).

51. For a discussion of the importance of global approaches to public health, see chapter 10, *infra*.

52. LAWRENCE O. GOSTIN, PUBLIC HEALTH LAW: POWER, DUTY, RESTRAINT 155–61 (2d. ed. 2008).

53. Pure Food Act, Ch. 3915, 34 Stat. 768 (1906).

54. United States v. Darby, 32 U.S. 100 (1941); Charles C. Steward Mach. Co. v. Davis, 301 U.S. 548 (1937).

55. 312 U.S. at 100; NLRB v. Jones & Laughlin Steel Corp., 301 U.S. 1 (1937); 301 U.S. at 548.

56. Susan Wall, *Transformations in Public Health Systems*, 17 HEALTH AFFAIRS 69 (1998).

57. U.S. CONST. ART. VI, CL. 2.

58. For example, the Employee Retirement Income Security Act of 1974, known as ERISA, explicitly precludes state regulation of self-insured employee benefit plans, including health plans, leaving states with only limited authority over employer-provided health insurance. *See* 29 U.S.C. § 1144 (a)(2000).

59. For a discussion of some of the reasons why this might be the case, see Roderick M. Hills, Jr., *Against Preemption: How Federalism Can Improve the National Legislative Process*, 82 N. Y. U. L. Rev. 1, 10–16 (2007).

60. Geier v. Am. Honda Motor Co., Inc. 529 U.S. 861, 884 (2000).

61. Stacy Allen Carroll, *Federal Preemption of State Products Liability Claims: Adding Clarity and Respect for State Sovereignty to the Analysis of Federal Preemption*, 36 Ga. L. Rev. 797, 800 (2002); Jean Macchiaroli Eggen, *The Normalization of Product Preemption Doctrine*, 57 Ala. L. Rev. 725, 726 (2006); Lars Noah, *Reconceptualizing Federal Preemption of Tort Claims as the Government Standards Defense*, 37 Wm. & Mary L. Rev. 903, 905 (1996).

62. *Requirements on Content and Format of Labeling for Human Prescription Drug and Biological Products*, 71 Fed. Reg. 3, 922, 3, 933–36 (Jan. 24, 2006) (to be codified at 21 C.F.R. pts 201, 314, 601).

63. Medtronic, Inc. v. Lohr, 518 U.S. 470 (1996).

64. *E.g.*, 529 U.S. at 861.

65. 552 U.S.__, 128 S.Ct. 989 (2008) (construing 49 U.S.C. § 14501(c)(1)).

66. *Id.* at 996.

67. Riegel v. Medtronic, Inc., 552 U.S. __, 128 S.Ct. 999 (2008).

68. Warner-Lambert Co. v. Kent, __ U.S. __, 128 S.Ct. 1168 (2008) (*aff'd mem*).

69. See note 61, *supra*.

70. 514 U.S. 549 (1995).

71. Heart of Atlanta Hotel, Inc. v. United States, 379 U.S. 241 (1964); Wickard v. Filburn, 317 U.S. 111 (1942).

72. Pub. L. 101–647, 104 Stat. 4789, 4844–845 (1990).

73. 514 U.S. at 562–65.

74. *Id.* at 567.

75. 529 U.S. 598 (2000).

76. P.L. 103–322, 108 Stat. 1941 (1994).

77. 529 at 628 (Souter, J., dissenting).

78. 545 U.S. 1 (2005).

79. *Id.* at 2210.

80. *Id.* at 33, 36 (Scalia, J., concurring).

81. *Id.* at 42–43 (O'Connor, J., dissenting).

82. *Id.* at 45.

83. 505 U.S. 144 (1992).

84. 521 U.S. 898 (1997).

85. *Id.* at 940 (Stevens, J., dissenting).

86. Charles C. Steward Mach. Co. v. Davis, 301 U.S. 548, 590 (1937).

87. New York v. United States, 505 U.S. 144 (1992).

88. 483 U.S. 203 (1987).

89. *Id.*

90. Arlington Central School Dist. Bd. of Educ. v. Murphy, 548 U.S. 291 (2006).

91. *E.g.*, Virginia Dep't of Educ. v. Riley, 106 F. 3d 559, 570–72 (4th Cir. 1997) (en banc); United States v. Sabri, 183 F. Supp. 2d 1145, 1155–159 (D. Minn. 2002),

rev'd in part, 326 F. 3d 937 (8th Cir. 2003), *aff'd mem.* 541 U.S. 600 (2004); Lynn A. Baker & Michael N. Berman, *Getting Off the Dole: Why the Court Should Abandon Its Spending Doctrine and How a Too-Clever Congress Could Provoke It to Do So*, 78 IND. L. J. 459, 471–74 (2003).

92. Nicole Huberfeld, *Clear Notice for Conditions on Spending, Unclear Implications for States in Federal Healthcare Programs*, 86 N.C.L. REV. 441, 476 (2008).

93. 514 U.S. at 581.

94. 42 U.S. C. § 710. *See* Christopher Trenholm et al., *Impacts of Four Title V, Section 510 Abstinence Education Program, Final Report* (2007), http://aspe.hhs.gov/hsp/abstinence07/report.pdf (last visited Mar. 3, 2008).

95. *Cf.* ANTONIN SCALIA, A MATTER OF INTERPRETATION: FEDERAL COURTS AND THE LAW 37–41 (Amy Gutmann ed., 1997) (offering a textualist theory of statutory and constitutional interpretation).

96. Ryan, *supra* note 2, at 24–25.

97. GORDON S. WOOD, THE CREATION OF THE AMERICAN REPUBLIC, 1776–1787 345–46 (1969).

98. THE FEDERALIST No. 51, at 291 (James Madison) (Clinton Rossiter ed., 1999).

99. 514 U.S. at 568, 576 (Kennedy, J., concurring).

100. 505 U.S. at 168–69.

101. THE FEDERALIST No. 15 (Alexander Hamilton) (Clinton Rossiter ed., 1999).

102. THE FEDERALIST No. 3 (John Jay) (Clinton Rossiter ed., 1999).

103. New State Ice Co. v. Liebmann, 285 U.S. 262, 311 (1932) (Brandeis, J. dissenting).

104. This argument is compatible with Hills's argument that state regulations can help to place health and safety issues on Congress's agenda. *See* Hills, *supra* note at 59, at 19–20.

105. U.S. Cancer Statistics Working Group, *United States Cancer Statistics:* 1999–2002 *Incidence and Mortality Web-Based Report* (2005), http://www.cdc.gov/cancer/npcr/uscs (last visited Oct. 10, 2008).

106. Centers for Disease Control and Prevention, *Women and Heart Disease Fact Sheet, Death Rates for Diseases of the Heart per 100,000 Women, 2002*, http://www.cdc.gov/DHDSP/library/fs_women_heart.htm (last visited Oct. 10, 2008).

107. *See* American Lung Association, *The State of the Air 2005*, http://environment.about.com/od/healthenvironment/a/stateofair.htm (last visited Oct. 10, 2008).

108. Cooley v. Board of Wardens, 53 U.S. (12 How.) 299, 319–20 (1852).

109. *See* David P. Fidler, *A Globalized Theory of Public Health Law*, 30 J.L. MED. & ETHICS 150, 157 (2002). For a further discussion, see chapter 10, *infra*.

110. *E.g.*, Rowe, 128 S.Ct. at 989.

CHAPTER 5

Individual Rights, Population Health, and Due Process

Achieving a just balance between constitutionally protected
rights and the powers and duties of the state to defend and
advance the public's health poses an enduring problem for
public health law.

—Lawrence O. Gostin, *Public Health Law:*
Power, Duty, Restraint

IN THE FALL OF 2001, as the nation struggled to come to terms with the
terrible events of 9/11, and anthrax spread through the United States
mail, the CDC commissioned the Center for Law and the Public's
Health at Georgetown and Johns Hopkins Universities to draft a model
state law updating and clarifying emergency powers that states could use
during a public health emergency. The subsequent publication of the
Model State Emergency Health Powers Act (MSEHPA), which sought to
give governors extraordinary powers and contained substantial provisions
authorizing isolation, quarantine, and mandatory medical examinations
and treatment, prompted a heated debate about the roles of government
coercion and individual liberty in public health protection.[1]

Although fears of bioterrorism have since receded somewhat, the controversy generated by the MSEHPA has not. Indeed, as the years have progressed, new public health threats—SARS (severe acute respiratory
syndrome), pandemic influenza, extensively drug-resistant tuberculosis—

have come to the fore. As they have done so, the debate about restrictive public health laws and civil liberties has continued. For example, during the SARS outbreak in 2003, the focus turned to the government's power to halt travel and impose wide-scale quarantines, as was done in parts of Asia and Canada.[2] Two years later, as the federal government planned its response to a possible influenza pandemic, President George W. Bush stated that he would consider using the military to enforce quarantines.[3] A few weeks later, CDC published proposed new quarantine regulations that would have expanded its power to detain individuals who were thought to have an infectious disease.[4]

By the spring of 2007, attention turned to drug-resistant tuberculosis when Atlanta attorney Andrew Speaker became the first American in more than forty years to be subject to a federal quarantine.[5] Speaker had been on his honeymoon in Europe when the CDC asked him to stay put after incorrectly diagnosing him with extensively drug-resistant tuberculosis (TB). Fearing isolation in a European hospital, Speaker evaded his inclusion on the no-fly list and border guards ordered to detain him by traveling to Prague and then to Montreal before driving into the United States. Once in New York, Speaker was detained and eventually flown to Denver for treatment. While he was there, Congress held hearings on the fiasco. The thrust of those hearings and the media coverage was clear: Speaker's actions demonstrated that public health protection requires tough laws.[6] In a dangerous age, when viruses can spread around the world in hours, many presumed that liberty must be exchanged for public health protection.

Is that in fact the case? If the protection and promotion of population health is a critical goal for the law, does that mean that individual rights must necessarily give way to tough public health measures? Does a population perspective compel a cramped view of individual liberty?

This chapter looks at those questions in the context of quarantine, one of the oldest and most coercive types of public health laws.[7] It first asks whether individual liberty and protection of population health are necessarily at odds. It then applies a population-based critique to due process law. This approach emphasizes the complementary relationship between individual liberty and population health and stresses the importance of using public health laws that broadly address population-based problems.

While validating the importance of public health protection, courts applying a population approach would look more critically than they now do at whether particular deprivations of individual liberty, such as quarantine, are actually an effective and least restrictive means of protecting the health of affected populations. This discussion paves the way for considering in later chapters the relationship between individual liberty and population health in other contexts.

INDIVIDUAL RIGHTS AND PUBLIC HEALTH: DO THEY CLASH?

Population-based legal theory postulates that law *ought* to protect and promote the health of populations. But at what cost to the interests and dignity of individuals or vulnerable populations?

In some sense, all enforceable laws limit the liberty of individuals. Some theorists, however, subscribe to what may be termed the conventional view, that there is an "inherent tension" between protecting the health of populations and the rights and interests of individuals.[8] This is the view reflected in the MSEHPA and other post-9/11 efforts to toughen public health laws.[9] It is also the view implicit in the remarks of Representative Bennie Thompson (D-MS), chair of the House Homeland Security Committee, when he asked in reaction to the case of Andrew Speaker, "When are we going to stop dodging bullets and start protecting Americans?"[10]

More deeply, the conventional view resonates with widely held liberal notions about individual autonomy, the role of individual choice in determining individual health, and the relationship of individuals to populations. If individuals are assumed to be the masters of their own health, and if populations are viewed as mere aggregations of individuals, then the health of populations can be seen as a function of individual choices. Hence, protecting population health appears to require the restriction of individual choices that pose dangers to others, such as Speaker's choice to fly across the Atlantic with TB. As Lawrence Gostin, the principal drafter of the MSEHPA has forcibly argued, classical liberal theory supports the restriction of individual behaviors that pose a significant risk to others.[11] According to Gostin, "infectious disease regulations targeted towards individuals who pose risks of tangible and immediate harm to others . . . are well within traditional liberal understandings of the legitimate role of the state. Consequently, liberals would be expected to support liberty-limiting infectious disease control measures (e.g., vaccination, physical examination, treatment and quarantine) at least in high-risk circumstances."[12]

Yet, from a population perspective that is mindful of the interdependence of health and the social roots of individual preferences, the story seems more complex. First, in a world in which hundreds of thousands of people have drug-resistant forms of TB, and untold numbers travel with the disease every day, the focus on one man, Speaker, and the need to restrain him seems distracting if not strange.[13] Second, because individual choices are themselves partially constructed by the environment, including the legal environment, the emphasis on restricting, if not punishing, individual choices as if they were made in a vacuum, rather than seeking to change the environment in which individuals exercise and develop their choices, seems ill directed. Once we recognize the population basis of the problem and the potential strength of population-based interventions, the claim that public health protection requires the restriction of individual liberty becomes both theoretically and empirically problematic.

Nevertheless, history cautions that public health laws have often focused on and have frequently scapegoated particular individuals and vulnerable populations. The Nazis, after all, perpetrated some of their earliest atrocities in the name of promoting the health and vigor of their race.[14] In this country, a similar enthusiasm for eugenics led to the forced sterilization of Carrie Buck and thousands of other poor, young women.[15] Years later, in the infamous Tuskegee Study, the U.S. Public Health Service misled and failed to treat poor, mostly black, men with syphilis in an effort to learn more about that disease.[16]

These well-known abuses are not isolated cases. Throughout history, infectious epidemics have been frequently met with discrimination and gross denials of individual liberty. In the early twentieth century, for example, public health officials in San Francisco greeted the appearance of bubonic plague with racially based vaccination and quarantine programs, overlooking the rights, needs, and dignity of San Francisco's Chinese American residents.[17] During this same period, public health officials in Boston responded to an outbreak of smallpox by bringing guards to the railroad yards and forcibly vaccinating "Italians, negroes (sic) and other employees."[18]

The question raised by such examples is whether the conventional view is correct: does public health protection necessarily require limiting individual liberty? Or, does public health protection provide a pretext for the abridgment of individual rights and the mistreatment of minorities? In fact, the population perspective suggests that the conflict between individual liberty and population health is neither as inevitable nor as deep as the conventional view suggests. After all, as discussed in chapter 1, many of the most important public health efforts of the nineteenth century promoted public health by using law to provide clean water, safe homes, and wholesome foods.[19] Although these efforts necessarily relied to some degree on the coercive power of the state in that they depended ultimately on the government's ability to tax and regulate, the coercion of individuals was certainly not a central feature of these reforms. Rather, they used law to alter the environment faced by broad populations. The effective limitation of individual rights was trivial, at least compared with quarantine and like laws that severely restrict the movement and autonomy of individuals.

Certainly in the late nineteenth and early twentieth centuries, public health practitioners increasingly turned their attention to the role that individuals played in the spread of disease. It was during this period that mandatory vaccination, contact tracing, and even isolation and quarantine were widely used. Still, even in this period, when public health officials felt most confident about using law in a paternalistic and often highly coercive manner, many advocates emphasized the importance of educating rather than coercing the public.[20]

By the time of the HIV epidemic in the 1980s and 1990s, public health officials in the United States and in many other nations concluded that they had to work with rather than against high-risk populations to have to have any success in stemming the epidemic.[21] Some scholars contend that the approach taken with respect to HIV was "exceptional"[22] and deviated from the historic public health approach, but the historical record, as we have seen, presents a more mixed picture.[23]

Advocates of environmental changes or voluntary approaches argue that they are both more respectful of autonomy and more apt to be effective than heavy-handed restrictions of liberty.[24] To explain that somewhat counterintuitive conclusion, opponents of coercive public health laws point to the important role that trust plays in promoting population health.

According to Patricia Illingworth, trust is a social good that facilitates reciprocity and social cooperation.[25] As such, trust may be essential for the successful implementation of policies that require individuals to act for the good of others or, as Thomas Glass and Monica Schoch-Spana have written, "the public will not take the pill if it does not trust the doctor."[26] Thus highly coercive or discriminatory policies that erode the trust of affected groups may actually undermine rather than promote population health. For example, when Milwaukee public health officials responded to an 1894 smallpox outbreak by forcibly moving immigrants and poor residents to a smallpox hospital, a riot ensued.[27] More recently, peasants and farmers rioted in China when health officials proposed quarantining asymptomatic individuals during the SARS outbreak.[28]

A related but more fundamental argument against the conventional view was articulated by Jonathan Mann, who was heavily influenced by his work with the HIV epidemic in Africa. Mann argued that respect for human rights, by which he meant the universal moral rights reflected in international law, helps promote, not undermine, the health of populations.[29] This is so for several reasons. First, some deprivations of human rights, such as genocide or torture, directly harm health. Second, sometimes the health of a population cannot be improved unless and until some human rights are secured. Mann noticed, for example, that campaigns to stop the spread of HIV in Africa were often ineffective when women lacked control over their sexual experiences. In the case of HIV, rights of sexual freedom and equality for women serve not as limits on but as foundations for population health.

Further support for Mann's observation comes in the work of social epidemiologists who have noted the intriguing association between equality and population health. Although it is well known that a society's health is correlated with its overall wealth, several studies have suggested that the distribution of wealth within a society, or the degree of inequality within it, also influences its health.[30] If this so-called relative-income hypothesis is correct, then, as Norman Daniels and colleagues have argued, "justice [may be] good for our health."[31] In other words, laws and policies that curtail discrimination and oppression may protect the health of different populations within a society. Conversely, highly coercive laws or those that reinforce an unequal distribution of resources may undermine population health.

Ultimately the question whether the conventional view is correct, and the protection of population health relies more on laws that starkly limit individual liberty or on respect for liberty and equality, is an empirical one that depends on multiple factors, including the nature of the health threat, whether the law is based on a sound scientific understanding of the epidemiology, and the existing relationship between a particular population and its government. Calls for voluntary quarantines may thus have been more effective when SARS struck Toronto than they would be in the United States because cooperation and social solidarity are more pronounced in Canada than in the United States.[32]

In any case, the argument that trust, cooperation, nondiscrimination, and respect for liberty may promote population health does not deny that conflicts sometimes exist between laws that promote a population's health and individual liberties. Rather, it reminds us that population health does not necessarily depend on pointing the strong arm of the state at particular individuals. Some conflicts between population health and individual liberty may be inevitable, but they are not the key to the relationship between population health and law.

Positive and Negative Rights

The discussion so far has presupposed specific understandings of the terms *liberty* and *rights*. Indeed, the dispute between those who hold and those who reject the conventional view derives largely from differing conceptions of liberty and rights. When proponents of the conventional view assume the inevitability of a clash between individual rights and population health, they rely on two assumptions about individual liberty and rights, both of which stand in sharp contrast to the tenets of the population perspective. First, proponents of the conventional view assume that liberty and rights are primarily negative, relating to individuals' desires to be left unrestrained. Second, proponents presuppose that individuals use their liberty and legal rights to make choices that are exogenous to social life.

These assumptions are closely connected to what C. B. Macpherson has coined *possessive individualism*, which holds that each individual is a "proprietor of his own person and capacities, owing nothing to society for them."[33] From this perspective, the autonomous choice that an individual seeks to exercise is independent from both the environment and the populations of which the individual is a member. Moreover, because possessive individualism values autonomy so highly, it posits that individuals have a moral right or claim to exercise their autonomy, except under limited circumstances, such as when their actions harm another.[34] Interestingly, once such liberties are coined rights, it becomes easy to assume that they are or at least ought to be recognized as such by the law. Hence, even if a court has not found a right of an individual to defy a motorcycle helmet law or to ignore a compulsory vaccination law, civil libertarians can and do criticize such laws as infringing on individual rights.

The population perspective paints a very different picture. Rather than framing choices as exogenous to social life, and liberty as protecting an individual's interest in being left alone, the perspective emphasizes the role that populations play in influencing individual choices, opportunities, and risks. Hence, scholars that share many of the views of the population perspective, such as Jonathan Mann or Norman Daniels, are less apt than traditional liberals to envision rights as trumps against the state. They emphasize instead so-called positive rights, which provide individuals with what they need to realize their own preferences. As a result, when Mann and Daniels argue that rights are necessary or at least conducive to public health, they are not referring simply to the negative rights traditionally recognized by a liberal state, but also to theoretical positive rights, such as those to education or public health, that could enhance the opportunities available to individuals and improve the social determinants of health.[35]

A positive right to population health protection would differ from a traditional negative right not only because it would presuppose an action rather than restraint on the part of government but also because it would be less individualistic. Indeed, the recognition of a positive right to population health necessarily assumes that individuals cannot fulfill all of their goals, which presumably includes being healthy, without the assistance or support of others. In addition, the recognition of positive rights is based on the premise that individuals cannot satisfy their own preferences or choices wholly apart from the populations in which they exist. Thus, the claim for a right to promotion of population health sees individuals as interdependent and situated within populations.

The distinction between positive and negative rights helps explain the debate between adherents of the conventional view and their critics. It also suggests that each side of the debate is in part correct. Holders of the conventional view rightly observe that laws that promote population health frequently invade or conflict with negative liberties, including those that have been recognized as rights by positive law in the Unites States. On the other hand, critics of the conventional view observe with equal veracity that such laws may, at times, support positive rights to population health.

This analysis suggests several points critical to a discussion of constitutional rights and population health. First, laws that are enacted in the name of public health can be viewed from a liberal, individualistic perspective as potential infringements on individual liberty. Yet, to the extent that such laws promote the health of populations (and of course, that a law is claimed to do so does not mean that it does so), they can also be seen as supporting the positive right to population health. Finally, that both statements are true helps explain why the relationship between individual rights and population health is both complex and problematic. In American domestic law, it typically falls to constitutional law, particularly under the due process clauses of the Fifth and Fourteenth Amendments, to mediate and resolve these tensions.

THE POLICE POWER AND DUE PROCESS

Conflicts between individual interests and public health have always existed, but they have not always been understood as raising constitutional questions. In the antebellum period, the federal government enacted relatively few laws relating to public health. States, on the other hand, instituted a wide variety of measures aimed at protecting the public's health, from quarantines to laws regulating the practice of trades.[36] Occasionally, these laws were challenged in court as violating an individual's rights. Almost always these challenges were in state court based on state statutory or common law grounds. The U.S. Constitution was not implicated because it was not viewed as giving individuals many rights against their states.

One of the earliest appellate cases to deal with the clash between individual liberty and a core public health law was heard by the Massachusetts Supreme Judicial Court. In *In re Vandine*, Justice Putnam upheld a Boston sanitary ordinance requiring individuals who collected house dirt and offal to be licensed.[37] Recognizing that "every regulation of trade is in some sense a restraint upon it,"[38] Justice Putnam noted that "the great object of the city is to preserve the health of the inhabitants."[39] Because house dirt and offal were "sources of contagion and disease," the court agreed that the city could require a license. Moreover, the court suggested, there could be no right to disregard a law designed to protect public health.

The court's approach in *Vandine* was followed in the more famous *Commonwealth v. Alger*.[40] *Alger* challenged a Massachusetts statute that prohibited the erection of a wharf beyond certain harbor lines. In finding that the statute did not derogate the defendant's property rights, Chief Justice Shaw commented on the nature of the state's police power, noting that "rights of property, like all other social and conventional rights, are subject to such reasonable limitations in their enjoyment, as shall prevent them from being injurious, and to such reasonable restraints and regulations established by law, as the legislature, under the governing and controlling power vested in them by the constitution, may think necessary and expedient."[41] The chief justice then explained that when the police power was used to limit an individual's use of property, the state was not taking property, it was instead simply limiting a use that was noxious or injurious. Under the common law maxim, *sic utere tuo, ut alienum non laedas* (use your own property so as not to injure others), individuals had no right to harm others.[42]

It was only after the Civil War and the ratification of the Fourteenth Amendment that cases such as *Alger* or *Vandine* could be litigated under the federal constitution and clothed in the language of constitutional rights. Ratified in 1868 and enacted largely to ensure the constitutionality of the Civil Rights Act of 1866, the Fourteenth Amendment contained new and broad promises of individual rights that could be used to limit the police power of the states.[43] Most important, Section 1 echoed the Fifth Amendment's guarantee of due process of law by stating that "no State shall make or enforce any law which shall abridge the privileges or immunities of citizens of the United States; nor shall any State deprive any person of life, liberty, or property, without due process of law; nor deny to any person within its jurisdiction the equal protection of the laws."[44] With the enactment of the Fourteenth Amendment, individuals who felt that state police power laws infringed on their liberty could now assert that the Constitution gave them a legal right to trump the state.

The first set of Supreme Court cases making such Fourteenth Amendment claims resembled *Vandine* in numerous respects. In the so-called

Slaughter-House cases, the Court considered a challenge by a group of butchers to a Louisiana statute that regulated slaughtering in New Orleans and required, among other things, that all butchering occur on property operated by the Crescent City Livestock Company.[45] According to the butchers, the state had violated their privileges and immunities as citizens of Louisiana as well as their rights to due process and equal protection of the law by granting Crescent City a monopoly. Chief Justice Miller's majority opinion rejected all of these claims.

In the most famous part of the opinion, the Chief Justice provided a narrow construction to the Fourteenth Amendment's Privileges and Immunities Clause, finding that it applied only to federally granted privileges, not to privileges of state citizenship.[46] To some commentators, this interpretation eviscerated the amendment's capacity to redress the discrimination that freedmen faced in the former confederate states.[47] For our purposes, however, the more significant part of Chief Justice's Miller opinion is the brief introduction that focused on the nature of the police power and its relationship to the new constitutional amendment.

In his introduction, Chief Justice Miller noted that "from its very nature, [the police power is] incapable of any very exact definition or limitation."[48] Nevertheless, on that power "depends the security of social order, the life and health of the citizen, the comfort of an existence in a thickly populated community."[49] Hence, the chief justice argued, a state's exercise of that power must be upheld by a court, "unless some restraint in the exercise of that power be found in the constitution of that State or in the amendments to the Constitution of the United States."[50]

Applying those principles to the Louisiana law before him, Chief Justice Miller had no doubt that the law was a proper exercise of the police power. He quoted the great New York jurist Chancellor Kent: "'Unwholesome trades, slaughter-houses, operations offensive to the senses, the deposit of powder, the application of steam power to propel cars, the building with combustible materials, and the burial of the dead, may all,' says Chancellor Kent, 'be interdicted by law, in the midst of dense masses of population, on the general and rational principle, that every person ought so to use his property as not to injure his neighbors; and that private interests must be made subservient to the general interests of the community.'"[51]

Miller then asserted that the regulation of butchering and the inspection of animals to be killed for meat are among the "most necessary" exercises of the police power and that unless a challenger could show that the state had exercised its power in an impermissible way, the statute must be found constitutional.[52] That conclusion applied whether the challenge was under the Fourteenth Amendment's Privilege and Immunities Clause, its Due Process Clause, or its Equal Protection Clause. In all cases, a law that was within the boundaries of the police power because it sought to prevent harm to the community was constitutional.

Given that the case was decided when many still believed that the miasma from decaying animals caused disease and that New Orleans, in particular, suffered from horrific epidemics of yellow fever, Miller's conclusion was not surprising.[53] A few points, however, are worth emphasizing. First, the Court accepted that a challenge to a traditional state public health measure could be brought under the Fourteenth Amendment. By so deciding, the Court paved the way for further federal constitutional review of laws designed to protect public health. Yet the Court followed the reasoning of earlier common law cases such as *Commonwealth v. Alger* in presuming that constitutional rights could not trump the police power because the former ended where the latter began.

In two separate dissents, Justices Bradley and Field offered a very different analysis. Although they accepted Chief Justice Miller's conclusion that the Fourteenth Amendment did not preclude states from using the police power to protect public health, they questioned whether the Louisiana statute was a legitimate exercise of that power.

According to Justice Field, only two aspects of the Louisiana law qualified as a legitimate exercise of the police power: those requiring the landing and slaughtering of animals below the City of New Orleans and those requiring the inspection of the animals. The monopoly provisions, on the other hand, were not necessary for sanitation or health and therefore were not a bona fide exercise of the police power.[54] According to Justice Field, "under the pretence of prescribing a police regulation the State cannot be permitted to encroach upon any of the just rights of the citizen, which the Constitution intended to secure against abridgement."[55] Most important, to Justice Field, the Fourteenth Amendment was designed to "give practical effect to the declaration of 1776 of inalienable rights, rights which are the gift of the Creator, which the law does not confer, but only recognizes" and which include the right to pursue one's calling in conformity with legitimate police power regulations.[56] In other words, the Fourteenth

Amendment constitutionalized natural law rights and empowered courts to protect those rights against the state. This view implies that there may be times when the police power, or at least government actions undertaken in its name, will need to be limited to protect inalienable rights.

In his dissent, Justice Bradley advanced the same theme. To him, the Fourteenth Amendment codified certain individual rights created by natural law: "The right of personal security, the right of personal liberty, the right of private property. . . . These are the fundamental rights which can only be taken away by due process of law, and which can only be interfered with, or the enjoyment of which can only be modified, by lawful regulations necessary or proper for the mutual good of all."[57] Like Justice Field, Justice Bradley viewed these rights as pre-social, external limits on state power.

The contrast between Justice Miller's majority opinion and the dissenting opinions in *Slaughter-House* illustrates two very different approaches to how courts can apply the Fourteenth Amendment to state laws that purport to protect public health. Chief Justice Miller's approach was traditionalist, grounded in common law assumptions about the relationship of individual rights and the police power. This view incorporated existing notions about the police power into Fourteenth Amendment doctrine, assuming that if a law was reasonably aimed at protecting public health, it did not violate the Fourteenth Amendment. Perhaps more important, the traditional view accepted the importance of the police power and assumed that litigants who challenged an exercise of the police power had the burden of establishing that it was, as Justice Harlan suggested in *Jacobson v. Massachusetts*, "unreasonable, arbitrary and oppressive."[58]

As Lawrence Gostin suggests, this approach reflects the influence of social compact theory.[59] It views the police power as prior to liberty. Hence, reasonable exercises of the police power cannot limit liberty. Less obviously, although traditionalist judges did not speak of positive rights, their emphasis on the importance of the police power and their view of public health protection as a necessity, provides at least rhetorical support for asserting a positive duty on the part of the state to protect population health.[60]

In sharp contrast, the dissenting opinions in *Slaughter-House* were more protective of negative individual liberty and less supportive of government interventions aimed at promoting public health. This view achieved its greatest influence during the previously discussed *Lochner* period,[61] though echoes of it remain in more recent cases.[62] For present purposes, several distinctions between the *Lochner*-era and traditional approaches are worth emphasizing. First, the *Lochner* approach was predicated on the existence of clear boundaries between the police power and individual liberty. Second, the *Lochner* approach accepted that individuals have pre-existing rights. Third, the doctrine assumed that those rights were not limited to those enumerated within the Constitution but instead encompassed a larger set of negative liberties derivable from natural law. Finally, the approach postulated that it was the responsibility of the judiciary to protect such rights from an overreaching state. As a result, the courts became border guards entrusted to keep the police power within its limited terrain.

Both the traditional and *Lochner* approaches were subject to sharp attack by the legal realists and were ultimately rejected during the New Deal. In the wake of Roosevelt's court-packing plan, the Supreme Court adopted a third, still influential approach that relied far less on either traditional conceptions of the police power or natural rights. This approach granted public health protection a far lesser role on the constitutional stage.[63]

The New Deal approach is well illustrated by the Supreme Court's analysis in *Williamson v. Lee Optical*, which affirmed a state law prohibiting opticians from fitting prescription lenses without a prescription.[64] The state argued that its law was designed to protect the health of eyeglass users and thus was within the state's police power. Under a traditional approach, the Court would likely have affirmed the state law simply because it was a traditional and reasonable exercise of the police power. In contrast, under the *Lochner* approach, the Court would have been far more skeptical of the state's assertion of authority and more protective of the right of an optician to practice his or her profession. Nevertheless, because the regulation concerned health, the Court may have still concluded that the state regulation fell on the police power side of the police power–individual rights boundary. Under either approach, that the state law targeted health would have been critical to the case's outcome.

Not so under the New Deal approach. Reacting to the *Lochner*-era Court's willingness to place strict boundaries on the police power in order to protect so-called fundamental rights, the *Williamson* Court went to the opposite extreme, granting even greater deference to the state than the traditionalists did. According to Justice Douglas, "the Oklahoma law may exact a needless, wasteful requirement in many cases. But it is for the legislature, not the courts, to balance the advantages and disadvantages of the new requirement."[65] As long as there was "an evil at hand for correction, and it might be thought that the particular legislative measure was a rational way to correct it," the state law would be upheld.[66]

The New Deal Court thus differed from the earlier approaches in several critical ways. First, in contrast to *Lochner*, the Court did not see its role as protecting individual rights against the police power. Nor did it put the burden on the state to defend its regulation. Rather, in *Williamson*, the Court held that as long as the state had a rational basis, the legislation would be upheld.

Although the deference the New Deal Court gave to the state bears some resemblance to that accorded by the traditional approach, there are subtle but important differences. Under the traditional approach two questions were critical: did the state purport to pursue a legitimate police power goal, such as the promotion or protection of public health, and if so, did it do so in a reasonable manner?[67] In asking the latter question, the Court did not second-guess the legislature. For example, in *Jacobson v. Massachusetts*, the Court made clear that it would not strike down a statute simply because an alternative public health theory could be presented that questioned the appropriateness of the state's vaccine law.[68] In contrast, after the New Deal, the Court no longer paid much attention to whether the state sought a traditional police power objective. Nor did the Court demand that the statute constitute a reasonable effort to achieve the state's goal. Rather, the Court applied the more lenient rationality standard, under which the statute was found constitutional as long as there was a hypothetical justification for it. Empirical evidence was not essential.

Thus the New Deal Court was far more deferential to state legislatures than earlier courts had been. At the same time, the New Deal approach was also less mindful of the importance of public health to constitutional decision making. After the New Deal, the actual or even potential efficacy or relationship of the state's law to population health was no longer essential or even relevant to the law's constitutionality. At the same time, the language in traditionalist opinions that could be read as endorsing the importance of population health was gone. In effect, all affirmative state goals were treated as the same—merely as outcomes of legislative determinations. Missing was any appreciation of the importance of population health protection to the development of or justification for the police power. Missing also was an understanding of the role that populations play in framing individual interests and liberties as well as epidemiology's value in helping courts review state infringements on liberty.

CONTEMPORARY DUE PROCESS LAW

The New Deal jurisprudence left major questions unanswered: were there any limits to the police power? If the courts would no longer assume a clear boundary between appropriate, that is, traditional, exercises of the police power and the realm of individual liberty, was there any room left for judicial protection of rights under the due process clause?

Almost immediately it became clear that the answers to both questions were yes. Despite the majoritarianism of the New Deal jurisprudence, the Court did not abandon the due process clause or cease to protect individual rights. Rather, it focused its protection on some favored rights and continued to neglect the importance of population health.

One influential approach to deciding what rights should be protected was offered in *United States v. Carolene Products Co.*, a 1938 case involving a federal rather than state law.[69] In its decision, the Supreme Court rejected a Fifth Amendment due process challenge to a federal statute regulating so-called filled milk. In so doing, Justice Stone inserted his famous footnote 4 that set forth criteria for determining when courts should provide a "narrower scope for operation of the presumption of constitutionality," in other words, for deciding when courts should protect individual rights.[70] Less deference, he suggested, might be appropriate when the legislation "appears on its face to be within a specific prohibition of the Constitution, such as those of the first ten Amendments," when the legislation "restricts those political processes which can ordinarily be expected to bring about repeal of undesirable legislation," or when it is directed at particular racial, religious, or "discrete and insular minorities."[71]

Significantly, the framework that Justice Stone proposed offered no role for an assessment of the nature of the state's goal or its efficacy. Rather, the level of judicial review would depend solely on the nature of the individual or group interest that was infringed upon. To be sure, by suggesting that enhanced judicial review was appropriate when a law was directed at vulnerable groups, Justice Stone seemed to recognize, as a judge using population-based legal analysis would, that laws can target particular groups. However, what Justice Stone did not see, and what the Court has too often failed to appreciate in the following decades, is that laws that are not aimed at different groups may still have important disparate impacts on different populations. Moreover, populations consist not only of specified and discrete groups, but also varied and overlapping groups.

In the years since *Carolene Products* and the New Deal, the Court largely adopted Justice Stone's footnote 4 suggestion and incorporated most but not all of the rights enumerated in the Bill of Rights into the Due Process Clause of the Fourteenth Amendment.[72] Likewise, under its equal protection analysis, the Court came to apply strict scrutiny to laws that were directed at racial or ethnic minorities.[73] Moreover, as is well known, the Court decided in the 1970s to provide so-called intermediate scrutiny to laws that discriminate on the basis of gender.[74]

More controversial has been the Supreme Court's determination that the due process clause protects other so-called fundamental rights, including the right to privacy.[75] The debate over the Court's fundamental rights jurisprudence has been heated. Some justices and scholars, known often as originalists, have argued that the set of fundamental rights should be limited to those rights recognized by the Framers of the Fourteenth Amendment. Others have argued that the Constitution's text is purposefully open-ended and that it is necessarily the job of courts to look to the broader principles set forth in the Constitution and in the nation's legal heritage, and perhaps even in international legal principles, to determine what rights are fundamental. In the background of these debates are deep cultural and social divisions within society as well as the long-standing controversy about the role of courts in a democratic polity.

For our purposes, these heated debates are less important than that in most cases the key question becomes the nature of the individual claim—does it warrant recognition as a constitutionally protected right—rather than the aim or impact of the state's action on population health. Thus frequently the determination of whether a right is deemed fundamental is effectively dispositive of a case regardless of the law's merits.[76]

For example, in *Abigail Alliance for Better Access to Developmental Drugs v. Von Eschenbach*, the D.C. Court of Appeals considered the claim that a dying individual has a constitutional right under the Due Process Clause to use investigational drugs that have yet to be licensed by the Food and Drug Administration.[77] The court's majority found against the claimants on theory that there was "no fundamental right . . . of access to experimental drugs for the terminally ill."[78] In reaching this decision, the court looked to the "nation's history, legal traditions, and practices" and emphasized that American governments have historically regulated drugs to ensure safety to individual users.[79] In addition and in full accordance with the post–New Deal approach to the due process clause, the court noted that "the democratic branches are better suited to decide the proper balance between the uncertain risks and benefits of medical technology, and are entitled to deference in doing so."[80] In contrast, the dissent argued that the nation's legal history established a fundamental and personal right of dying individuals to use experimental drugs.[81]

What neither the majority nor the dissent explored was the decision's ramifications for drug safety and thereby the health of different populations. Nor did any of the judges ask whether the FDA's regulatory scheme served to enhance the positive liberty of individuals who require and use prescription drugs. Thus the court never asked whether the law added to or diminished liberty. Rather, the discussion was limited to whether the negative, individual right that the plaintiff to sought to have recognized was fundamental.

Even when courts do not emphasize the fundamental nature of the individual right at issue, they still tend to focus on the individual nature of the claim and harm. For example, in *Lawrence v. Texas*, which struck down laws criminalizing sodomy between consenting adults, Justice Kennedy wrote, "Liberty presumes an autonomy of self that includes freedom of thought, belief, expression, and certain intimate conduct. The instant case involves liberty of the person both in its spatial and more transcendent dimensions."[82] Thus although Justice Kennedy did not focus on the fundamental nature of the right at hand, he still emphasized the importance of individual autonomy, rather than the impact of the state's law on an already stigmatized population.[83] In contrast, in dissent Justice Scalia challenged the constitutional worthiness of the individual claim.[84] Arguing that neither history nor precedent supported finding a fundamental right of adults to engage in sodomy, Justice Scalia argued that the law was constitutional merely to express the disdain of the majority of people in Texas for same-sex sodomy. Justice Scalia did not care, however, if the state law failed to provide any empirically verifiable benefit to any population, nor did he care if laws against sodomy harmed a population. Rather, he would have upheld the law simply because the individual claim was not a historically recognized, fundamental right.[85]

Only occasionally in recent decades have the Supreme Court justices suggested that the relationship between autonomy and state action might be deeper and more complex than is usually portrayed. For example, in *Washington v. Glucksberg*, the majority upheld a state's ban on physician-assisted suicide by concluding that there was no historical or legal basis for finding that an individual had a fundamental right to assistance in committing suicide.[86] In a concurring opinion, however, Justice Souter suggested that the question before the Court could not be resolved simply on the basis of the historical pedigree of the individual's claim: "Just as results in substantive due process cases are tied to the selections of statements of the competing interests, the acceptability of the results is a function of the good reasons for the selections made. It is here that the value of common-law method becomes apparent, for the usual thinking of the common law is suspicious of the all-or-nothing analysis that tends to produce legal petrifaction instead of an evolving boundary between the domains of old principles. Common law method tends to pay respect instead to detail."[87]

Following that advice, Justice Souter looked closely at the rationales for the state's law. Finding that the law helped protect vulnerable patients from involuntary euthanasia, he concluded that the law should be upheld. But he suggested that his conclusion was not necessarily a final one. Because he saw the analysis as depending on facts and contexts that could change, he concluded that the answer as to whether the law was constitutional could change. In effect, the empirical world mattered.

Although distinct doctrinally, Justice Souter's approach in *Glucksberg* has much in common with an earlier line of Supreme Court cases that includes *O'Connor v. Donaldson*,[88] which held that illness alone does not justify commitment, and *Addington v. Texas*,[89] which held that a person cannot be civilly committed unless the state proves by clear and convincing evidence that the individual is dangerous to him- or herself or others. In these cases, which lie at the intersection between substantive and so-called procedural due process, the state unquestionably infringed on an individual's negative liberty. Yet, without ever deciding whether the liberty at issue was fundamental, the Court placed limits on when and how the state may civilly commit someone. In so doing, the Court effectively recognized that the state's goal matters. Likewise, by stressing in *Addington* the importance of procedural protections to determine whether a particular commitment would meet a state's goal, the Court implicitly accepted that the state's evidence matters. Still, as shall be suggested, these cases fall far short of applying a population approach that looks deeply at the nature of the impact of the state's laws on varying populations.

In many ways, however, the civil commitment cases are an anomaly; they do not represent the core of substantive due process law. The cases that do, such as *Glucksberg*, emphasize the nature of the right of an individual as an individual rather than the relationship between the individual and the multiple populations in which his or her health and well-being is determined. As a result, the question whether a state's law actually promotes or even undermines the health of populations is rarely central to a court's analysis. This means that states have less need to attend to empirical evidence and consider whether a law is actually well suited to the goals its advocates claim. Lawmakers can take credit for protecting public health by enacting laws, such as those that criminalize sexual activity for individuals who are HIV positive or ban partial birth abortions, without having to demonstrate that the laws actually serve their intended purpose.[90] Grandstanding suffices.

In addition, to the extent that judicial doctrines express and inculcate public values, the majoritarianism of the post–New Deal doctrine imparts a problematic message: the improvement of the health of populations is neither a serious nor an important public value. In contrast to earlier cases such as *Slaughter-House*, *Jacobson*, and even *Lochner*, courts today do not treat the advancement of population health as either a central goal of law or a critical factor in constitutional cases. As a result, there is little in contemporary opinions from which to conclude that the Constitution creates any duties, even only moral duties, on the part of states to promote population health.[91]

The result is a doctrine that all too often fails to consider the diversity of populations as well as the negative and positive aspects of liberty. In contemporary due process cases, courts generally defer to the state or focus on an abstract and arid determination of the "fundamentalness" of the individual right. Lost in the fray is the critical recognition that an individual interest does not and cannot stand totally apart from the interests of the varied populations to which the individual belongs. Lost also is a meaningful assessment of the nature and impact of the state's action on the relevant populations.

A POPULATION-BASED DUE PROCESS

To see how a population-based legal approach would alter the analysis of cases arising under the Due Process Clause, consider the constitutional status of quarantine. Although public health practitioners distinguish quarantine from the isolation of people who are ill, legal discussions have generally applied the term *quarantine* to any restriction of an individual's movement or contact with others to prevent the spread of an infectious disease. Hence quarantine undeniably limits an individual's negative liberty in the name of public health.

Historically courts have been quick to assume that states have the power to impose a quarantine to prevent the spread of a disease. Indeed, during the traditionalist period, when the scope of the police power was equated with efforts to protect public health, courts were emphatic about the state's power to quarantine. For example, in 1876, the Supreme Court of Maine rejected a constitutional challenge to the removal of a sick child from its mother to a smallpox hospital: "It is unquestionable, that the legislature can confer police powers upon public officers, for the protection of the public health. The maxim *salus populi suprema lex* is the law of all courts and countries. The individual right sinks in the necessity to provide for the public good."[92]

During the mid-twentieth century, after the development of antibiotics and vaccines that proved effective against many infectious diseases, quarantine was less often needed or used. During this period, the post–New Deal approach to the Due Process Clause made the once simple identification of quarantine with the police power an inadequate answer to the question whether quarantine was constitutional.[93]

Surprisingly, under contemporary doctrine, the constitutionality of quarantine remains elusive. On the one hand, quarantine limits a long-recognized, thus likely to be found fundamental, aspect of individual liberty—freedom of movement. On the other hand, the practice of quarantine is well established in the law and no court has questioned that it may be used under some circumstances. Perhaps for this reason, courts have wisely resisted the temptation to apply the all-or-nothing approach suggested by mainstream substantive due process analysis. Instead, following the lead of the West Virginia Supreme Court of Appeals,[94] modern courts have looked to the civil commitment cases and have focused on two factors: whether the state has afforded the individual with adequate procedural protections and, less often, whether the state has shown that quarantine is the least restrictive alternative.[95]

Although commentators have focused much of their discussion of quarantine on its applicability in a massive public health emergency, such as the type that the MSEHPA was designed to address, much of the case law arises from an epidemic of multidrug-resistant tuberculosis in the early 1990s. At the time, many public health officials attributed the outbreak to the confluence of the HIV epidemic (people who are HIV positive are much more likely to develop active tuberculosis if they are infected), homelessness, the rise of immigration from TB-endemic regions, and the erosion of tuberculosis control programs in earlier years. Worried that some individuals would fail to adhere to the long course of TB treatment and develop and spread multidrug-resistant TB, which is both difficult and costly to treat, officials in many states ordered the quarantine of so-called noncompliant patients.[96]

City of Newark v. J.S. exemplifies how courts handled such cases.[97] J. S. was a homeless African American man who was HIV positive and infectious with tuberculosis. There was evidence that he had previously tried to leave the hospital against medical advice. He had also failed to comply with either infection-control guidelines or his prescribed treatment. In multiple ways he was the type of patient whom public health officials tend to see as creating a menace.

In an interesting and lengthy opinion written after the commitment order had been issued, the New Jersey Superior Court analyzed J. S.'s rights under the Due Process Clause as well as the Americans with Disabilities Act (ADA).[98] In many ways the opinion took a population perspective. First, the court recognized both the legitimacy and importance of the state's goal of preventing the spread of an infectious disease, noting that isolation and quarantine are archetypical exercises of the police power.[99] Thus, in contradiction to the mainline of due process doctrine, the court did not focus on a determination of whether the state was violating a fundamental liberty. Perhaps more interestingly, and again in contrast to many due process cases, the court emphasized the importance of the public health evidence, noting in its discussion of the ADA claim that though "opinions of public health officials must be respected, their decisions must be based upon the latest knowledge of epidemiology, virology, bacteriology, and public health."[100] The court thus made clear that the scientific evidence mattered. The legal outcome did not depend simply on the legal categories given to the state's power or the individual's claim.

Most important, in deciding that both the Due Process Clause and the ADA permitted the state to quarantine J. S. only if that was the least restrictive alternative, the court noted the complex and complementary relationship between the promotion of population health and the advancement of liberty: "Good public health practice considers human rights so there is no conflict. Since coercion is a difficult and expensive means to enforce behaviors, voluntary compliance is the public health goal. Compliance is more likely when authorities demonstrate sensitivity to human rights."[101] To ensure such sensitivity, the court held that J. S. was entitled to the procedural guarantees generally provided to people who were committed due to mental illness. In addition, the court clarified that J. S. could not be medicated against his will and could be detained only until he had three negative sputum tests in a row. Once he was no longer infectious, he had to be released.

By seeking a middle ground that attempted to reconcile individual rights with public health protection, and by recognizing that the former may advance the latter, the court's opinion in *J.S.* provides a starting point for a viable population-based approach to the relationship between individual liberty and protection of population health. But it is only a starting point.

In contrast to the New Jersey court in *J.S.*, and indeed to almost all courts that have considered quarantine cases in recent years,[102] a population-based analysis would look more skeptically at the state's claim that it was seeking to protect the public's health, questioning the assumption that the state was acting on behalf of and in furtherance of the interests of the public, as if there were a single population facing a single, unified risk. In fact, there were different populations that faced very different risks and J. S. was a member of many of the populations most at risk. Thus the question should not have been whether detaining J. S. protected the public, but rather whether it was the least restrictive way of helping those populations at the greatest risk of TB. From a population perspective, this question is critical not only because it keeps courts mindful of the dangers of invidious discrimination (a very real danger in the case of detaining noncompliant TB patients),[103] but also because it also reminds courts that conflicts that are perceived to pit the rights of lone individuals against the public are seldom that simple. More often, as was true in *J.S.* and in most litigated quarantine cases, different communities have different interests, values, and risks. Thus when a state claims that a law is enacted to protect the public's health, caution is in order.

This caution does not mean that courts adopting a public health perspective should disregard the presumption of constitutionality granted to acts of the legislature. In a democratic system the laws enacted by legislative bodies must be taken prima facie as the actions of the public even if they really are merely the actions of the majority or the political winners. Legislation always has winners and losers. This reality is the strongest justification for the highly deferential form of review exemplified by *Williamson v. Lee Optical*.

Nevertheless, though a recognition that there are multiple populations differentially situated with respect to any exercise of the police power should not legitimize the judiciary's casual disregard of the democratic process, it should lead courts to ask if the population whose liberty is denied receives a benefit, or an increase in their positive liberty from the deprivation. In the case of J. S., the relevant question is whether the communities at high risk for TB are the ones who would benefit from his isolation. Another question is whether those who might be isolated would receive benefits, such as medical care for all their health needs, while they were isolated. Or is one population seeking to externalize the costs of reducing its risks by disregarding the interests of another, more vulnerable population? In effect, is a population at relatively low risk of contracting TB seeking to further lower its risk by imposing the high cost of detention on others who are already at greater risk?[104] If so, the reconciliation between rights and public health that the *J.S.* court lauded might not be so simple. Indeed, unless there were a significant overlap between the population benefited and that harmed, neither a social compact nor Rawlsian perspective could support the deprivation of liberty, because an individual behind a veil of ignorance would not limit his or her autonomy for the good of a group to which he or she does not belong.[105] Implicit in this discussion is the critical premise that liberty must be understood in both its negative and positive components and that both are appropriately part of a due process analysis. In other words, if we accept that protection of population health is not only a positive good but, as Justice Harlan pointed out in *Jacobson,* a critical rationale for the empowerment of the state, and that it is the role of the courts to review denials of liberty under the Due Process Clause, then a court should be obliged to consider whether or to what extent the challenged state action has deprived an individual of both negative and positive liberty. This suggests that deprivations of negative liberty can, in a sense, be offset by increases in positive liberty. Conversely, as suggested, if the state deprives an individual or population of negative liberty to protect the health or safety of other populations, there can be no positive liberty gained to justify the deprivation of negative liberty.

This discussion points to another way in which a population-based approach would part company from the analysis offered by the *J.S.* court. In *J.S.,* the court assumed that isolation was the least restrictive alternative because J. S. was infected with active TB and was homeless. (Indeed, the court suggested that a different outcome might have been in order had J. S. had a home to go to.) By so doing, the court applied the least restrictive alternative test narrowly, taking J. S.'s social environment as a given, ignoring what the state could or should do to change that environment.

But from a population perspective, this approach is unduly restricted. It locates the source of risk in the actions or choices of a single, noncompliant individual, such as J. S., but ignores the social factors that make it difficult for populations to adhere to their medication regime. It also fails to ask whether the detention of one individual would in fact help or harm the health of others. For example, if both HIV status and homelessness were significant risk factors for TB, a truly less restrictive and more effective policy might provide housing for homeless HIV patients. Such a policy, by reaching a broader population, and working with rather than against those who are at risk for TB, might lead to a greater reduction in the prevalence of TB than would the detention of a few people like J. S. At the least, a court could and should find that the absence of such truly less restrictive policies raises serious questions about whether the detention of any particular individual such as J. S. is in fact well suited to reducing the threat to the population's health.

Hence, from a population perspective, the question that must be asked is not whether there is a less restrictive way to reduce the risk posed by any one individual, but whether any feasible intervention is less restrictive of negative liberty and more supportive of positive liberty. To answer that question courts would have to consider the broad social factors that may affect both the risk posed by the individual and the efficacy of the state's chosen approach to protect public health. For example, in *Best v. St. Vincent's Hospital*, a federal magistrate suggested that directly observed therapy (DOT), a policy that requires TB patients to take their medication under observation, was a less restrictive way of reducing the risk of TB than was quarantine.[106] Although the court did not explicitly demand that DOT be made available before the state could quarantine an individual who was infected with TB, the court's opinion supports the inference that the imposition of a quarantine in the absence of less restrictive population approaches such as DOT would be constitutionally problematic.

Thus a court can and should inquire about the existence of broader, population-based alternatives before quickly affirming the imposition of a highly coercive measure on any particular individual. Although such an examination may well lead courts to the outer boundaries of their own institutional competence, raising questions that the New Deal Court sought to avoid about public health policies and the allocation of state tax dollars,[107] courts can and, from a population perspective, should nevertheless do what courts have always done: consider the appropriateness of any individual confinement. In so doing they would not establish or demand any particular alternative population-based program, but they would require states to recognize and address the broader nature of a problem before shifting the burden of prevention to any particular vulnerable person. Thus a mandatory quarantine for pandemic influenza or a bioterrorism event may be more constitutionally defensible if the government has put in place other less restrictive policies, such as stockpiling vaccines and providing income supports for people who stay at home, than if the government responds merely by confining some individual or group that has been exposed to the pathogen.

Finally, to ensure the reciprocity and trust that support population health, a population-based approach to quarantine or any due process case would put a premium on three related attributes: accountability, transparency, and participation. Although population health protection sometimes requires governments to limit negative liberty, courts under a population approach would look to see if the populations affected are treated as participants and stakeholders in interventions that affect their health and liberty. This would necessitate that restraints on liberty be transparent and justifiable to the populations most affected.

Judicial review, by providing a forum to contest police power actions, offers one important forum for such dialog and accountability. But courts can and should encourage the establishment of better and richer forums. For example, instead of interpreting the Due Process Clause as demanding only individual hearings when constitutionally recognized rights are abridged, courts applying a population-based perspective might find that coercive public health policies developed in the open and with the participation of affected communities are entitled to greater deference than those formulated less transparently and inclusively.[108]

In addition, under a population-based approach, the court's examination of the nature and impact of the state law on populations would consider empirical evidence on the nature of the state's goal and the potential efficacy of its approach to the populations at issue. In effect, the stringency or bite of review would depend on multiple factors, including the importance and nature of the state interest, the strength of the individual and group interest, and the extent to which the state offers a positive benefit to the individual or group that alleges harm. Thus judicial review would not be tiered, but would instead, as Justice Souter suggested in *Glucksberg,* be applied along a continuum. The most deferential form of review would be applied when the state has the most critical interests and the individual the most trivial. Alternatively, courts would apply the most the stringent review when the state interest is the least apt to benefit the affected population and the individual interests are substantial. Although the recognition of this spectrum would defy easy predictability, there is no reason to assume that this approach would be more indeterminate than the current doctrine's query as to whether the rights claimed are fundamental.

Moreover, in time, a population-based analysis would lead to the development of a body of law that could help to define the necessary and proper goals for states. This enterprise would necessarily be normative and presuppose that promotion of population health is an appropriate, indeed critical, goal for a political entity. But it would also be empirical and would appreciate that not all laws purporting to protect population health are in fact well designed to do so.

Finally, the population approach would reframe the debate about public health and individual rights. Rather than emphasizing, as the conventional view does, the many conflicts between individuals and public health, it would stress the ways in which individual and population interests coincide. By recognizing that law can provide a forum for debate, discussion, and dialog on how the well-being of diverse and often disagreeing populations can be advanced, while providing judicial review to ensure that actions taken in the name of population health have some possibility of achieving that goal, a population-based approach to due process law may help promote policies that are both more effective and less restrictive of individual rights than those emphasized since 9/11.

NOTES

1. The Center for Law and the Public's Health at Georgetown and Johns Hopkins Universities, *The Model State Emergency Health Powers Act* (Dec. 21, 2001), http://www.publichealthlaw.net/MSEHPA/MSEHPA2.pdf (last visited Oct. 10, 2008). In support of the Model Act, see Lawrence O. Gostin et al., *The Model State Emergency Health Powers Act: Planning for and Response to Bioterrorism and Naturally Occurring Infectious Diseases*, 288 JAMA 622, 622 (2002). For an example of criticism of the act, see George J. Annas, *Bioterrorism, Public Health, and Civil Liberties*, 346 N. ENG. J. MED. 1337 (2002).

2. For a discussion of the SARS outbreak and the issues it raised in the United States, see Mark Rothstein, *SARS, Public Health, and Global Governance: Are Traditional Public Health Strategies Consistent with Contemporary American Values?*, 77 TEMP. L. REV. 175 *passim* (2004).

3. David Brown, *Military's Role in Flu Pandemic: "Troops Might Be Used to Effect a Quarantine," Bush Says*, WASHINGTON POST, Oct. 5, 2005, at A-05.

4. 70 Fed. Reg. 71, 892, 71, 903 78192 at § 70.16 (Nov. 30, 2005).

5. *See* Wendy E. Parmet, *Perspective: Legal Power and Legal Rights: Isolation and Quarantine in the Case of Drug-Resistant Tuberculosis*, 357 N. ENG. J. MED. 433, 433 (2007).

6. *Id.*

7. For a fuller discussion of quarantine, see Wendy E. Parmet, *AIDS and Quarantine: The Revival of an Archaic Doctrine*, 14 HOFSTRA L. REV. 53, 55–71 (1985).

8. James Colgrove and Ronald Bayer, *Manifold Restraints: Liberty, Public Health and the Legacy of Jacobson v. Massachusetts*, 95 AM. J. PUB. H. 571, 575 (2005).

9. Lawrence O. Gostin, *The Model State Public Health Powers Emergency Act: Public Health and Civil Liberties in a Time of Terrorism*, 13 HEALTH MATRIX 3, 13 (2003).

10. Parmet, *supra* note 5, at 433.

11. Lawrence O. Gostin, *When Terrorism Threatens Health: How Far Are Limitations on Personal and Economic Liberties Justified?*, 55 FLA. L. REV. 1105, 1147 (2003).

12. *Id.* at 1148 (citation omitted).

13. For a discussion of the drug-resistant TB problem, *see* WHO/IUATLD Global Project on Anti-Tuberculosis Drug Resistance Surveillance, *Anti-Tuberculosis Drug Resistance in the World*, Report No. 4 (2008), http://www.who.int/tb/publications/2008/drs_report4_26feb08.pdf (last visited Oct. 10, 2008).

14. Matthew Lippman, *War Crimes Prosecutions of Nazi Health Professionals and the Contemporary Protection of Human Rights*, 21 T. MARSHALL L. REV. 11, 14–21 (1995).

15. WILLIAM E. LEUCHTENBURG, THE SUPREME COURT REBORN: THE CONSTITUTIONAL REVOLUTION IN THE AGE OF ROOSEVELT 3–25 (1995).

16. U.S. Public Health Service, U.S. Dep't of Health, Education and Welfare, *Final Report of the Tuskegee Syphilis Study Ad Hoc Advisory Committee* (1973).

17. NAYAN SHAH, CONTAGIOUS DIVIDES: EPIDEMICS AND RACE IN SAN FRANCISCO'S CHINATOWN 120–57 (2001).

18. *Workmen Vaccinated*, BOSTON HERALD, Mar. 16, 1902, at 10.

19. *See* chapter 1, *supra*.

20. Keith Tones, *Health Promotion, Health Education and the Public Health*, in 1 OXFORD TEXTBOOK OF PUBLIC HEALTH (R. Detels et al. eds., 4th ed. 2002). *See also* George Dock, *Compulsory Vaccination, Antivaccination, and Organized Vaccination*, 133 A.J. MED. SCIENCES 218 (1907).

21. Scott Burris, *Public Health, 'AIDS Exceptionalism' and the Law*, 27 J. MARSHALL L. REV. 251, 259–61 (1994).

22. Ronald Bayer, *Public Health Policy and the AIDS Epidemic: An End to AIDS Exceptionalism?*, 324 N. ENG. J. MED. 1500, 1501 (1991).

23. Burris, *supra*, note 21, at 254–58.

24. George J. Annas, *Puppy Love: Bioterrorism, Civil Rights, and Public Health*, 55 FLA. L. REV. 1171, 1179 (2003).

25. PATRICIA ILLINGWORTH, TRUSTING MEDICINE: THE MORAL COSTS OF MANAGED CARE 94 (2005).

26. Thomas A. Glass & Monica Schoch-Spana, *Bioterrorism and the People: How to Vaccinate a City against Panic*, 34 CLINICAL INFECTIOUS DISEASES 217, 221 (2002) (emphasis omitted).

27. Judith W. Leavitt, *Public Resistance or Cooperation? A Tale of Smallpox in Two Cities*, 1 BIOSECURITY AND BIOTERRORISM 185, 185 (2003).

28. Lesley A. Jacobs, *Rights and Quarantine during the SARS Global Health Crisis: Differentiated Legal Consciousness in Hong Kong, Shanghai and Toronto*, 41 LAW & SOC'Y REV. 511, 529 (2007).

29. Jonathan M. Mann, *Medicine and Public Health, Ethics and Human Rights*, 27 HASTINGS CTR. REP. 6, 6–14 (1997). For a further discussion of human rights, see chapter 10, *infra*.

30. NORMAN DANIELS, BRUCE KENNEDY AND ICHIRO KWACHI, IS INEQUALITY BAD FOR OUR HEALTH? 3–33 (2000).

31. *Id.*

32. Rothstein, *supra note* 2, at 182–92.

33. C. B. MACPHERSON, THE POLITICAL THEORY OF POSSESSIVE INDIVIDUALISM: HOBBES TO LOCKE 3 (1962).

34. JOHN STUART MILL, ON LIBERTY 13 (Currin V. Shields ed., 1956).

35. For further discussion of the role of positive rights in population health, see chapter 6, *infra*. The argument here is related but not identical to that developed in chapter 1 as to why promoting population health is a positive social good.

36. William J. Novak, *Governance, Police, and American Liberal Mythology, in* PUBLIC HEALTH LAW AND ETHICS: A READER 186, 187 (Lawrence O. Gostin ed., 2002).

37. 23 Mass. 187 (1828).

38. *Id.* at 190–91.

39. *Id.* at 192.

40. 61 Mass. (7 Cush.) 53 (1851).

41. *Id.* at 85.

42. *Id.* at 86.

43. PAUL BREST ET AL., PROCESSES OF CONSTITUTIONAL DECISIONMAKING: CASES AND MATERIALS 246–48 (4th ed. 2000).

44. U.S. CONS'T Amend. V.

45. 83 U.S. (16 Wall.) 36 (1873).

46. *Id.* at 74.

47. *See, e.g.*, David Currie, *The Constitution in the Supreme Court: Limitations on State Power, 1865–1873*, 51 U. CHI. L. REV. 329, 348 (1984).

48. 83 U.S. at 62.

49. *Id.*

50. *Id.* at 66.

51. *Id.* at 62 (quoting JAMES KENT, 2 COMMENTARIES ON AMERICAN LAW, at 340).

52. *Id.* at 63.

53. Wendy E. Parmet, *From Slaughter-House to Lochner: The Rise and Fall of the Constitutionalization of Public Health*, 40 AMER. J.L. HIST. 476, 481–86 (1996).

54. 83 U.S. at 87 (Field, J., dissenting).

55. *Id.*

56. *Id.* at 105

57. *Id.* at 112, 116 (Bradley, J., dissenting).

58. 197 U.S. 11, 26 (1905).

59. *See* Lawrence O. Gostin, Public Health Law: Power, Duty, Restraint 123 (2d ed. 2008) (discussing Jacobson v. Massachusetts).

60. *See* 197 U.S. at 27.

61. Lochner v. New York, 198 U.S. 45 (1905); *see* chapter 2, *supra*.

62. *E.g.*, Roe v. Wade, 410 U.S. 113 (1973); Griswold v. Connecticut, 381 U.S. 479 (1965).

63. *See* chapter 2, *supra*.

64. 348 U.S. 483 (1955).

65. *Id.* at 487.

66. *Id.* at 488.

67. Jacobson v. Massachusetts, 197 U.S. at 25.

68. *Id.* at 30.

69. United States v. Carolene Products Co., 304 U.S. 144 (1938). For a discussion of the importance of *Carolene Products*, see John Hart Ely, Democracy and Distrust 75 (1980).

70. 304 U.S. at 152–53 n.4.

71. *Id.*

72. Lawrence H. Tribe, American Constitutional Law 772 (2d ed. 1988).

73. Korematsu v. United States, 323 U.S. 214 (1944).

74. Craig v. Boren, 429 U.S. 190 (1976).

75. Planned Parenthood v. Casey, 505 U.S. 833 (1992); Roe v. Wade, 410 U.S. 113 (1973).

76. *E.g.*, Washington v. Glucksburg, 521 U.S. 702 (1997). This is not always so. In *Gonzales v. Carhart*, 550 U.S. __, 127 S.Ct. 1610 (2007), the Supreme Court upheld the Partial-Birth Abortion Act without denying that a right to an abortion was fundamental. The Court reached its decision in part based on the view that the Act did not in fact infringe upon the protected right. Interestingly, the Court also stated that courts should defer to legislative determinations in the face of medical uncertainty. *See id.* at 1636.

77. 495 F.3d 695 (D.C. Cir. 2007) (en banc).

78. *Id.* at 697.

79. *Id.* at 703–10 (quoting Washington v. Glucksberg 521 U.S. 702, 710 (1997)). The court also rejected the contention that the common law defenses of self-defense and necessity evidenced a fundamental right to take experimental drugs in the face of death.

80. *Id.* at 713. Interestingly, the court cited *Jacobson v. Massachusetts*, 197 U.S. 11, 30 (1905) for that proposition.

81. 495 F.3d. at 714, 714–22 (Rogers, J., dissenting).

82. 539 U.S. 558, 562 (2003).

83. Although Justice Kennedy spoke of stigma, his concern was clearly placed on the stigma that private individuals suffered as a result of the criminalization of their private behavior. The focus remained on the individual nature of the harm. *See id.* at 575.

84. *Id. at* 586, 594–99 (Scalia, J., dissenting).
85. *Id. at* 594–99.
86. Washington v. Glucksberg, 521 U.S. 702 (1997).
87. *Id.* at 752, 770 (Souter, J., concurring).
88. 422 U.S. 563 (1975).
89. 441 U.S. 418 (1979).
90. *See* Gonzales v. Carhart, 550 U.S. 124 (2007).
91. *See* chapter 6, *infra.*
92. Haverty v. Bass, 66 Me. 71, 73–74 (1876).
93. Parmet, *supra* note 6, at 75–77.
94. Greene v. Edwards, 263 S.E.2d 661 (W. Va. 1980).
95. Although there is strong reason to believe that the Constitution permits the quarantining of individuals only when it is the least restrictive alternative, there is no authoritative appellate court opinion so holding and many of the quarantine cases rely on state statutory grounds. For a fuller discussion of quarantine law, see Michelle A. Daubert, *Pandemic Fears and Contemporary Quarantine: Protecting Liberty Through a Continuum of Due Process Rights,* 54 Buff. L. Rev. 1299 *passim* (2007).
96. Karen H. Rothenberg and Elizabeth C. Lovoy, *Something Old, Something New: The Challenge of Tuberculosis in the Age of AIDS,* 42 Buff. L. Rev. 715, 730–31 (1994).
97. 652 A.2d 265, 267–68 (N.J. Super. Ct. Law Div. 1993).
98. 42 U.S.C. §§ 12101–213.
99. 652 A.2d at 271.
100. *Id.* at 274.
101. *Id.* at 276.
102. *E.g.,* City of New York v. Antoinette R., 630 N.Y.S.2d 1008 (N.Y. Sup. Ct. 1995); City of New York v. Doe, 614 N.Y.S.2d 8 (N.Y. App. Div. 1994).
103. Daniel Markovits, *Expert Testimony: Bridging Bioethics and Evidence Law: Quarantines and Distributive Justice,* 33 J.L. Med. & Ethics 323, 323 (2005).
104. For a fuller discussion of the distributive impact of quarantine, see *id.*
105. John Rawls, A Theory of Justice, 136–42 (1971).
106. 2003 U.S. Dist. Lexis 11354 (S.D.N.Y. 2003).
107. For a fuller discussion of the institutional competence issues raised by this discussion, see chapter 6, *infra.*
108. This suggestion reflects traditional understandings that legislation enacted by a democratically accountable body is entitled to greater deference than administratively promulgated regulations, whereas administrative regulations that have been subject to a publicly open process, and hence are quasi-legislative, are entitled to greater deference than informal, interpretative regulations that have not been subject to public input.

CHAPTER 6

A Right to Die? Further Reflections on Due Process Rights

> When Is There a Constitutional 'Right to Die'? When Is There a Constitutional 'Right to Live?'
>
> —Yale Kamisar, *Georgia Law Journal*

OFTEN THE AMERICAN legal and political systems seem to pay more attention to matters affecting the few than to threats endangering large populations.[1] So it seemed in 2005, when the fate of one woman in a persistent vegetative state, Terri Schiavo, commanded the attention not only of the media but also of all three branches of government in both Florida and Washington, D.C.[2] As legislators and courts debated Schiavo's rights, countless other nameless and faceless individuals died from diseases and accidents that could have been, but were not, prevented. Likewise, surprisingly little attention or preparation was paid to a host of other dangers that threatened to kill thousands or even millions of people.[3]

Why was that so? This chapter argues that a partial answer relates to the failure of due process law to adopt a population perspective.

DUE PROCESS AND "THE RIGHT TO DIE"

The roots of the constitutional debate over end-of-life decision making, the legal issue central to the Schiavo controversy, go back to the 1970s. As

141

noted in chapter 5, after the New Deal, the Supreme Court adopted a new approach to reviewing state police power actions under the Due Process Clause, one that focused on the nature and legal status of the individual interest at stake. If the interest was found to be a fundamental right or one otherwise worthy of judicial protection, courts reviewed the state action rigorously, often applying what is known as strict scrutiny, a form of review that requires the state to justify its regulation as necessary for a "compelling state purpose." On the other hand, if the individual interest was found less worthy of judicial protection, courts generally deferred to the state, typically applying the highly deferential "rational relationship" test used in cases such as *Williamson v. Lee Optical.*[4]

Constitutional law's movement from a methodology that emphasized the nature of a state's goal to one that focused on individual interests had parallels in the worlds of public health and medicine. After the advent of the germ theory in the late 1800s, the field of public health slowly began to shift its gaze away from social and environmental determinants of health to the impact of individual decisions and choices. Initially this development led some public health practitioners to view individuals as vectors of contagion who had to be subject to coercive police powers.[5] As the prevalence of infectious killers declined during the epidemiological transition, however, public health increasingly turned its attention to the so-called chronic diseases of affluence, such as coronary artery disease and cancer. As these diseases took center stage, public health practitioners began to emphasize the role of individual lifestyle choices in establishing an individual's risk of disease.[6]

The new focus on so-called individual choices coincided with the increasing preeminence of the medical profession and the decreasing prestige of the field of public health.[7] Throughout the twentieth century, medical science became increasingly adept at diagnosing and ameliorating individual health problems. As it did so, illness came to be viewed as an individual, clinical condition that could be cured by medical interventions. And, as Rand Rosenblatt has noted, there was far more money to be made from medical treatment than from population-level interventions.[8] Thus perhaps it should not be surprising that by the mid-twentieth century, the field of medicine had overshadowed the field of public health not only in terms of dollars spent but also in terms of status.

As medicine gained prestige and influence, a new field, bioethics, developed to respond to the ethical conundrums created by modern medicine. As Leslie Francis and her colleagues have pointed out, that bioethics emerged as a field in the brief period after the decline of the old infectious epidemics and before the advent of the HIV epidemic greatly influenced both the field's agenda and its perspective.[9] Hence, much of the early work of bioethics focused on ethical dilemmas that arose from clinical encounters between individual patients and health care providers. To a large degree, this work was reactive in that it opposed medicine's strong tradition of paternalism. Spurred by the authority-questioning ethos of the 1960s and 1970s, and the civil and women's rights movements, bioethics initially focused on the rights of patients to make their own decisions.[10]

As feminist bioethicists have stressed, the field's emphasis on individual self-determination overlooked the importance of relationships and the role of caring.[11] It also caused bioethics to pay too little attention to the influence of a patient's race, class, and cultural identity as well as society's reaction to such factors. More broadly, bioethics initially failed to consider that individuals are situated in multiple populations and that both their health care needs and their health care choices are influenced and affected by population factors. Instead, the field of bioethics relied heavily on rights talk, and gave considerable attention to negative, legal rights. Indeed, since its inception, bioethics has had a close and reciprocal relationship with law.[12] For example, bioethicists frequently cite and rely on legal decisions to support their claims.[13]

Two legal developments were closely associated with the emergence of the field of bioethics. Perhaps most important was the transformation of the common law of informed consent from a relatively narrow legal principle to a bold, legal doctrine central to the physician-patient relationship. In the early 1970s, several prominent courts reformulated the tort of informed consent to require physicians to inform patients about what a reasonable patient, as opposed to a reasonable physician, would want to be told about the nature and risks of a medical procedure.[14] Implicit in this new standard with its apparent departure from paternalism was the belief that patients had a legal right to determine whether to have a particular medical procedure.[15] After all, if patients had no such right, why would it matter if they were not given adequate information to make a choice?[16]

As the concept of informed consent as a facilitator for individual choice became pervasive in law and bioethics, the Supreme Court began to constitutionalize the idea that individuals, as users of health care, have the right to control what happens to their own body. An important early case was *Griswold v. Connecticut*, in which the Supreme Court struck down a Connecticut ban on using birth control as violating a right to privacy implicit in the "penumbras, formed by emanations" from the specific guarantees in the Bill of Rights.[17] Less than ten years later, in its most controversial decision in a generation, *Roe v. Wade*, the Supreme Court, relocated that right to privacy to the Due Process Clause of the Fourteenth Amendment.[18] The Court's decision in *Roe* both reflected and amplified an understanding of the relationship between individuals, their health, and their legal rights similar to that expressed in the informed consent cases: that health and well-being depended most significantly on private, individual choices. Moreover, *Roe* and its progeny made clear that at least sometimes the Constitution guarantees individuals a fundamental right to exercise choices about their health care. And, although *Planned Parenthood v. Casey* subsequently modified the Court's approach to abortion by replacing strict scrutiny of state abortion regulations with a more state-friendly undue burden standard, the decisive three-judge joint opinion in that case reaffirmed *Roe*'s core tenet, that the Constitution protects a woman's choice.[19]

The epidemiological, public health, and medical changes that had helped to spur the concept of patient choice in both the reproductive rights and informed consent cases also affected legal and social perceptions of death and dying. As the President's Commission for the Study of Ethical Problems in Medicine and Biomedical and Behavioral Research stated in its very influential 1983 report, "Frequent dramatic breakthroughs— insulin, antibiotics, resuscitation, chemotherapy, kidney dialysis, and organ transplantation, to name but a few—have made it possible to retard and even to reverse many conditions that were until recently regarded as fatal. Matters once the province of fate became viewed as a matter of human choice, a development that had profound ethical and legal implications."[20]

Once death, or at least the time and place of death, became viewed as subject to human agency, the issue of who can decide whether a person must be treated or be allowed to die was bound to come before the courts and be framed as a constitutional question. And so it was. The first case to raise the issue was *In re Quinlan*.[21] Like so many of the subsequent right to die cases, *Quinlan* concerned the fate of a young woman, Karen Ann Quinlan, who was in a persistent vegetative state, an extremely rare condition with an estimated prevalence in the 1990s of between 10,000 to 25,000 adults in the United States.[22] Quinlan's condition was caused by a far more common public health problem, especially for those in her age group: drug and alcohol abuse.[23]

Arising in the 1970s, when medical care received more attention than population-based public health interventions, neither the New Jersey court that decided *Quinlan* nor the public debate about it centered on the cause of Quinlan's condition or on what could be done to prevent young people from overdosing. Rather, the *Quinlan* case directed attention to the personal tragedy as well as the somewhat broader, but still quite narrow, question of whether individuals have the right to reject life-sustaining treatment, or more specifically, as in the *Quinlan* case, to be removed from a ventilator. To some, especially religious conservatives, the answers were clear: life must always be valued and the decision to terminate treatment was morally tantamount to murder. To others, the prolongation of life after consciousness had ceased to be possible epitomized the dehumanization of death and humanity's failure to control its own technology. (A different critique that saw the issue in light of society's treatment of persons with disabilities was not then commonly articulated; it would find its voice later.[24]) As ethicists, theologians, and the public debated these perspectives and arguments, most bioethicists emphasized the individual issues and rights at stake.

So did the New Jersey Supreme Court. In a complex opinion, the court found that competent individuals have a constitutional right to privacy that grants them a right to decide to discontinue lifesaving treatment.[25] Because competent individuals have such a right, the court surmised, incompetent persons must have it too. For Quinlan this meant that her father, who was her guardian, could assert her right.[26] However, the court added, this right should generally be exercised in consultation between Quinlan's family, physicians, and the hospital's ethics committee. Only if all concurred that there was no reasonable possibility that Quinlan would emerge from her comatose condition could life support be withdrawn without risk of liability.[27]

Although the New Jersey court's opinion was tentative, predicating the right to withdraw life support on not only approval from an ethics committee but also on a finding that Quinlan would not regain consciousness, later courts described the right more clearly.[28] In general, state courts concurred with two central premises: first, individuals have a constitutional right to determine whether to have life-saving treatment, including ventilation and assisted feeding, and, second, that individual right survives beyond an individual's incapacity.[29] The various state courts that decided right to die cases did disagree, however, on how courts should determine the choice of an individual who was not competent.[30] Likewise, advocates and state legislatures debated which form of advanced directive, that is, a living will or a durable power of attorney, was preferable for conveying the wishes of an individual who was no longer competent.[31] Almost all lawmakers and bioethicists agreed, however, that the law should respect the choices of competent individuals.

In 1990, the United States Supreme Court took up the question of end-of-life care in *Cruzan v. Director, Missouri Department of Health*.[32] The facts in *Cruzan* were simple, but again compelling. In 1983, like approximately 3 million other Americans a year, Nancy Ann Cruzan was injured in a car accident.[33] Unlike the more than 35,000 who die as a result, she survived, but in a persistent vegetative state, relying on a feeding and hydration tube to receive nourishment.[34]

After some time, Nancy Cruzan's parents, acting as her guardians, asked the state hospital where she resided to remove the feeding tube that kept her alive. The hospital refused to remove the tube without a court order. Eventually the family went to court, where the attorney general, representing the state, objected to the tube's removal.[35] Although the trial court granted the family's request, the Missouri Supreme Court overturned that decision, holding that the state's interest in protecting Cruzan's life outweighed the burden that treatment imposed on her because she was unconscious and therefore oblivious of the treatment.[36]

The question before the United States Supreme Court was whether the Missouri Court's decision violated Cruzan's right to due process. Writing for a 5–4 majority, Chief Justice Rehnquist began by reviewing the common law of informed consent and noting that "the logical corollary of the doctrine of informed consent is that the patient generally possesses the right not to consent, that is, to refuse treatment."[37] He then went on to cite

Jacobson v. Massachusetts for the "the principle that a competent person has a constitutionally protected liberty interest in refusing unwanted medical treatment."[38] This reference was surprising because *Jacobson*, of course, rejected the plaintiff's claim to a constitutional right to refuse a smallpox vaccination. More important, Chief Justice Rehnquist's use of the term *liberty interest* as opposed to *constitutional* or *fundamental right* showed that the Chief Justice's majority was not prepared to find a fundamental constitutional right to reject medical treatment.

The *Cruzan* majority was willing, however, to assume "for purposes of this case" that "the United States Constitution would grant a competent person a constitutionally protected right to refuse lifesaving hydration and nutrition."[39] Yet that assumption did not resolve the question as to what standard a state must apply in determining the wishes of an incompetent person such as Cruzan. Indeed, as the Court saw it, it was beside the point to speak about the right of an incompetent person to reject treatment precisely because "an incompetent person is not able to make an informed and voluntary choice. . . . Such a 'right' must be exercised for her, if at all, by some sort of surrogate."[40] The real question, therefore, was what standard of evidence or type of procedure the state could use to determine whether the surrogate's decision conformed to the wishes of the incompetent patient. Given that the choice was between life and death, and that not all surrogates could be trusted fully to protect patients, the Court concluded that Missouri did not violate the Constitution by requiring clear and convincing evidence that a patient would wish to end treatment.[41]

The Court's opinion in *Cruzan* was narrow and written carefully to avoid a firm ruling on whether an individual had a constitutional right to reject treatment. Justice O'Connor's concurring opinion, however, was far broader and more declarative. It was also critical because she cast the decisive fifth vote. She stated firmly, "the liberty guaranteed by the Due Process Clause must protect, if it protects anything, an individual's deeply personal decision to reject medical treatment, including the artificial delivery of food and water."[42] She then went on to say that the majority's opinion did not preclude the Court from determining later that the Constitution requires states to implement the decisions of a duly appointed surrogate and that states, as "laboratories of democracy," could develop other approaches for protecting an incompetent patient's liberty interest in refusing medical care.[43]

When combined with the four dissenting justices who believed that Missouri had violated Cruzan's constitutional rights, Justice O'Connor's view that competent individuals have a constitutional right to reject treatment meant that five justices, a majority of the Court, recognized that competent individuals have a constitutional right to reject lifesaving treatment.[44] Critically, this right was understood and defined by the justices, state courts, and most bioethicists as the right of a lone individual to exercise the choice to cease treatment and die.

Positive Rights to Care and Protection

Rights, as we have seen, come in many varieties and may mean many things.[45] To Chief Justice Rehnquist, the right at issue in *Cruzan* was primarily a procedural due process right relating to the standard of proof that a court must use to determine whether a decision to terminate life-sustaining treatment represents the choice of the affected patient. To the dissenting justices in *Cruzan* as well as to Justice O'Connor, the right at issue was bolder and more substantive; it set a clear limit on the state's ability to prohibit patients from rejecting medical treatment. Thus, to Justice O'Connor and the dissenters, rights were negative trumps on the police power of the state, trumps that protected the autonomy of individuals, qua individuals.

The inaptly named right to die, however, was never really as absolute as the name implies. Even understood as a negative right of autonomy, the right was at best only a partial, limited trump. That the Supreme Court would see it so was made clear seven years after *Cruzan*, when the Court turned its attention to physician-assisted suicide. In *Washington v. Glucksberg* a unanimous Supreme Court rejected the claim that the state of Washington's prohibition against physician-assisted suicide impermissibly infringed upon the Due Process Clause.[46] Once again, Chief Justice Rehnquist wrote the majority opinion. This time, however, his analysis was different. He began by arguing that in a substantive due process case the Court must begin by determining whether the right claimed was fundamental. To do that, the chief justice contended, the Court must examine "our Nation's history, legal traditions and practices."[47] Looking to that history, he noted that "for over 700 years, the Anglo-American common-law tradition has punished or otherwise disapproved of both suicide and assisting suicide."[48] As a result, he concluded that the proffered right to assisted suicide was not grounded in the nation's legal history and could not be considered fundamental.

As for *Cruzan*, Chief Justice Rehnquist argued that to the extent that it recognized a constitutional right, that right was limited to the right of a competent person to reject "lifesaving hydration and nutrition."[49] That right did not apply to assisted suicide. He concluded by noting that because there was no fundamental right to assisted suicide, the state's ban on it had to be upheld as long as it was rational. Because the ban could serve the state's interest in furthering life and protecting vulnerable groups from being coerced into suicide, the law was rational and hence constitutional.[50]

Chief Justice Rehnquist's majority opinion in *Glucksberg* demonstrates some of the limits of the negative right to reject treatment: it does not extend to end-of-life scenarios in which the individual does not want to reject treatment but desires, instead, the availability of another type of treatment or action. In other words, the right to reject treatment, premised as it is on the assumption that negative rights are simply rights to be left alone, is not readily applicable when the individual is not seeking to be left alone, but instead seeks to receive the assistance of another.

The chief justice's application of the rational relationship test suggests another, more glaring deficit of the type of negative right recognized in *Cruzan:* its failure to consider the varying circumstances and vulnerabilities of those claiming the right. The so-called right-to-refuse treatment assumes that individual autonomy can be vindicated simply by leaving individuals alone. That presupposition, however, fails to recognize that people, especially at the end of life, are seldom in a position to achieve what they desire by simply being left alone. Indeed, as the President's Commission for the Study of Ethical Problems in Medicine and Biomedical and Behavioral Research noted back in 1983, the very question of whether there are rights at the end of life arose in part because "death is less of a private matter than it once was."[51] As people near the end of life, they often depend on their health-care providers, friends, and family. To assume that the most necessary or important right is the right to be left alone is to remove individuals from the circumstances of their lives and of their dying. Likewise, the assumption ignores the different circumstances that distinct populations face when they approach their death.

Perhaps Chief Justice Rehnquist gleaned those limitations on conventional negative rights when he rejected the claim to a right to physician-assisted suicide and cited the vulnerabilities of those who might exercise the right. If so, he never went further and adopted a population approach that situates negative individual rights in the context of population factors and notes the interconnection between positive and negative rights. To the contrary, his tenure on the Court is notable for his rejection of a population-based approach.

To understand more clearly how a population perspective might bear on the question of end-of-life care, it is useful to review briefly some cases that now seem like antique relics, but which once held a promise of ushering in the recognition of constitutionally protected positive rights. Interestingly, these cases were decided in the same era in which courts developed rights protecting patient autonomy, an era in which medical decisions were widely viewed as personal, intimate, and worthy of privacy. This was also the same time when the federal government became increasingly involved in financing medical services, most notably in 1965 by establishing both the Medicare and Medicaid programs. It was also a time when it seemed plausible to imagine that the Supreme Court would find a constitutional right to government-financed health care.

One especially interesting case from this period was *Memorial Hospital v. Maricopa County*, in which the Supreme Court held that the so-called right to travel prohibited the imposition of a durational residency requirement for accessing nonemergency, publicly provided medical care.[52] Though not creating a positive constitutional right to health care per se, Justice Thurgood Marshall's opinion for the Court reasoned that because the provision of health care was critical to an individual's ability to exercise other constitutionally protected choices, such as whether to move across state lines, governments had to be extra scrupulous in refusing to provide health care to some people while providing it to others. This analysis suggested that at least as long as the government was involved in providing health care, as it clearly is, courts might strictly review limitations that the state placed upon coverage.

From a population perspective, in which the deprivation of negative liberty must be assessed in relationship to the provision of positive liberty to the affected population, two other cases from the period are also noteworthy.[53] In *Estelle v. Gamble*, the Supreme Court, in an opinion by Justice Marshall, held that deliberate indifference to the medical needs of prisoners could violate the Eighth and Fourteenth Amendments.[54] This case suggested that, at least in some limited circumstances, the Court would predicate the deprivation of negative liberty on the provision of a positive right to the population at issue. Also interesting was *Youngberg v. Romeo*, in which the Supreme Court, in an opinion by Justice Powell, found that a civilly committed retarded man had a right under the Due Process Clause to enough medical care and training so that he could function within an institution free from bodily restraints.[55] Justice Powell's majority opinion, however, refused to find any general right of habilitation from the state, even though as Justice Blackmun pointed out in his concurring opinion, the state accepted custody precisely to provide "care and treatment."[56] Indeed, the majority's refusal to proclaim a clear right of care and treatment in *Youngberg* showed the Court's discomfort with recognizing affirmative or positive rights, even on behalf of people totally dependent on the state.

Many reasons have been and can be given for the Court's reluctance to recognize positive rights that would help secure an individual's ability to fulfill his or her autonomous choices. Most significant is that positive rights, such as a right to population health protection, appear more open-ended and less easily enforceable than negative rights that limit the government's action. What, after all, would it mean to say that an individual has a constitutional right to health care? Would it require the state to provide the individual with health insurance? How extensive would that insurance have to be? Or would the right require the state to actually provide health care, perhaps by establishing public hospitals? Would the state have to ensure that these hospitals offered state-of-the-art care?

And what about a broader right to protection of population health? Would it require the state to undertake every conceivable public health intervention? Clearly, such a right would be boundless because, as noted in chapter 2, almost all laws influence the health of populations.[57] Moreover, any such right would necessarily demand the expenditure of limited resources. Therefore, difficult trade-offs would be required. Vaccination or clean water? Seat belt laws or more extensive inspections of restaurants?

To many commentators, such trade-offs should be made by elected officials and appointed regulatory experts, not unelected courts, which lack not only electoral accountability but scientific expertise.

Other arguments against the recognition of positive rights to population health emphasize that the text of the Due Process Clause proscribes deprivations by the government; it does not explicitly prescribe obligations of the government.[58] Moreover, the recognition of positive rights appears dissonant to a judiciary and legal profession reared in a common law tradition that generally fails to impose duties on individuals to take actions to help others.[59] In addition, positive rights strike many critics as redistributive (who, after all, will pay for all that public health protection or universal health insurance?) and hence contrary to prevailing capitalistic norms, norms which the Supreme Court has seemed to embrace in recent decades when Republican presidents placed conservative jurists on the Court. As Cass Sunstein has observed, elections matter.[60]

This is not the place to review all of the arguments for and against the constitutional recognition of positive rights. Nevertheless, from a population perspective, three observations are relevant. The first concerns the preeminent role of courts in the American polity. As noted, some of the critical arguments against positive rights focus on the difficulty that courts would have in enforcing such rights, as well as the questionable appropriateness of asking courts to make complex, policy-laden decisions. These problems, however, arise partially because the American constitutional tradition presupposes an identity between constitutional rights and judicially enforceable guarantees. If the legal system accepted a looser relationship between rights and judicial enforcement, for example, by following international human rights law and viewing some rights as partially aspirational, the arguments that reject positive rights on the basis of the competence and role of the courts would lose weight.[61]

Second, arguments against positive rights tend to presuppose a clear distinction between positive and negative rights even though none exists. As Stephen Holmes and Cass Sunstein have noted, most so-called negative rights obligate the government to undertake actions and incur expenses, for example, by establishing a judicial system to vindicate claims of deprivation of property.[62] Moreover, although the Supreme Court has rejected positive rights broadly, it has recognized, as noted, some modest, context-specific positive rights. Thus in addition to requiring states to provide health care to prisoners, the Court has required states to provide lawyers to indigent defendants and has required states to extend health care and welfare to new residents when such benefits are also available to established residents. [63] In addition, some state courts, armed with constitutional texts that are far more explicit and expansive in their declaration of government obligations than the federal Constitution is, have been more willing than has the Supreme Court to enunciate relatively clear positive rights, especially with respect to education.[64] Thus it is false to proclaim that there is no place in American constitutional jurisprudence for positive rights.

Nevertheless, there can be little doubt that by the 1980s the U.S. Supreme Court had come to see due process rights as primarily negative, individualistic trumps. This view was starkly evident when the Court held that the right to an abortion did not compel states to provide indigent women with the means to pay for one.[65] Articulating a strongly individualistic ethos, in which individuals are alone held responsible for their circumstances, Justice Powell wrote for the Court in *Maher v. Roe* that the state's failure to include abortions within the scope of services covered by the Medicaid program "places no obstacles—absolute or otherwise—in the pregnant woman's path to an abortion. An indigent woman who desires an abortion suffers no disadvantage as a consequence of Connecticut's decision to fund childbirth [and not abortion]. . . . The indigency that may make it difficult—and in some cases, perhaps, impossible—for some women to have abortions is neither created nor in any way affected by the Connecticut regulation."[66] A similar understanding of individuals as solely responsible for their own fate was further evident in *DeShaney v. Winnebago County Department of Social Services*.[67] In *DeShaney* the Court reviewed the case of Joshua DeShaney, a small boy who, like over 160,000 other children per year,[68] was physically abused, brutally beaten by his father after the Winnebago County Department of Social Services returned him to his father's custody.[69] Seeking damages for the alleged violation of his rights to due process, his mother sued the county. Writing for the majority, Chief Justice Rehnquist rejected the claim: "Nothing in the language of the Due Process Clause itself requires the State to protect the life, liberty and property of its citizens against invasion by private actors. The Clause is phrased as a limitation on the State's power to act, not as a guarantee of certain minimal levels of safety and security."[70]

Notably absent from the Court's discussion was any echo of Justice Harlan's reminder in *Jacobson* that protection from harm was one of the reasons why we have governments. Absent also was language similar to Chief Justice Rehnquist's later comments in *Cruzan* that there are "some unfortunate situations in which family members will not act to protect [someone who is incompetent]. A State is entitled to guard against potential abuses in such situations."[71] Nor did the chief justice recall, as he did in *Glucksberg*, that some citizens are more vulnerable to abuse than others are. Rather, he held firm to the conventional view that the rights of individuals are pitted against the actions of the state.

In the years since *DeShaney*, the Supreme Court has continued to assert that the Fourteenth Amendment does not provide any general obligation on the part of the state to protect the health or well-being of its citizens. For example, although the Court in *DeShaney* left open the question of whether the procedural protections of the Due Process Clause might apply when a state law created an entitlement to care and protection, the Court later appeared to reject that possibility. In 2005 in *Town of Castle Rock v. Gonzales*, the Court considered a town's failure to enforce a domestic abuse restraining order.[72] Despite the fact that the precedent made clear that state law determined whether an interest qualifies as an entitlement warranting procedural due process, Justice Scalia's majority opinion held that no deference was owed to the state in concluding that a restraining order did not constitute a constitutionally protected interest.[73] According to Justice Scalia, because a restraining order depends on police enforcement and police actions are generally left to police discretion, and a restraining order has no ascertainable monetary value, it does not create an entitlement triggering procedural due process protection.[74] In other words, the individual's interest in having the state protect her from a dangerous and abusive partner is so diffuse and discretionary that it defies characterization as a constitutionally recognized entitlement. Thus, though the Constitution provides protections for individuals who wish to reject treatment when it is offered, those individuals or populations that seek the protection of the state can find no constitutional solace.

The juxtaposition of a limited right-to-reject treatment and the absence of any positive right to care or protection casts an interesting light on contemporary American jurisprudence and demonstrates vividly constitutional law's failure to appreciate the reciprocal and interdependent nature of negative and positive rights, an interdependency compelled by the fact that individuals do not live alone and cannot exercise meaningful choices apart from their social and physical circumstances. By failing to recognize that individuals live in, face health risks in, and die in populations, contemporary constitutional law offers rights that are shallow and often worth little. Such rights provide no foundation for furthering the state's ethical obligation to protect the health of populations. Nor do they offer individuals a meaningful choice.

Consider, for example, the decision of the California Court of Appeals in *Bouvia v. Superior Court*.[75] *Bouvia* differed from most right to die cases because the plaintiff, Elizabeth Bouvia, was competent. Indeed, the court found that she was "intelligent, very mentally competent."[76] However, Bouvia had a severe case of cerebral palsy and required a nasogastric feeding tube to be properly nourished. She was also hospitalized, but only because no more appropriate place for her to live was available. With no better place to live than a hospital, the recently divorced woman asked that her feeding tube be disconnected. Given the life she had, she chose death.

In its opinion affirming Bouvia's right to have the feeding tube removed, the California Court of Appeals emphasized the indignity of Bouvia's position and her right to make her own decisions regarding her treatment.[77] However, as disability rights theorists have noted, the court's opinion is troubling because it suggested that living with cerebral palsy is an unthinkable indignity.[78] Moreover, the court seemed to believe that cerebral palsy was horrific precisely because it caused Bouvia to be dependent on others. Yet, in making this assumption, the court gave no recognition to the fact that in many ways, and at some times, everyone is dependent on another. Likewise, in affirming Bouvia's choice, the court failed to consider just how limited was the choice it was giving her. For example, although the court noted that housing was not available to Bouvia, the court did not consider whether a right to choose should include a right to choose to live outside of a hospital.[79] Rather, the only choice protected by the law was the choice to die.

With this view of rights, the only right available to people who are physically dependent on medical support to live is the right to reject whatever treatment is offered, if it is offered. Such a conception of rights respects autonomy only if autonomy is viewed as little more than the absence of governmental or medical interference. If respect for autonomy means something more, such as respect for the choices and preferences of individuals including their preference for a healthy life, the rights recognized in *Bouvia* fail utterly to protect autonomy. They also fail to protect or promote the health of populations.

APPLYING A POPULATION PERSPECTIVE

The end-of-life dramas in cases such as *Quinlan*, *Cruzan*, and *Bouvia* raise important challenges for a population-based legal analysis. A population perspective, it will be recalled, considers the advancement of population health as a central goal of an ethical legal system. Understood simplistically, this could be taken to suggest that the law should seek to aim for the continuation of life, no matter what. After all, all other things being equal, the life expectancy of some specific populations, for example, the population of people in a persistent vegetative state, might increase dramatically if there were no right to die. So understood, of course, a population perspective would come perilously close to echoing the medical paternalism that bioethics and the patients' rights movement railed against. More important, it would privilege one narrow measurement of population health, life expectancy, over other, equally deserving measures.

Life expectancy is without question a critical indicator of the health of a population. Indeed, a quick comparison of life expectancies between countries, say Sweden and Nigeria, says much about the relative well-being of the residents of those two nations. Life expectancy is also both more readily available and more objective than most other measures of health.

The right to die cases, however, should serve to remind public health advocates that life expectancy is not the sole criterion by which to judge the health of a population. Quality of life also matters. In some situations, epidemiological data, including data about the mental health status of the relevant population, are available to shed light on quality of life. Fortuitously, populations tend to live longer, suffer from less disease, and experience less mental illness when their qualities of life are positive. Broad population statistics, however, cannot offer much insight into the quality of life for those who are unconscious or at the end of life. When cognitive life is over or death is near, quality must be appreciated, as the right to die cases rightly recognize, in a much more nuanced and subjective manner.

Health economists often measure quality of life by determining the economic value or price that people place on particular health conditions. Although these so-called quality-adjusted life years, or QALY scales, can be useful in shedding some light on the relative worth of different medical or regulatory interventions, they have proven highly problematic.[80] This is first because they invariably rely on a variety of inherently subjective and economically dependent variables. Thus QALY scales partially reflect socially created preferences. For example, the improvement in the quality of life attained by using Botox for cosmetic enhancement is hardly an objective, socially exogenous value. Rather, the value of Botox reflects both the social value placed on having young-looking skin in a particular society and the wealth of the population that is studied. More troubling is the fact that quality of life measurements reflect both the ignorance and bias that a society has towards individuals with disabilities. Indeed, quality of life measurements tend to devalue the quality of living with a disability.[81] Finally, QALYs are influenced by the existing distribution of resources since individuals with greater wealth will generally exhibit a greater willingness to pay to reduce pain or improve health.[82]

The difficulty of developing objective and unbiased quality of life measures for end-of-life interventions points to an additional and more pressing reason why a population perspective need not argue for continuation of life support technologies in all circumstances. The clinical medical interventions at issue in cases such as *Quinlan* and *Cruzan* are inherently more intimate and subjective than many of the other interventions, legal and medical, considered elsewhere in this volume. This is not only because, as Justice O'Connor has stated, "death will be different for each of us."[83] It is also because many of the rationales for public health interventions discussed in chapter 1 simply do not apply when death is imminent.

Not only does the decision to terminate life support not directly affect the health or well-being of strangers, but many of the collective action problems that may undermine a population's health in the absence of concerted interventions generally do not apply in these cases. To put it another way, there is no reason to believe that a law requiring the continuation of life support over the wishes of a patient and her family would lead to a meaningful improvement in a population's health, other than by increasing the life expectancy of the population of people on life support. On the other hand, because the death of individuals greatly affects their family and friends, overall population health is probably best advanced by leaving the decision to those most directly affected. This suggests that when individuals have never been or never will again be competent, more weight should be placed on the views of those close to them than contemporary doctrine, which emphasizes the patient's solitary choice, now does. Of course, this approach does not answer the problem of what should happen in cases such as *Schiavo* where families fight, but that problem is hardly a new one for courts, which have been dealing with family disputes for millennia.

The primary contribution of the population perspective to end-of-life jurisprudence is not, however, the conclusion that courts should consider the beliefs and feelings of family members and caretakers. Rather, it is the reminder that the independence prized in end-of-life cases is chimerical. Only when the law understands and takes account of the ubiquity of dependency, and that the opportunities people have and the choices they are offered are in part a function of factors outside their control, can the law respect individual autonomy, whether at the end of life or elsewhere in the life span.

The field of public health teaches that when it comes to life, health, and ultimately death, dependency, at least in a statistical sense, is the norm. An individual's health or well-being is generally a function of numerous interacting factors, including the individual's genes (which result from the distribution of genes in the population into which the individual was born), the environment in which the individual lives, and the choices or behaviors of both the individual and others within his or her relevant populations. Although individuals often can make choices that increase or reduce the probability of their own disease or premature death, they cannot control many of the risks they face. Likewise, the choices before them are always limited by constraints outside their control. Thus, though some individuals can heed a warning to evacuate a city before an impending hurricane, others cannot, either because they lack mobility given their physical or economic circumstances (including the circumstances of those who depend on them), or because thousands of others are seeking to escape at the same time, making timely evacuation impossible.[84] In these circumstances, as in many others, if the right to choose is simply a negative, individual right, then it is a hallow right indeed.

Likewise, the population perspective reminds us that the levels of risk that an individual faces are always determined, at least in part, and often in large measure, at a population level. Thus though an individual may be able to choose what treatment to accept or reject after a terrible car accident, the individual cannot fully control the risk he or she faces by driving. Nor can a lone individual control the risk that a natural disaster will devastate a city.[85] As a result, the most critical choices, such as lowering the risk of disease or injury, can never be realized solely by recognizing individualistic rights. Indeed, for a rights-based legal system to vindicate the important choice of whether to lower a risk, it would have to embrace, at least to a limited degree, what the Court rejected in *DeShaney*, a positive obligation on the part of the state (which may or may not be individually enforceable) to reduce the population's risk.

Consider again the facts of *Cruzan*. The issue presented before the Court was personally compelling but extremely narrow in its scope. The Court focused on Nancy Cruzan's right to die but was oblivious to whether she had a right to live more safely, in other words, whether she had a right to face a lower risk of traumatic brain injury following a car accident or a lower risk of collision in the first place. True, in some sense such questions supply the routine fare of tort litigation, but following cases such as *DeShaney*, they are viewed as outside the domain of constitutional analysis.[86] Hence the government's failure to enforce highway laws or require additional safety mechanisms in automobiles is not seen as the denial of a constitutionally binding right. As a result, although the government must respect and heed Cruzan's rights, it is her right to drive on highly risky roads and to choose to terminate her medical care that constitutional law respects. Nancy Cruzan had no constitutionally protected choice to drive safely even though such a right would have been essential to the full vindication of her autonomy.

From a population perspective, the individual choices trumpeted in the end-of-life case law and proclaimed by *DeShaney* to be the only choices constitutionally recognized help too few and come too late. Although the choice to reject medical treatment may be vitally important for an individual as a final expression of his or her dignity and in a response to subjective experiences of pain, that choice can only be exercised after other critical choices about how to live long and well are past. And many of these choices are not individual choices; they are choices for populations that can be realized only with the benefit of population-wide interventions. What, then, are the lessons of a population-based perspective for end of life jurisprudence? One important lesson is that the stark denial of rights to government protection enunciated by cases such as *Maher* and *DeShaney* needs to be reconsidered. From a population perspective, the assumptions of individual responsibility and choice articulated in those cases are misleading. Such assumptions ignore the reality that the risks individuals face are determined in part at a population level and that social intervention alone can change the odds and give individuals more meaningful choices. Hence the liberty extolled in *Cruzan* and due process law more broadly will remain thin and unfulfilled until the courts change course and pay more attention to population-level choices and the positive interventions that enable them.

Significantly, the recognition of the importance of positive rights to population-level interventions does not require courts to declare a constitutional right to either a wide array of social programs or specific public health interventions. The problems of judicial competence and limitations on resources discussed caution against any such pronouncement. However, even without declaring specific positive rights, courts can and should defend positive liberty. For example, as discussed in chapter 5, and as suggested by *Youngberg* and *Estelle v. Gamble*, courts can evaluate the state's deprivation of negative liberty by assessing it in relationship to the enhancement of positive liberty. After all, institutional concerns would not have prevented the court in *Bouvia* from requiring the state to provide Elizabeth Bouvia with more housing assistance as a precondition for denying her negative right to terminate care. Nor did problems of justiciability compel the Supreme Court to issue as stark a declaration as it did in *DeShaney*. To the contrary, a court worried about justiciability, yet cognizant of the shallowness of individualistic, negative rights, could easily have recognized a limited obligation on the part of the state to protect children already in state custody.[87]

Perhaps more important, a population-based perspective can influence the language courts use in end-of-life decisions. The atomistic and negative rhetoric courts espouse, however understandable it may be in terms of institutional concerns, does not simply affect individual constitutional cases. Although there is little doubt that the constitutional doctrines described reflect deeper cultural norms, they also shape cultural norms and thereby political understandings.[88] David Rothman, for example, has persuasively argued that legal reasoning and legal decisions have played a highly influential role in the development of the modern field of bioethics, and to that, one may add, health-care practice.[89] There is little reason to think that the influence has been confined to the health-care and bioethics professions. As Mark Tushnet noted years ago, the predominance of negative rights in American jurisprudence "creates an ideological barrier to the extension of positive rights in our culture."[90] Cases such as *Quinlan, Cruzan,* and *Schiavo* receive extraordinary attention in the media. They become the fulcrum not only for public debate but also for political mobilization, divisive politics, and legislative action.[91] By so doing, they help to reinforce society's understanding of the relationship between individuals, populations, health, and death. Thus a jurisprudence that talks in terms of an individual's right to choose to end treatment without any regard to the social factors that necessitated such treatment implicitly reinforces a social and political culture that deemphasizes the protection of population health. As a result, the media and body politic focuses on the sad case of Terri Schiavo but fails to attend to myriad population-level risks, including those posed by hurricanes, global warming, and emerging infections. Hence the right to die may have a more ominous impact than its advocates ever intended.

A population-based approach to end-of-life cases would not alone ensure the dramatic alternation of national priorities. Nor would it end the media's thirst for personal-interest stories. Nevertheless, in a nation in which constitutional law plays a pivotal and central role in civic discourse, a population-based approach would refocus constitutional law and hence move public debate to the larger, population context of the personal stories that make the headlines. And a population approach would make explicit that the risks an individual faces in life near death are not solely the result of personal choices. Such an approach would help ensure that the most fundamental law, constitutional law, would not frame issues in their narrowest and most trivial posture.

NOTES

1. This chapter is based in part on Wendy E. Parmet, *Terri and Katrina: A Population-Based Perspective on the Constitutional Right to Reject Treatment,* 15 TEMP. POL. & CIV. RTS. L. REV. 395 (2006).

2. George J. Annas, *"I Want to Live:" Medicine Betrayed by Ideology in the Political Debate over Terri Schiavo*, 35 STETSON L. REV. 49, 49–66 (2005).

3. For a discussion of why not enough attention is paid to such catastrophes, see RICHARD A. POSNER, CATASTROPHE: RISK AND RESPONSE 92–138 (2004). For a discussion of why we tend to focus on low probability events that affect identifiable people while underestimating high probability events that affect many more people, see Cass R. Sunstein, *Probability Neglect: Emotions, Worst Cases, and Law*, 112 YALE L.J. 61, 70–86 (2002).

4. 348 U.S. 483 (1955).

5. PETER BALDWIN, DISEASE AND DEMOCRACY: THE INDUSTRIALIZED WORLD FACES AIDS 14 (2005).

6. Wendy K. Mariner, *Law and Public Health: Beyond Emergency Preparedness*, 38 J. HEALTH L. 247, 258–60 (2005).

7. Anthony Robbins and Phyllis Freeman, *Public Health and Medicine: Synergistic Science and Conflicting Cultures*, 65 THE PHAROS 22, 25 (Autumn 2002).

8. Rand Rosenblatt, *The Four Ages of Health Law*, 14 Health Matrix 155, 158–59 (2004).

9. Leslie Francis et al., *How Infectious Disease Got Left Out—And What This Omission Might Have Meant for Bioethics*, 19 BIOETHICS 307, 307–08 (Nov. 2005).

10. O. Carter Snead, *The (Surprising) Truth about* Schiavo: *A Defeat for the Cause of Autonomy* (Notre Dame Legal Studies Research Paper No. 06–06, 2005), http://ssrn.com/abstract=886373 (last visited Oct. 10, 2008).

11. Anne Dogchin, *Feminist Bioethics, in* Stanford Encyclopedia of Philosophy (Edward N. Zalta ed., 2004), http://plato.stanford.edu/entries/feminist-bioethics/ (last visited Oct. 10, 2008).

12. The close relationship between law and bioethics is portrayed in GEORGE J. ANNAS, STANDARD OF CARE: THE LAW OF AMERICAN BIOETHICS *passim* (1993).

13. David Rothman, *The Origins and Consequences of Patient Autonomy: A 25-Year Retrospective, in* ETHICAL HEALTH CARE 91–97 (Patricia Illingworth & Wendy E. Parmet eds., 2005).

14. Canterbury v. Spence, 464 F.2d 772, 786–87 (D.C. Cir. 1972); Cobbs v. Grant, 502 P.2d 1, 11 (Cal. 1972).

15. *E.g.*, Norwood Hosp. v. Munoz, 564 N.E.2d 1017 (Mass. 1991).

16. Wendy E. Parmet, *Informed Consent and Public Health: Are They Compatible When It Comes to Vaccines?*, 8 J. Health Care L. & Pol'y 71, 82–84 (2005).

17. 381 U.S. 479, 484 (1965).

18. 410 U.S. 113 (1973).

19. 505 U.S. 833, 843, 869–79 (1992). More recently, the Court's opinion in *Gonzales v. Carhart*, 550 U.S. __ , 127 S.Ct. 1610 (2007), has cast even greater doubt on the stability of the constitutional protection for abortion rights.

20. PRESIDENT'S COMM. FOR THE STUDY OF ETHICAL PROBLEMS IN MED. AND BIOMEDICAL AND BEHAVIORAL RESEARCH, DECIDING TO FORGO LIFE-SUSTAINING TREATMENT, ETHICAL, MEDICAL, AND LEGAL ISSUES IN TREATMENT DECISIONS 1 (1983).

21. In re Quinlan, 355 A.2d 647 (N.J. 1976).

22. On gender disparities in right to die cases, see Allison August and Stephen Miles, *Courts, Gender and the 'Right to Die'*, 18 L. MED. & HEALTH CARE, 85, 85–95 (1990). For a discussion of the prevalence of the persistent vegetative state, see Adam Zeman, *Persistent Vegetative State*, 350 THE LANCET 795, 795–99 (1997). For a further discussion of the condition, see *Editorial—The Persistent Vegetative State*, 310 BRITISH MED. J. 341, 341–42 (1995).

23. For a discussion of the prevalence of drug and alcohol abuse, see National Institute of Alcohol Abuse and Alcoholism, 2001–2002 National Epidemiological Survey on Alcohol and Related Conditions; National Institutes of Drug Use, *Drug Abuse and Addiction Research, The Sixth Triennial Report to Congress*, http://www.drugabuse.gov/STRC/Prevalence.html (last visited Oct. 10, 2008).

24. *E.g., Issues Surrounding Terri Schindler-Schiavo are Disability Rights Issues, Say National Disability Organizations,* July 8, 2005, http://www.raggededgemagazine.com/schiavostatement.html (last visited Oct. 10, 2008).

25. 355 A.2d at 647.

26. *Id.* at 664.

27. *Id.* at 671.

28. *E.g.*, In re Conroy, 486 A.2d 1209 (N.J. 1985); In re Martin, 538 N.W.2d 399 (Mich. 1995).

29. Alan Meisel and Cathy Cerminara, THE RIGHT TO DIE: THE LAW OF END-OF-LIFE DECISIONMAKING 202 (2006).

30. *See* note 28, *supra.*

31. *See* BARRY R. FURROW ET AL., BIOETHICS: HEALTH CASE LAW AND ETHICS 282–88 (4th ed. 2001); Mark C. Rahdert, *The Schiavo Litigation: A Case Study for Federalism*, 15 TEMP. POL. & CIV. RTS. L. REV. 423, 423 n.6 (2006) (citing state statutes).

32. 497 U.S. 261 (1990).

33. U.S. Dep't of Transportation, National Center for Statistics and Analysis, *Traffic Safety Facts* 2004: *A Compilation of Motor Vehicle Crash Data from the Fatality Analysis Reporting System and General System*, http://www-nrd.nhtsa.dot.gov/pdf/nrd-30/NCSA/TSSFAnn/TSF2004.pdf at 15 (last visited Oct. 10, 2008).

34. *Id.*

35. William H. Colby, *Conference on the Law of Death and Dying: From Quinlan to Cruzan to Schiavo: What Have We Learned?*, 37 LOY. U. CHI. L.J. 279, 284–85 (2006).

36. Cruzan v. Harmon, 760 S.W.2d 408 (Mo. 1988), *aff'd sub nom*, Cruzan v. Director, Missouri Dep't of Health, 497 U.S. 261 (1990).

37. 497 U.S. 261, 270 (1990).

38. *Id.* at 278.

39. *Id.* at 279.

40. *Id.* at 280.

41. *Id.* at 281–83.

42. *Id.* at 287, 289 (O'Connor, J., concurring).

43. *Id.* at 292 (O'Connor, J., concurring).

44. 497 U.S. at 301 (Brennan, J. dissenting); 497 U.S. at 330 (Stevens, J., dissenting).

45. *See* chapter 5, *supra*.

46. 521 U.S. 702 (1997); Vacco v. Quill, 521 U.S. 793 (1997) (companion case finding that New York's prohibition against physician-assisted suicide does not violate the Equal Protection Clause).

47. 521 U.S. at 710.

48. *Id*. at 711.

49. *Id*.at 723.

50. *Id*. at 731–32.

51. PRESIDENT'S COMM. FOR THE STUDY OF ETHICAL PROBLEMS IN MEDICINE AND BIOMEDICAL AND BEHAVIORAL RESEARCH, DECIDING TO FORGO LIFE-SUSTAINING TREATMENT, *supra* note 20, at 1.

52. 415 U.S. 250 (1974).

53. *See* chapter 5, *supra*.

54. 429 U.S. 97 (1976).

55. 457 U.S. 307, 324 (1982).

56. *Id*. at 317–20; *Id*. at 325, 326 (Blackmun, J., concurring) (citing Pennsylvania Mental Health and Mental Retardation Act of 1966, Pa. Stat. Ann., Tit. 50 § 4406(b) (Purdon 1969)).

57. *See* chapter 2, *supra*.

58. DeShaney v. Winnebago Cty. Dep't Soc. Servs. 489 U.S. 189, 195–97 (1989).

59. *See* Cass R. Sunstein, *Lochner's Legacy*, 87 COLUM. L. REV. 873, 885–90 (1987). For a further discussion of the common law's no duty rule, see chapter 9, *infra*.

60. Cass R. Sunstein, *Why Does the American Constitution Lack Social and Economic Guarantees?*, 56 SYRACUSE L. REV. 1, 22 (2005).

61. *See, e.g.*, *International Covenant on Economic, Social and Cultural Rights, Art.* 2, (1966), in HEALTH AND HUMAN RIGHTS: BASIC INTERNATIONAL DOCUMENTS (Stephen P. Marks ed., 2006), at 4, 5.

62. STEPHEN HOLMES & CASS R. SUNSTEIN, THE COST OF RIGHTS: WHY LIBERTY DEPENDS ON TAXES 45–47 (1999).

63. *E.g.*, Saenz v. Roe, 526 U.S. 489 (1999) (state law limiting welfare benefits for new residents violates right to travel); Memorial Hosp. v. Maricopa Cty., 415 U.S. 250 (1974) (state residency requirement for receiving free nonemergency health care violates the Equal Protection Clause); Gideon v. Wainwright, 372 U.S. 335 (1963) (finding that the Sixth Amendment requires states to provide indigent defendants with counsel).

64. *E.g.*, McDuffy v. Sec. Office of Educ., 615 N.E.2d 526 (Mass. 1993) (limited by Hancock v. Comm'r of Educ., 822 N.E.2d 1134 (Mass. 2005)).

65. *See, e.g.*, Harris v. MacCrae, 448 U.S. 297, 318 (1980) (upholding Hyde Amendment's restrictions on funding of medically necessary abortions); Maher v. Roe, 432 U.S. 464 (1977) (upholding Connecticut restriction on Medicaid funding of elective abortions).

66. 432 U.S. at 474.

67. 489 U.S. 189 (1989).

68. U.S. Dep't Health and Human Services, Admin. for Children and Families, *Child Maltreatment 2003*, http://acf.hhs.fov/programs/cb/pubs/cm03/index.htm (last visited Oct. 10, 2008).

69. 489 U.S. at 191–93.

70. *Id.* at 195.

71. 497 U.S. at 281 (quoting In re Jobes, 529 A.2d 434, 447 (N.J. 1987)).

72. 545 U.S. 748 (2005).

73. *Id.* at 756.

74. *Id.* at 756–67.

75. 179 Cal. App. 3d 1127 (Cal. App. 2d Dist. 1986).

76. *Id.* at 1136.

77. *Id.* at 1144–45.

78. *See* Adam A. Milani, *Better off Dead than Disabled?: Should Courts Recognize a "Wrongful Living" Cause of Action When Doctors Fail to Follow Patients' Advanced Directives?*, 54 WASH. & LEE L. REV. 149, 203–04 (1997).

79. 179 Cal. App. 3d at 1145.

80. For a discussion of QALY scales, see Matthew D. Adler, *QALYs and Policy Evaluation: A New Perspective*, 6 YALE J. HEALTH POL'Y & ETHICS 1 (2006).

81. Samuel R. Bagenstos, *The Americans with Disabilities Act as Risk Regulation*, 101 COLUM. L. REV. 1479, 1508 (2001).

82. Adler, *supra* note 80, at 10.

83. Glucksberg, 521 U.S. 702, 736 (O'Connor, J., concurring).

84. Bill Murphy, *Hurricane's Aftermath: Lessons from Florida: Texas Urged to Build Better Houses: Conference Offers Suggestions for Avoiding Rita's Evacuation Crisis: Lessoning Damage*, HOUSTON CHRONICLE, Oct. 29, 2005, at B-3 (noting that after the evacuation gridlock resulting from Hurricane Rita, Texas is considering amending its building code to require more hurricane-resistant structures).

85. For a discussion of the population-level threats that accompanied Hurricane Katrina and that ensue in the wake of many natural disasters, see P. Gregg Greenbough & Thomas D. Kirsh, *Public Health Responses: Assessing Needs*, 353 NEW ENG. J. MED. 1544, 1544–46 (2005).

86. *See* chapter 9, *infra*.

87. *See, e.g.*, 489 U.S. at 203, 205 (Brennan, J., dissenting).

88. *See, e.g.*, Leland Ware, *Brown at 50: School Desegregation from Reconstruction to Resegregation*, 16 U. FLA. J.L. & PUB. POL'Y 267, 292–95 (2005) (reassessing the cultural and social impact of *Brown v. Board of Education* and citing the scholarly literature on the subject).

89. Rothman, *supra* note 13, at 79–91.

90. Mark Tushnet, *An Essay on Rights*, 62 TEX. L. REV. 1363, 1363 (1984).

91. *See* Joshua E. Perry, *Biblical BioPolitics: Judicial Process, Religious Rhetoric, Terri Schiavo and Beyond* 27–43 (Vanderbilt Pub. Law Research Paper No. 05–02, 2005), http://ssrn.com/abstract=775587 (last visited June 1, 2008); Wendy E. Parmet and Richard A. Daynard, *The New Public Health Litigation*, 21 ANNUAL REV. PUB. HEALTH 437, 455 (2000).

CHAPTER 7

The First Amendment and the Obesity Epidemic

Congress shall make no law . . . abridging the freedom of speech.

—First Amendment, U.S. Constitution

FREEDOM OF SPEECH, secured by the First Amendment, is a bedrock principle of both American democracy and constitutional law.[1] It is a principle that courts, including the Supreme Court, have come to regard very seriously. Indeed, if any constitutional right is treated as creating a strict limit on the power of the state, it is the First Amendment's protection of speech.

Yet, in our so-called information age, speech is also a powerful determinant of population health. In myriad ways, speech can and does promote population health, providing individuals and populations with information they can use to keep themselves healthy and, more important and less obvious, providing them with information they can use to mobilize around public policies that can promote their health. But speech can also harm the health of populations, both by enticing individuals to engage in risky behaviors and by shaping an unhealthy environment.

Given how important speech is to population health, it might appear that a clash between free speech and population health is inevitable, that courts must choose between validating the First Amendment and permitting the government to protect population health. At times this will

166

undoubtedly be the case. But, as we have seen, by emphasizing the inter-dependence of health and the relationship between individuals and the multiple populations they form, as well as the importance of empirical evidence, population-based legal analysis can help courts safeguard both individual rights and population health.

This chapter illustrates the application of population-based legal analysis to the supposed conflict between individual rights and free speech in the context of one particular public health threat, childhood obesity, and one particular type of speech that has been implicated in the childhood obesity epidemic, commercial speech. The chapter suggests how a population-based approach might reconcile respect for speech with protecting the health of children. As we shall see, such a reconciliation is not easy. A population perspective does not provide a definitive answer to all of the "small questions [that] will not go away" concerning commercial speech.[2] It does, however, offer important insight into how courts can safeguard both free speech and population health.

CHILDHOOD OBESITY AS A POPULATION PROBLEM

For children, obesity is defined as a body mass index (BMI) at or above the ninety-fifth percentile of the age- and gender-specific BMI charts prepared by the CDC.[3] Although genetic factors may play a role in predisposing individual children to obesity, genetics alone cannot explain the dramatic increase in the prevalence of obesity among children that has occurred both in the United States and around the world in recent decades.[4] According to a 2007 report by the Institute of Medicine, "between 1963 and 2004, obesity rates quadrupled for older children, ages 6 to 11 years (from 4 to 19 percent), and tripled for adolescents, ages 12 to 19 years (from 5 to 17 percent). Between 1971 and 2004, obesity rates increased from 5 to 14 percent in 2- to 5-year-olds."[5]

Among certain populations of children, the prevalence of obesity is especially high. For example, in 2003 and 2004, 20.0 percent of non-Hispanic black children were considered overweight (a term that some researchers use in lieu of the term *obesity*) and 35.1 percent were at risk of becoming overweight.[6] Even more alarming is the fact that 40 percent of non-Hispanic, black, female children were at risk of being overweight.[7]

American Indian children also have particularly high rates of obesity, with studies showing rates of 20 or 21 percent.[8] Children with physical or developmental disabilities or other health care needs also appear to have an especially high prevalence of being overweight.[9]

Although obese children are often healthy, they face higher risks than their nonobese peers for many health problems. Perhaps most worrisome is their heightened risk for type II diabetes, a disease that is becoming relatively common among adolescents even though it was once seen almost exclusively in adults and was therefore known as adult onset diabetes.[10] In addition, obese adolescents are more prone than their peers to emotional and behavioral problems and more likely to develop psychopathologies.[11] Also, overweight and obese children are more likely than their peers to be the victims of verbal bullying and physical aggression.[12] Increases in BMI are also associated with increases in blood pressure, leading to what researchers have termed "an evolving epidemic of cardiovascular risk in youth."[13]

Children who are obese or overweight also face an increased risk of numerous health problems, including coronary heart disease, later in their lives.[14] They are also more likely to be overweight or obese as adults,[15] thereby enhancing their risk of "type 2 diabetes; endometrial, colon, postmenopausal breast, and other cancers; and certain musculoskeletal disorders, such as knee osteoarthritis."[16] These prospects have prompted some researchers to predict that the epidemic of childhood obesity may lead to a decline in life expectancy in the United States.[17]

Despite the rise of obesity among children and the related dire health consequences that have been predicted, some scholars have questioned whether the obesity problem is appropriately viewed as a population health problem. Richard Epstein writes, for example, that "whatever the problems with obesity, it is not a communicable disease, with the fears and pandemonium that real epidemics let loose in their wake. The attempts to describe it as a public health problem therefore expand the definition of public health to cover a wide range of decisions and actions that have none of the functions of public goods. There are no collective action problems, for I can go on a diet while you decide to binge, or the reverse."[18]

Epstein is certainly correct that overweight and obesity do not create collective action problems of the same nature or degree as infectious diseases do. Nevertheless, there are important reasons why obesity, especially in children, should be viewed as a public health issue and therefore one about which the law should be concerned. Most obviously, children are a vulnerable population in which the state has a particularly acute interest, traditionally recognized by the *parens patriae* power.[19] This is not to say that any particular legal intervention is justified to protect children, or that parents should not, in the first instance, be left to make decisions for their children. Indeed, the courts have recognized that parents have a fundamental liberty interest in the care and custody of their children.[20] It is merely to explain why childhood obesity is a matter of public as well as private concern.

In addition, obesity creates significant public costs. In 2003, direct costs associated with overweight and obesity totaled $75 billion.[21] Some $39 billion was spent by Medicare and Medicaid alone for obesity-related health care costs.[22] The increased prevalence of obesity also contributes to the increase in private health insurance costs.[23] Hence obesity's burden does not simply fall on individuals who make their own choices about what to eat or how often to exercise, but as well on the shoulders of a far broader population.

Libertarian and free market critics are apt to respond by claiming that obesity and other so-called lifestyle health problems create public costs only because society, foolishly they would say, insures individual health care costs. If that reliance were reduced, individuals would bear the costs of their own health decisions. This would negate much of the public cost of unhealthy decisions and at the same time reduce the moral hazard created by insurance. From this perspective, obesity is a public health problem only because the public chooses to bear the costs.

As discussed in chapter 8, policies that seek to shift the costs of health care onto individuals can in fact undermine the health of populations. Here, it is enough to say that even if health insurance creates a moral hazard that exacerbates the obesity problem, the abolition of health insurance is not a politically feasible option.[24] As a result, the public has and will continue to have an economic interest in the obesity epidemic.

More important, the free market and libertarian analyses of the obesity problem overstate the role of individual choice in determining the prevalence of obesity in a population. As Adam Benforado and colleagues have explained, claims that obesity results from individual choices overemphasize the role of individual disposition and "under-appreciate the role of situation, environment, and context in accounting for human behavior."[25] Although it may be accurate to say that individuals have considerable choices about what and how much they eat, and how much energy they expend, those choices exist within a social, cultural, economic, and even legal context that frames the preferences and decisions that individuals make.[26]

A recent study published in *The New England Journal of Medicine* highlights the importance of social framing and suggests that perhaps obesity is not all that different from an infectious disease after all. Using data from the famed Framingham Heart Study, Nicholas Christakis and James Fowler found that an individual's risk of being obese increased if she or he had a friend who was obese and that "obesity may spread in social networks in a quantifiable and discernable pattern that depends on the nature of social ties."[27] Although the mechanism for this effect remains unknown, Christakis and Fowler speculated that a friend's obesity alters an individual's norms, expectations, and ultimately behavior. If their findings hold, obesity is in a sense infectious.[28]

Scholars have also implicated a number of environmental factors, beyond the choice of any one individual, that increase the risk of obesity. For example, individuals in the developed world now face an overabundance of cheap, highly caloric food. Especially troubling to many observers is the ubiquity of high-fructose corn syrup.[29] According to James Tillotson, the excess of cheap, highly caloric food is not the result of chance: "Successful government agricultural policies have resulted in the availability of relatively inexpensive basic agricultural commodities (grains, meats, fats and oils, and dairy products) to American food-processing industries. In turn, this has lowered purchase costs for individuals and has created an environment of economical and plentiful daily food."[30]

Other scholars have pointed to additional social and environmental factors. For example, some researchers relate the obesity epidemic to the decline of agricultural work, the rise of suburbia and the increased reliance on the automobile, all of which reduce the number of calories that people burn.[31] Still others have noted the role of the school lunch program and the poor-quality food it serves.[32] Without questioning the role of these factors and others, it seems clear that speech, especially the commercial speech of food companies, has also played a role in altering the preferences and norms of populations.[33] The next section reviews some of the empirical evidence for that assertion and considers more carefully the ways in which speech can influence a population's health.

THE ROLE OF SPEECH

Modern America is awash in speech relating to food, diet, exercise, and weight. Some of this speech comes from public health experts and officials and is disseminated by the media, government websites, and product labels. Such health-promoting speech may be unclear or confusing, especially when, as in the case of nutrition, the advice offered appears to change almost weekly. Nevertheless, it may also be useful and give individuals information with which to make the type of informed choices that Epstein would encourage. Unfortunately, studies have shown that health-promoting speech, unless it is very clear and highly visible, is rarely effective.[34] Few people change their habits or lifestyles simply because of a warning label or newspaper article, never mind a lecture given in a health class. Information generally has to be given in a more vivid and salient manner, as marketers well know.

The concept of bounded rationality, put forth by behavioral analysts, offers some insight into the reasons for the ineffectiveness of many efforts to improve health by supplying individuals with information about the risks and benefits of particular activities.[35] As behavior analysts have shown, people do not act in an entirely rational manner, nor in a completely irrational one. They instead "are predictably irrational."[36] They rely on cues or heuristics to process information. [37]

One heuristic particularly relevant to the impact of speech pertaining to health is the availability heuristic. According to behavior analysts, individuals tend to consider a possibility more likely to occur based on the ease in which it comes to mind. The more vivid, emotive, or common the speech is about an event, the more people are apt to think the event is commonplace or likely to occur, regardless of evidence to the contrary.[38] On the other hand, information provided occasionally and without great visibility is apt to be disregarded.

Advertisers take advantage of the availability heuristic when they saturate the culture with marketing, giving the appearance that their products are more common and prized in a particular culture or community than they actually are. The food industry has been especially adept at using this approach, marketing its products pervasively, especially to children, creating the illusion that high-sugar, low-nutrition products are everywhere, always in use, and very desirable.[39]

The food industry spends great sums of money on advertising, much of it aimed at children. According to Juliet Schor and Margaret Ford, food and beverage companies are estimated to spend roughly $10 billion per year in advertising aimed at children.[40] The Kaiser Family Foundation reports that in 2005, children ages two through seven saw an average of 13,904 advertisements on television per year; children between the ages of eight through twelve saw an average of 30,155 advertisements per year.[41] Food advertisements make up the largest category of advertisements aimed at children.[42] Half of all advertising time on children's shows is spent on food advertisements,[43] mostly for highly processed food of poor nutritional quality.[44]

Food companies use a wide variety of other promotional and marketing techniques to make their products appear both ubiquitous and desirable. According to a report by the Federal Trade Commission and the U.S. Department of Health and Human Services, food companies spend a substantial amount on "a variety of promotions, contests, sweepstakes, and similar activities."[45] Some, for example, pay retailers to place their products in locations particularly accessible to children; companies also place prizes in food and link particular food products to popular children's television, movie, or book characters.[46] In recent years, food companies have also created websites with interactive games, contests, and downloadable screensavers or pictures.[47]

Some of the food advertising aimed at children occurs in schools, a closed environment in which children are captive listeners. For example, Channel One is piped into eight thousand middle and high schools throughout the country, reaching 6 million students.[48] Schools with Channel One contracts are required to show a twelve-minute news broadcast in its entirety including two minutes of commercials,[49] the majority of which are for fast foods.[50] As Adam Benforado and his colleagues noted, marketing in school is "not just about maximizing vending machine purchases or selling more chicken nuggets in the lunch line. It is about normalizing fast food and gaining lifetime customers."[51]

Food advertising can provide children and their parents with information relevant to the choices they will make. More frequently, advertising helps shape the environment in which food choices are made. By creating the perception of what is culturally desirable, advertising helps to alter a child's preferences not simply by informing the child about the virtues of the advertised product but also by creating an environment in which "everyone else does it." [52] As a result, children's choices change because the norms of the population they care about, their peer group, changes. Similarly, because commercial speech affects the perception of what behaviors are normative in a population, it can also alter the preferences of individuals, affecting their choices and reinforcing the cultural message about what others do. In a world in which children think that all of their peers eat a certain snack food or drink a particular soda, and in which those foods are readily available, abstention from those choices becomes very difficult indeed.

Unfortunately, the pervasiveness of food advertising and the culture it spawns makes studying its population-level impact problematic. Although researchers have shown an association between television viewing and obesity,[53] as well as a relationship between exposure to advertising and increased requests for advertised foods,[54] none have demonstrated a direct causal link between food advertising and obesity at the population level. Possibly, this is because too many variables confound the relationships between exposure to advertising, children's food behaviors, and obesity. Television is a primary source of exposure to advertising; it is also strongly associated with physical inactivity and consumption of snack food, which in turn contribute to the imbalance that causes obesity.[55] Teasing out the impact of advertising from the effect of television is a major methodological challenge.[56] Nonetheless, recent reports from the World Health Organization and the Institute of Medicine conclude that the existing evidence suggests a probable relationship between food advertising and childhood obesity.[57] This conclusion lends strong support to the idea that modern American culture places children at an especially high risk for obesity (though other cultures are catching up), creating what some have termed a toxic environment.[58] Although speech is certainly not the only cause of this environment, it is likely more than a trivial factor, and one that reaches broad populations of children.

THE COMMERCIAL SPEECH DOCTRINE

The potential of speech, particularly commercial speech, to create an environment conducive to childhood obesity creates a tension between the First Amendment and the protection of children's health. This tension has been exacerbated by recent developments in the so-called commercial speech doctrine.

Between the *Lochner* era and 1975, regulations of commercial speech, an amorphous term that includes advertising and promotional material, were considered exempt from the First Amendment, subject only to the highly deferential rational basis test. This allowed governments broad latitude to regulate speech regardless of its impact on population health. Then, in *Bigelow v. Virginia*,[59] the Supreme Court struck down a Virginia statute that made it illegal for any publication to encourage or promote an abortion in the state. [60] Recognizing the role that speech can play in informing individuals and communities about their health care choices, the Court distinguished prior law and found the First Amendment applicable to the regulation of paid advertisements.

The following year, in *Virginia State Board of Pharmacy v. Virginia Citizens Consumer Council*, the Court struck down another Virginia law, this one banning the advertising of drug prices.[61] In its opinion, the Court noted the difficulty of distinguishing commercial speech from other forms of speech and suggested that consumers may have "as keen, if not [a] keener" interest in receiving commercial information than in receiving other forms of information.[62] Moreover, the Court suggested, the state's ban could harm the poor, sick, and aged who could benefit from price information.[63] The Court added that to seek to protect people from their own poor choices, as the state had attempted to do, would be "highly paternalistic."[64]

In effect, the *Virginia Board of Pharmacy* Court believed that the First Amendment created a judicially protected right to advertise not because of the importance of the advertiser's interest but to serve the interests of consumers. As the Court saw it, the advertising at issue offered individuals information they could use to make informed choices about their health. Less explicitly stated, but clearly evident in the Court's opinion, was the belief that price advertising could spur price competition and lower the price of drugs, allowing poor consumers to purchase medications that they could not otherwise afford. In other words, despite the Court's disdain for pater-nalism, it seemed to appreciate that the commercial speech being banned would not simply provide rational individuals with a choice; it would help change for the better the environment in which choices are made.

Taken together, *Bigelow* and *Virginia State Board of Pharmacy* demon-strate the complexity of the relationship between commercial speech, the First Amendment, and population health. In both cases, the Court empha-sized the difficulty of distinguishing commercial speech from other forms of speech as well as the potential value of commercial speech to the popu-lation of listeners. Nevertheless, the Court also recognized that commercial speech was in some ways different from other forms of speech and thus warranted less constitutional protection.[65] What would happen if the com-mercial speech at issue was found to harm, rather than aid, the health of populations, the Court did not say.

A potential answer to that question came in 1980 in *Central Hudson Gas & Electric Corp. v. Public Service Commission of New York*, a case chal-lenging a New York law prohibiting utilities from advertising aimed at stimulating the use of energy.[66] Recognizing the distinctions between com-mercial speech and other forms of protected speech, the Supreme Court offered a four-prong test for analyzing state restrictions on commercial speech. Under this *Central Hudson* test, the Court first asks whether the regulated speech promotes legal activity and, if so, whether the speech is truthful and not misleading.[67] If the answers to both questions are yes, the Court finds the speech worthy of protection and moves to the second part of the test. This prong asks whether the government regulation serves a substantial interest.[68] Under the third prong, the Court asks whether the regulation directly advances the state's interest.[69] The fourth prong asks whether the regulation is more expansive or burdensome than is necessary.[70]

Since it was decided, many Supreme Court justices have been highly critical of the *Central Hudson* test.[71] In a separate opinion, Justice Blackmun argued that the state should not be allowed to "manipulate" individual choices or regulate speech, "absent clear and present danger."[72] Justice Rehnquist questioned the majority's faith in an unregulated "marketplace of ideas,"[73] arguing that "there is no reason for believing that the market-place of ideas is free from market imperfections any more than there is to believe that the invisible hand will always lead to optimum economic decisions in the commercial market."[74] To Justice Rehnquist, by treating commercial speech akin to political speech, the majority had undermined the states' ability to promote the interests of their citizens.[75]

In recent years, other justices have criticized *Central Hudson's* approach to analyzing commercial speech. For example, Justice Thomas has argued that *Central Hudson* undermines the First Amendment by permitting states to regulate in order to manipulate consumer behavior.[76] In contrast, Justice Scalia has contended that the test has "nothing more than policy intuition to support it."[77] Given the Court's inconsistent application of the test over the years, this criticism is not without merit.[78]

Despite these criticisms, the Court has continued to rely on *Central Hudson*, though its application of the test has become increasingly rigorous.[79] Two cases that concern population health illustrate this shift and the Court's failure to apply a population approach.

Lorillard Tobacco Company v. Reilly questioned the constitutionality of Massachusetts regulations designed to shield children from advertisements for cigar and smokeless tobacco.[80] Writing for the Court, Justice O'Connor began by noting that the parties had conceded that the regulations pertained to truthful speech about a legal product and that the state had an important interest in preventing tobacco use by minors. As a result, only the third and fourth prongs of the *Central Hudson* test, asking whether the regulations directly advanced the state interest and were no more burdensome than was necessary, were at issue.[81]

In applying these parts of the *Central Hudson* test to the Massachusetts regulation, the Court noted the considerable body of empirical evidence demonstrating that advertising stimulates demand among minors for cigars and smokeless tobacco.[82] By so doing, the Court recognized that by associating products with desirable images, such as Joe Camel, advertising helps form preferences.[83] Nevertheless, the Court found the Massachusetts law to be overly broad and to place an unnecessary burden on tobacco retailers and manufacturers "in conveying truthful information about their products to adults, and adults [who] have a corresponding interest in receiving truthful information about tobacco products."[84] For example, the state's ban on outdoor advertisements within 1000 feet of a school or playground, the Court found, effectively prohibited advertising in most urban locations.[85] As a result, tobacco retailers would have little ability to advertise their goods to adults.

From a population-based perspective, the Court's analysis was problematic. In finding the state regulations to be overly broad, the Court ignored its earlier recognition that advertising does not simply inform individual choice, but also shapes the environment and forms preferences. The Court also never asked whether the state in fact had any less burdensome way of countering tobacco advertising's deleterious impact on the health of minors. Instead, the Court focused only on the interests of the sellers and buyers in disseminating and obtaining the information that the advertising offered.[86] By failing to ask whether the state had another means of protecting children's health, the Court turned *Central Hudson* into a strict scrutiny test that was close to impossible for the state to survive.

The rigor of the Court's *Central Hudson* test was again evident in *Thompson v. Western States Medical Center*.[87] In *Thompson*, pharmacists challenged the constitutionality of a federal law forbidding the advertising of compounded drugs that are otherwise exempt from the licensing requirements of the Food and Drug Administration Modernization Act of 1997.[88] Once again, in an opinion by Justice O'Connor, the Court applied *Central Hudson* in a manner resembling strict scrutiny, holding that the ban failed the fourth prong because the government did not show that it could not achieve its aims in a way that was less restrictive of speech.[89] In placing the burden clearly on the government, the Court posited several non–speech-related approaches that the government could have used to advance its goal. For example, the government could have banned the use of commercial-scale manufacturing or testing equipment by compounding pharmacists, or the government could have banned the sale of compounded drugs to wholesale or retail establishments.[90] Likewise, the Court surmised, the government could have capped the amount of compounding drugs sold by a pharmacist.[91]

As Justice Breyer explained in dissent, these alternatives probably would not have achieved the government's health goals.[92] Compounded drugs are risky because they have not been approved or tested for safety. For patients with contraindications to commercially available drugs, the extra risk may be warranted, but that would not be so for the typical consumer. As a result, the ban on advertising made sense as a way of preventing the escalation of demand, and therefore use, of risky medications. As Justice Breyer explained, "there is considerable evidence that consumer oriented advertising will create strong consumer-driven demand for a particular drug."[93]

The majority rejected Justice Breyer's argument, noting that the government had not suggested that point in its brief and that Justice Breyer expressed "a fear that people would make bad decisions if given truthful information."[94] In effect, the Court saw the sole purpose of commercial speech as the provision of information that individual, rational actors can use to make decisions that they believe to be within their own interest. In so doing, the Court overlooked the population-level, environmental impact of commercial speech on a population's health.

COMPELLED SPEECH

Speech influences the health of a population not only by its presence but also by its absence. By leaving crucial information out, especially in the presence of other information, commercial speech can mislead and create false impressions. Commercial speech can also deprive individuals and populations of information they could otherwise use to protect their health.

Governments have long sought to counter the deleterious impact of the absence of information by compelling the disclosure of risk-related information. For example, the federal Cigarette Labeling and Advertising Act requires specific warning labels to be affixed to cigarette packages and advertisements.[95] More generally, product liability law requires manufacturers to warn about some of the dangers associated with their goods. [96] Likewise, physicians and other health care professionals are required by the common law of informed consent to inform their patients about material risks and benefits of medical procedures.[97] All such information can help to inform an individual's choice. It also, like commercial speech, can enter the public realm and shape the environment in which populations form preferences and make decisions.

Although the practice of requiring the disclosure of health-related information is both long-standing and common, its relationship to the First Amendment's speech clause is uncertain. The source of the uncertainty is the compelled speech doctrine, which dates to the 1943 case, *West Virginia Board of Education v. Barnette*.[98] In *Barnette* the Supreme Court struck down a statute requiring schoolchildren to salute the flag while saying the Pledge of Allegiance. In so doing, the Court stated that "if there is any fixed star in our constitutional constellation, it is that no official, high or petty, can prescribe what shall be orthodox in politics, nationalism, religion, or other matters of opinion or force citizens to confess by word or act their faith therein. If there are any circumstances which permit an exception, they do not now occur to us."[99]

Subsequent cases have expanded the types of compelled speech protected by the First Amendment. For example, in *Village of Schaumburg v. Citizens for a Better Environment*,[100] and later, *Riley v. National Federation of the Blind of North Carolina, Inc.*,[101] the Court held that state laws requiring charities to disclose their financial solicitations were subject to full First Amendment protection. In *Riley*, in rejecting the state's claim that laws compelling speech should be treated differently from those prohibiting speech, the Supreme Court asserted "the First Amendment guarantees 'freedom of speech,' a term necessarily comprising the decision of both what to say and what not to say."[102] This view raises serious constitutional questions for laws (statutory, regulatory, or even common law) that compel the disclosure of health information.

From a population perspective, the application of the compelled speech doctrine to laws requiring the disclosure of health risks is highly problematic. Although their impact may be meager,[103] such laws can help empower individuals and populations both by giving them the information they need to reduce their risk of injury and by changing the social understanding of dangerous goods or activities. Hence compelled speech laws can at least modestly alter the risk that populations experience without infringing upon or coercing them. For example, a law that requires food packages to note if a food contains trans fats can provide consumers the information they need to exercise their preference not to ingest trans fats. In addition, by enhancing social awareness of the role trans fats plays in human health, the law may influence consumers to change their preferences without directly prohibiting them from buying or eating trans fats. Labeling laws thus help to implement voluntary, as opposed to coercive, population health policies. In so doing, they can promote positive liberty without undermining consumers' negative liberty.[104]

To be sure, labeling laws do infringe on the negative liberty of commercial speakers. They limit a speaker's liberty, however, far more modestly and far less restrictively than laws prohibiting either commercial speech or commercial activity. In effect, labeling laws can be viewed, as the Supreme Court viewed them in *Zauderer v. Office of Disciplinary Counsel*, as permissible less restrictive alternatives.[105] This may be especially true when the disclosure that is compelled is "purely factual and uncontroversial."[106] In such cases, the *Zauderer* Court stated, the law should be affirmed as long as it is "reasonably related to the State's interest in preventing deception of consumers."[107] Significantly, lower courts have applied this relatively lenient "reasonably related" standard beyond the case of deception and to the protection of population health. For an example particularly relevant to the obesity epidemic, the Federal District Court for the Southern District of New York recently struck down a First Amendment challenge to a new city regulation requiring chain restaurants to post the caloric content of menu items.[108]

The Supreme Court has also made clear that governments can tax entities to finance state-sponsored speech. Thus in *Johanns v. Livestock Marketing Association*,[109] the Court upheld the Beef Promotion and Research Act,[110] which assessed beef producers to finance the promotion of beef. In an opinion by Justice Scalia, the Court upheld the law (which certainly was not aimed at promoting health) on the ground that the compelled speech doctrine does not apply to taxes that finance speech by the government.[111] *Johanns* makes clear that the First Amendment does not prohibit the government from including nutrition education in the public school curriculum or from producing and disseminating its own warnings about the dangers of certain foods. However, by emphasizing the highly formal distinction between a tax financing government speech and an assessment supporting private speech, the Court in *Johanns* potentially cast further doubt on laws that compelled private actors to convey controversial messages. If so, the government's ability to shape the information environment may be limited to the reach of its own tax-supported public health campaigns. Given the pervasiveness of private marketing, it would not be surprising if the government's message was lost amidst that roar.

A POPULATION-BASED APPROACH

The starting point of a population-based approach to commercial speech is the recognition that protecting public health is an essential goal of law.

This, of course, does not mean that public health protection should always trump claims of free speech. As cases such as *Virginia State Board of Pharmacy* show, a state's claim that a regulation of speech protects public health is not always to be trusted. Moreover, as discussed in chapter 5, individual rights are generally compatible with and sometimes necessary for the protection of public health. This is not simply because speech, as free market advocates would claim, can provide individuals with important information that they can use to protect their own health. It is also because speech may facilitate or make possible the public discussion and community mobilization that are often critical to protecting a population's health. Think here of the important role that community mobilization played in the 1980s in focusing attention on and getting the government to respond to the HIV epidemic.[112] Moreover, speech can help foster public trust and social capital, both of which are positively associated with public health.[113] As Ellen Goodman reminds us: "communication is . . . embedded, lexically and conceptually, in community, communion and common."[114] Without speech, community, and therefore community well-being, are impossible.

Respect for population health, therefore, does not negate a concern for free speech. Nor does it suggest that courts should cease protecting commercial speech, because, as the Court correctly recognized in *Virginia State Board of Pharmacy*, commercial speech is not only difficult to distinguish from noncommercial speech, it can at times also advance population health. Nevertheless, as the Court stated, commercial speech is more "durable" than other forms of speech because it is propelled by the profit motive.[115] As a result, commercial speech can be especially pervasive and available, which gives it a particularly powerful ability to shape the environment and culture in ways that can undermine, as well as help, the health of populations. Hence, while providing protection for commercial speech, a population-based approach would follow the original intent of *Central Hudson* and apply something closer to a mid-level scrutiny, one that is mindful of the ways that speech can both help and harm populations. In effect, a population-based approach would avoid the type of absolute and formal distinctions evident in cases such as *Johanns* and emphasize instead the messy and all-too-important particulars of commercial speech regulations.

Such an approach is highly compatible with traditional understandings of the First Amendment. For example, in his famous dissent in *Abrams v. United States*, Justice Oliver Wendell Holmes Jr. explained that speech should be protected in part because society cannot know a priori which ideas are true and which are false.[116] Significantly, this justification for the protection of speech was consequentialist. Justice Holmes did not suggest that speech should receive broad protection because it is special or exceptional. He argued simply that speech should be given considerable constitutional protection because in a world in which human beings are fallible, the debate of ideas is the best way to determine which ideas are most worthy of adoption. This suggests that courts should provide meaningful protection for free speech and look carefully at government arguments for regulating it. It does not mean that the First Amendment creates any absolute, individual right.[117] As Justice Holmes saw it, the right to free speech was not a trump to public policy, rather its handmaiden.

In recent decades, many theorists have espoused a different rationale for the protection of speech, viewing it as designed to secure individual autonomy rather than the good of the body politic.[118] By so doing, they seem to assume that the regulation of speech necessarily limits individual liberty. The population perspective, however, reminds us that this is not necessarily the case. As suggested in chapter 6, to be meaningful, individual autonomy requires the recognition of positive liberty. More generally, individual liberty requires an environment in which individuals face reduced risks so that they can make authentic and meaningful choices about how to live their lives. After all, without population health protection, individuals cannot "develop their faculties,"[119] nor are they presented with choices that are meaningful to them. Thus respect for individual autonomy requires that individual rights to speech (especially when those rights are exercised not by individuals but by commercial entities) be reconciled with protection of population health. Otherwise, individuals cannot in fact be free.

This idea that freedom of speech must coexist with protection for population health is at times evident in the Supreme Court's own commercial speech cases. Indeed, in the earliest commercial speech cases, such as *Bigelow* and *Virginia Board of Pharmacy*, the state's restriction of speech was likely detrimental to, rather than protective of, population health. In those cases, the Court expanded its protection of commercial speech partially in an effort to assist public health, or at least access to health care. Moreover, in *Central Hudson* and its progeny, the Court recognized that government may at times limit commercial speech to advance legitimate goals, including the protection of health. Thus, despite the de facto appearance of strict scrutiny in the more recent commercial speech cases, the Court has continued to adhere to the position, compatible with a population perspective, that courts must reconcile the dangers posed by restricting commercial speech with those presented by the speech itself.

A population-based approach, however, would alter the way that the Court actually applies the *Central Hudson* test in two critical ways. First, it would focus the analysis on the impact of speech on populations, rather than on individuals. Courts would thus look more closely at the impact of the regulated speech on different affected populations, rather than solely or even primarily on the speaker. Second, a population approach would take empirical evidence seriously.

What would this approach mean in practice? Think about a hypothetical federal law that prohibited the advertising of high-calorie, low-nutrition food during television programs (broadcast or cable) that were aimed at children under the age of ten. Under the prevailing application of the *Central Hudson* test, as evidenced in *Lorillard*, as well as cases that have struck down regulations aimed at protecting children from pornography on the Internet,[120] such a regulation would likely be found to be unconstitutional. Under a population-based approach, the fate of such a law would be far less certain.

Consider first what it would mean to focus on populations. Under a population approach the court would have to consider the impact of the speech and the regulation on the multiple populations at special risk for the health problem at issue. Therefore, in the case of a regulation aimed at preventing childhood obesity, the particular vulnerabilities of young children would be central to all aspects of the analysis. Moreover, a population focus would recognize that food marketing does not simply provide children and their parents with messages. Rather, food advertising operates at a population level, altering the environment in ways that individuals cannot control. Although any one individual parent can turn off the television, or even throw it away, short of removing a child from the environment (perhaps the planet), a parent cannot shield him or her from the environmental impact and culture-altering effect of advertising. A typical child, after all, will want to eat what all of his or her peers want to eat even if the child has never seen the commercials that helped to influence the peers. Moreover, the weight of a child's peers may alter the child's sense of what weight is normal.[121]

In addition, a court applying a population-level analysis informed by epidemiology would understand the potential impact of determinants to which a population is widely exposed. Hence, even if advertising is not "the" cause of the obesity epidemic, indeed even if it only plays a minor role in determining the probability that any one child will be obese, across the population of children exposed to it directly and indirectly (through the behavior of their peers), advertising may significantly increase the number of cases of obesity. Thus in asking whether the regulation at hand relates to a population health problem that the state seeks to address, the court would keep its eye on advertising's population effects.

Finally, by appreciating the importance of population-level impacts and the role of the environment in creating risks of disease, a court would remember that individual choices alone cannot protect individuals from the negative impact of advertising. Gone would be the rather knee-jerk charge of paternalism and the argument, made by Justice Blackmun in *Virginia State Board of Pharmacy*, that a state should "assume that this information is not in itself harmful, that people will perceive their own interests if only they are well enough informed, and that the best means to that end is to open the channels of communication rather than to close them."[122] Instead, the Court would consider whether there were other interventions, less intrusive of speech, but equally protective of the health of populations, that could be enacted and achieve the desired population health goal.

In this regard, the effectiveness of laws warning about the health of the food being advertised, as well as the potential of health promotion campaigns, would need to be reviewed. It is less clear whether a court should go further and ask whether outright bans or taxes placed on the targeted food would constitute a permissible, less-restrictive alternative. Such policies might be less restrictive of speech, but far more onerous both for the producers and the public. Indeed, few public health experts concerned about obesity would suggest that unhealthy foods be banned altogether (imagine a world without birthday cakes); their taxation raises a more interesting, and frequently discussed, possibility.

Ultimately, under a population-based analysis, the review of a regulation of speech designed to reduce childhood obesity would consider the empirical evidence. However, because both speech and public health are valued and their specific relationship inevitably depends upon the particularities of the context, a court would resist the *Lorillard*-type of strict scrutiny in which the result is essentially preordained. Instead, a court would look at what is actually known about the scope of the obesity problem on the affected population (children under ten), the role that advertising plays in causing or aggravating that problem, the potential impact of the ban in the problem, the ability of parents and children to otherwise get information about food products, the harm that the ban would cause to the advertisers, and the public's ability to debate and consider the public health problem more generally. For many of these issues, there will be no data available and the analysis will necessarily be based on well-informed common sense. For other issues, however, there will be relevant, if not definitive, empirical evidence, which can and should guide the analysis. As a result, many possible restrictions of food-related commercial speech might fail constitutional muster. On the other hand, a narrowly drawn, evidence-based regulation might survive. Perhaps not.

To critics, the indeterminacy presented by this analysis creates a fatal flaw, leaving freedom of speech dependent on the uncertainty and messiness of the empirical world. But the alternative approach, protecting speech regardless of its impact on the health of populations, presents its own risks, especially in a world in which speech plays an increasingly large role in shaping the environment. In such a world, an individualistic and absolutist interpretation of the right to engage in commercial speech risks not only the health of children and other at-risk populations, but also the public goals that the First Amendment aims to safeguard. By eschewing absolutes and demanding that the analysis be informed by evidence and conducted in the very real world in which choices are formed, population-based legal analysis points the way to the reconciliation of public discourse, population health, and speech.

NOTES

1. This chapter is based in part on Wendy E. Parmet and Jason Smith, *Free Speech and Public Health: A Population-Based Approach to the First Amendment*, 39 Loy. L.A. L. Rev. 363 (2006).

2. Steven H. Shiffrin, *The First Amendment and Economic Regulation: Away from a General Theory of the First Amendment*, 78 Nw. U. L. Rev. 1212, 1216 (1984) (quoted

in David C. Vladeck, *The Difficult Case of Direct-to-Consumer Advertising*, 41 LOY. L.A. L. REV. 259, 262 (2007).

3. Inst. of Med., *Progress in Preventing Childhood Obesity: How Do We Measure Up?* 17 n.1 (2007).

4. Helen N. Lyon & Joel N. Hirschhorn, *Genetics of Common Forms of Obesity: A Brief Overview*, 82 A. J. CLINICAL NUTRITION 215S, 215S (July 2005). *See also* Sara Bleich et al., *Why Is the Developed World Obese*, 29 ANN. REV. PUB. HEALTH 273, 274 (2008).

5. INST. OF MED., *supra* note 3, at 24.

6. Cynthia L. Ogden, *Prevalence of Overweight and Obesity in the United States, 1999–2004*, 295 JAMA 1549, 1551 (2006).

7. *Id.*

8. INST. OF MED., *supra* note 3, at 77.

9. Paula M. Minihan, Sarah N. Fitch, & Aviva Must, *What Does the Epidemic of Childhood Obesity Mean for Children with Special Health Care Needs?*, 35 J.L. MED. & ETHICS 61, 64–66 (2007).

10. INST. OF MED., *supra* note 3, at 79.

11. See Serpil Erermis et al., *Is Obesity a Risk Factor for Psychopathology among Adolescents?*, 46 PEDIATRICS INT'L 296, 300 (2004).

12. *Id.* at 1193.

13. Jonathan M. Sorof et al., *Overweight, Ethnicity, and the Prevalence of Hypertension in School-Aged Children*, 113 PEDIATRICS 475, 475–82 (2004).

14. Jennifer L. Baker et al., *Childhood Body-Mass Index and the Risk of Coronary Heart Disease in Adulthood*, N. ENG. J. MED. 2329, 2330–35 (2007).

15. *Id.*

16. U.S. Dep't of Health and Human Services, *The Surgeon General's Call to Action to Prevent and Decrease Overweight and Obesity 2001*, at 8.

17. David S. Ludwig, *Perspective—Childhood Obesity: The Shape of Things to Come*, 23 N. ENG. J. MED. 2325, 2325 (2007). This view is controversial. See Katherine M. Flegel et al., *Cause-Specific Excess Deaths Associated with Underweight, Overweight, and Obesity*, 298 JAMA 2028, 2036 (2007); Katherine M. Flegal et al., *Excess Deaths Associated with Underweight, Overweight, and Obesity*, 293 JAMA 1861–67 (2005).

18. Richard A. Epstein, *Obesity Policy Choices: What (Not) to Do about Obesity: A Moderate Aristotelian Answer*, 93 GEO. L.J. 1361, 1368 (2005) (citations omitted).

19. LAWRENCE O. GOSTIN, PUBLIC HEALTH LAW: POWER, DUTY, RESTRAINT 80 (2d ed. 2008).

20. *E.g.*, Troxel v. Granville, 530 U.S. 57, 65 (2000).

21. Allison C. Morrill & Christopher Chinn, *The Obesity Epidemic in the United States*, 25 J. PUB. HEALTH POL'Y 353, 357 (2004).

22. Lisa Smith & Bryan A. Liang, *Childhood Obesity: A Public Health Problem Requiring a Policy Solution*, 9 MICH. ST. J. MED. & L. 7, 47 (2005).

23. *Id.* at 69–70.

24. *See, e.g.*, Robin Toner et al., *Most Support U.S. Guarantee of Health Care*, N.Y. TIMES, Mar. 2, 2007, at A-1.

25. Adam Benforado, Jon Hanson, & David Yosifon, *Broken Scales: Obesity and Justice in America*, 53 EMORY L.J. 1645, 1657–58 (2004).

26. Jess Alderman et al., *Application of Law to the Childhood Obesity Epidemic*, 35 J.L. MED. & ETHICS, 90, 90–92 (2007); Marlene B. Schwartz & Kelly D. Brownell, *Actions Necessary to Prevent Childhood Obesity: Creating the Climate for Change*, 35 J.L. MED. & ETHICS 78, 79–81 (2007).

27. Nicholas A. Christakis & James H. Fowler, *The Spread of Obesity in a Large Social Network over 32 Years*, 357 N. ENG. J. MED. 370, 377 (2007).

28. Some scholars quesstion the findings of Christakis and Fowler. For example, Cohen-Cole and Fletcher argue that Christakis and Fowler fail to take adequate account of contextual and environmental factors. Ethan Cohen-Cole & Jason Fletcher, *Is Obesity Contagious? Social Networks vs Environmental Factors in the Obesity Epidemic*, Quantitative Analysis Unit, Federal Reserve Bank of Boston Working Paper No. QAU08–2, http://ssrn.com/abstract = 109832 (last visited Nov. 1, 2008) (forthcoming in *J. Health Economics*). Even if this critique is accurate, it does not undermine the claim that the increase in obesity is due to social rather than individual factors.

29. MICHAEL POLLEN, THE OMNIVORE'S DILEMMA: A NATURAL HISTORY OF FOUR MEALS 100–119 (2006).

30. James E. Tillotson, *America's Obesity: Conflicting Public Policies, Industrial Economic Development, and Unintended Human Consequences*, 24 ANN. REV. NUTRITION 617, 620 (2004). *See also* MARION NESTLE, FOOD POLITICS: HOW THE FOOD INDUSTRY INFLUENCES NUTRITION AND HEALTH 93–110 (2002).

31. Bleich et al., *supra* note 4, at 24; Russ Lopez, *Urban Sprawl and Risk for Being Overweight or Obese*, 94 AM. J. PUB. HEALTH 1574 (2004).

32. Martha Y. Kubik et al., *The Association of the School Food Environment with Dietary Behaviors of Young Adolescents*, 93 AM. PUB. HEALTH 1168 (2003). In 2004 Congress enacted legislation requiring schools participating in the National School Lunch Program to develop and implement wellness plans. CHILD NUTRITION AND WIC REAUTHORIZATION ACT OF 2004, PUB. L. 108–265, 118 STAT. 729 (2004). For a fuller discussion of the laws regulating school lunches, see Alderman et al., *supra* note 26, at 92–95.

33. Juliet B. Schor & Margaret Ford, *From Tastes Great to Cool: Children's Food Marketing and the Rise of the Symbolic*, 35 J.L. MED. & ETHICS 10, 13–14 (2007).

34. *See* Robert C. Hornik, *Introduction, Public Health Communication: Making Sense of Contradictory Evidence*, in PUBLIC HEALTH COMMUNICATION, EVIDENCE FOR BEHAVIOR CHANGE 12 (Robert C. Hornik ed., 2002).

35. *See* Paul Horwitz, *Free Speech as Risk Analysis: Heuristics, Biases, and Institutions in the First Amendment*, 76 TEMP. L. REV. 1, 12 (2003). For a further discussion of cognitive heuristics and their implications for First Amendment theory, see Derek E. Bambauer, *Shopping Badly, Cognitive Biases, Communications and the Fallacy of the Marketplace of Ideas*, 77 U. COLO. L. REV. 649, 673–702 (2006).

36. Horwitz, *supra* note 35, at 6. *See also* DAN ARIELY, PREDICTABLY IRRATIONAL: THE HIDDEN FORCES THAT SHAPE OUR DECISIONS *passim* (2008).

37. Horwitz, *supra* note 35, at 12.

38. *Id.* at 15.

39. Schor & Ford, *supra* note 33, at 15–16.

40. *Id.* at 11.

41. KAISER FAMILY FOUNDATION, FOOD FOR THOUGHT: TELEVISION ADVERTISING TO CHILDREN IN THE UNITED STATES 2 (March 2007), http://www.kff.org/entmedia/upload/7618.pdf (last visited Oct. 10, 2008).

42. *Id.* at 3.

43. *Id.* at 8.

44. *Id.* at 3.

45. Federal Trade Comm'n & U.S. Dep't. of Health and Human Services, *Perspectives on Marketing, Self-Regulation & Childhood Obesity: A Report on a Joint Workshop of the Federal Trade Commission and the Department of Health and Human Services* (April, 2006), at 6.

46. *Id.*

47. *Id.*; KAISER FAMILY FOUNDATION, *supra* note 41, at 11–12.

48. ChannelOne.com, *Frequently Asked Questions*, http://www.channelone.com/static/faq/ (last visited Nov. 1, 2008).

49. SUSAN LINN, CONSUMING KIDS: THE HOSTILE TAKEOVER OF CHILDHOOD 82 (2004).

50. JULIET B. SCHOR, BORN TO BUY: THE COMMERCIALIZED CHILD AND THE NEW CONSUMER CULTURE 129 (2004).

51. Benforado, Hanson & Yosifan, *supra* note 25, at 1703.

52. Office of Communications, *Childhood Obesity-Food Advertising in Context* 110–14 (2004), http://www.ofcom.org.uk/research/tv/reports/food_ads/report.pdf (last visited Oct. 10, 2008).

53. Amy B. Jordan & Thomas N. Robinson, *Children, Television Viewing, and Weight Status: Summary and Recommendations from an Expert Panel*, 615 ANNALS AM. ACAD. POL. & SOC. SCI. 119, 120–22 (2008).

54. Katherine A. Coon & Katherine L. Tucker, *Television and Children's Consumption Pattern: A Review of the Literature*, 54 MINERVA PEDIATRICA 423, 423 (2002).

55. Steven L. Gortmaker & David S. Ludwig, *Programming Obesity in Childhood*, 364 LANCET 226, 226 (2004).

56. Jean L. Wiecha et al., *When Children Eat What They Watch: Impact of Television Viewing on Dietary Intake in Youth*, 160 ARCHIVES OF PEDIATRIC & ADOLESCENT MED. 436, 436, 441 (2006).

57. *See* INST. OF MED., FOOD MARKETING TO CHILDREN AND YOUTH: THREAT OR OPPORTUNITY? (2006); World Health Organization, *Joint WHO/FAO Expert Consultation on Diet, Nutrition and the Prevention of Chronic Disease* (WHO Technical Report Series 916, 2003), http://www.who.int/hpr/NPH/docs/who_fao_expert_report.pdf (last visited Oct. 10, 2008).

58. Schwartz & Brownell, *supra* note 25, at 80; Alice Escalante de Cruz, Stephanie Phillips, Mieke Visch, & Diane Saunders, *The Junk Food Generation: A Multi-Country Survey of the Influence of Television Advertisements on Children*, Consumers International (2004).

59. 421 U.S. 809 (1975).

60. *Id.* at 818.

61. 425 U.S. 748 (1976).

62. *Id.* at 763.

63. *Id.*

64. *Id.* at 770.

65. *Id.* at 771.

66. 447 U.S. 557 (1980).

67. *Id.* at 566.

68. *Id.*

69. *Id.*

70. *Id.*

71. *See, e.g.,* Elizabeth Blanks Hindman, *The Chickens Have Come Home to Roost: Individualism, Collectivism and Conflict in Commercial Speech Doctrine,* 9 Comm. L. & Pol'y 237, 252–69 (2004).

72. 447 U.S. at 573, 575 (Blackmun, J., dissenting).

73. *Id.* at 592 (Rehnquist, J., dissenting).

74. *Id.*

75. *Id.* at 594.

76. 44 Liquormart, Inc. v. Rhode Island, 517 U.S. 484, 518 (1996) (Thomas, J., concurring).

77. *Id.,* at 517 (Scalia, J., concurring).

78. *E.g.,* 517 U.S. at 484 (striking down state ban on alcohol advertising); Florida Bar v. Went For It, 515 U.S. 618 (1995) (upholding state bar rule prohibiting lawyers from sending communications to prospective clients soliciting representation in personal injury matters); United States v. Edge Broadcasting Co., 509 U.S. 418 (1993) (upholding federal law prohibiting the broadcast of lottery advertisements except for advertisements of state-run lotteries by stations licensed to a state that runs a lottery); Posadas de Puerto Rico Assocs. v. Tourism Co. of Puerto Rico, 478 U.S. 328 (1986) (upholding a ban on the advertising of casino gambling).

79. *Note—Making Sense of Hybrid Speech: A New Model for Commercial Speech and Expressive Conduct,* 118 Harv. L. Rev. 2836, 2852 (2005).

80. 533 U.S. 525 (2001).

81. *Id.* at 555.

82. *Id.* at 560–61.

83. *Id.* at 561.

84. *Id.* at 564.

85. *Id.* at 562.

86. *Id.*

87. 535 U.S. 357 (2002).

88. 21 U.S.C. § 353a (2000).

89. 535 U.S. at 371.

90. *Id.* at 372.

91. *Id.*

92. *Id.* at 378, 379 (Breyer, J., dissenting).

93. *Id.* at 383.

94. *Id.* at 374.

95. 15 U.S.C. 1333.

96. RESTATEMENT (THIRD) TORTS: PRODUCTS LIABILITY, § 2(c) (1998).

97. *See* BARRY FURROW ET AL., HEALTH LAW 310–43 (2d ed. 2000).

98. 319 U.S. 624 (1943).

99. *Id.* at 642.

100. 444 U.S. 620 (1980).

101. 487 U.S. 781 (1988).

102. *Id.* at 797.

103. *See* text accompanying note 34, *supra.*

104. *See* chapter 8, *supra.*

105. 471 U.S. 626 (1985). The Court in *Zauderer* upheld a state law requiring lawyers to include in their advertisements information about their fee agreements.

106. *Id.* at 651.

107. *Id.*

108. New York State Restaurant Ass'n v. New York City Bd. of Health, 2008 U.S. Dist. LEXIS 31451 (S.D.N.Y. April 16, 2008).

109. 544 U.S. 550 (2005).

110. 7 U.S.C. § 2901.

111. 544 U.S. at 559–60.

112. RONALD BAYER, PRIVATE ACTS, SOCIAL CONSEQUENCES 211–13 (1989); RAYMOND A. SMITH & PATRICIA D. SIPLON, DRUGS INTO BODIES: GLOBAL AIDS TREATMENT ACTIVISM 3–37 (2006).

113. This point is more fully developed in Wendy E. Parmet and Jason A. Smith, *Free Speech and Public Health: A Population-Based Approach to the First Amendment*, 39 LOYOLA L.A.L. REV. 363, 385–91 (2006).

114. Ellen P. Goodman, *Media Policy Out of the Box: Content Abundance, Attention Scarcity, and the Failures of Digital Markets*, 19 BERKELEY TECH. L.J. 1389, 1405 (2004).

115. *Virginia State Bd. of Pharmacy*, 425 U.S. at 771, n. 24.

116. Abrams v. United States, 250 U.S. 616, 630 (1919) (Holmes, J., dissenting).

117. Schenck v. United States, 249 U.S. 47, 52 (1919).

118. *E.g.*, Martin H. Redish, *The Value of Free Speech*, 130 U. PA. L. REV. 591, 593 (1982).

119. Whitney v. California, 274 U.S. 357, 371, 372 (Brandeis, J., concurring, 1927).

120. *E.g.*, Ashcroft v. American Civil Liberties Union, 542 U.S. 656 (2004).

121. *See* Christakis and Fowler, *supra* note 27, at 377.

122. *Virginia State Bd. of Pharmacy*, 425 U.S. at 770.

CHAPTER 8

A Population-Based Health Law

It is projected that a modern [influenza] pandemic could lead to the deaths of 200,000 to 2 million people in the United States alone.

—Homeland Security Council, *National Strategy for Pandemic Influenza: Implementation Plan*

SINCE 2001, public health officials have focused much of their attention on preparing for and responding to a public health emergency, a grave crisis that could quickly wrack massive havoc on the public's health.[1] Initially, in the wake of 9/11 and the subsequent anthrax attacks on the U.S. mail, bioterrorism received the lion's share of attention. Government spending on research related to bioterrorism mushroomed, the regulation of laboratories using dangerous pathogens was enhanced, vaccines and antitoxins were stockpiled, and model laws were drafted to expand state authority to quarantine, isolate, and forcibly treat individuals.[2] Later, during the lead-up to the invasion of Iraq, the federal government launched a program to vaccinate health and emergency personnel against smallpox in anticipation of a possible smallpox attack.[3]

As time passed, the public health emergency agenda broadened to encompass an all-hazards approach that includes natural disasters, such as hurricanes and naturally occurring epidemics. More recently, concern has centered on the possibility of an influenza pandemic, a threat that seemed especially alarming in 2005 given the rapid spread of the so-called

H5N1 avian influenza, a so-called bird flu that has proven highly lethal, though not readily transmissible among humans.[4]

In response to the possibility of an influenza pandemic, the federal government in 2005 developed a *National Strategy for Pandemic Influenza*.[5] Subsequently, the government issued additional implementation plans and updates.[6] Taken together, these documents offer a three-pillared approach that emphasizes preparedness and communication, surveillance and detection, and response and containment.[7] They call for increased federal support for vaccine research and development, stockpiling vaccines and antiviral medications, and enhanced international cooperation to detect and limit outbreaks of avian flu around the world. They also call on federal agencies, state and local governments, and private entities to engage in "preparedness."[8]

The plans paint a worrisome picture. They warn that up to two million Americans may die in a worst-case scenario,[9] that there will be shortages of vaccines and antiviral medications for years to come,[10] and that hospital beds and medical supplies will be in significant short supply if a pandemic strikes.[11] In addition, the plans caution that during a pandemic, the federal government will lack the capacity to provide the support that state and local governments may need.[12] In short, despite years of planning for a public health emergency and billions of dollars spent on preparedness, the federal government concedes that it will be unable to avert a major public health catastrophe should a pandemic occur. In effect, the government admits it will not be able to fulfill one of its most basic obligations.

Why is that so? As the previous chapters have argued, a population's health is determined by numerous social, economic, cultural, and environmental factors, including law. Although emergency measures and laws can bolster the government's ability to respond to a crisis, they alone cannot protect a population's health in either ordinary or emergency conditions. Rather, effective preparedness depends on a wide array of laws that promote and protect population health not only in emergencies but also in the calm periods between the storms.

In this regard, health law plays an important and often overlooked role. It helps shape the health care system, influencing whether that system has the capacity to respond to the challenges posed by a pandemic or other emergency, or whether it lacks essential attributes, such as resiliency and redundancy, leaving it overly dependent upon emergency measures, such as isolation and quarantine, when the worst-case scenario arises. Unfortunately, as the federal government's plans for an influenza pandemic unintentionally make clear, U.S. health law has failed to do its job. By ignoring the interdependency of health and the importance of populations, American health law has helped establish a health care system that is unprepared both for public health emergencies and the more common, everyday threats that populations face.

INFECTIONS AND THE INTERDEPENDENCY OF HEALTH

In the late nineteenth and early twentieth centuries, the developed world entered into an epidemiological transition.[13] Deaths from infectious diseases declined, as other diseases, particularly coronary artery disease and cancer, became the primary causes of death.[14] Still, infectious diseases did not really go away. In 1918 and 1919, years after public health officials boasted about their conquest of the most fearsome infectious diseases, humanity faced an influenza pandemic of astounding lethality. Epidemiologists now estimate that twenty to fifty million people died from the misnamed Spanish flu.[15] According to historian John Barry, the pandemic may have killed 8 to 10 percent of all young adults on the planet.[16] Subsequent less lethal, but still very deadly, influenza pandemics appeared in 1957 and 1968.[17] Even in a typical, nonpandemic flu year, influenza kills approximately 47,000 Americans.[18]

Influenza, however, is not the only infectious disease that continues to take an enormous toll. In the last twenty-eight years, HIV has spread around the globe and has claimed more than twenty million lives, leaving more than fourteen million children, most of them in Africa, without one or both parents.[19] Even today, despite the discovery of effective medications, AIDS, tuberculosis, and malaria together cause more than five hundred million illnesses a year and kill at least six million people.[20] More generally, infectious disease remains the leading cause of death for children and young adults throughout the developing world.[21]

In the last twenty years, epidemiologists have spoken about the problems of emerging and reemerging infections, infectious diseases that are either new to an area or are of renewed lethality. The list of such infections is long and includes HIV, Lyme disease, E-coli 0157:h7, Legionnaires' disease, and more recently SARS. The reasons for reemergence are many but, not surprisingly, human activity often is involved. According to the Institute of Medicine, "emergence is especially complicated by social, political, and economic factors—including the development of megacities, the disruption of global ecosystems, the expansion of international travel and commerce, and poverty—which ensure that infectious diseases will continue to plague us."[22] In addition, practices relating to the prescription of antibiotic and antiviral medications, and the lack of effective infection control in health care settings, have also been associated with the spread of drug-resistant infections, such as methicillan-resistant Staphylococcus aureus, commonly known as MRSA.[23] In other words, the emergence and reemergence of infectious disease depends on broad, indeed global, environmental factors outside of the control of any individual or nation.

The continuing threat of infection should remind us that any one individual's disease can affect others. In the case of highly contagious diseases, like influenza, the effect is direct and obvious. One person's illness can spread easily to others. Moreover, the higher the prevalence of an infection in a population, the greater the risk is to others in that population. From this a critical but often overlooked point follows: the prevention or treatment of disease in any one individual helps to reduce the risks to others in the population. Hence a population has a strong self-interest in preventing or treating individuals with infectious diseases.

Fortunately, few infections are as highly contagious as influenza. Some, like HIV, can only be transmitted through intimate, blood-to-blood, or sexual contact. Others, like malaria, require a nonhuman vector, such as a mosquito. Still others are waterborne. In such cases, an individual does not "catch" the disease simply from being in the same room with an infected person, making highly restrictive policies such as isolation and quarantine particularly inappropriate. Nevertheless, the general points discussed in conjunction with influenza remain valid. Infection creates a risk or cost external to others while its prevention or treatment creates a benefit to others.[24]

Of course, as suggested in chapter 7, the same could be said for many behaviors, or so-called lifestyle choices. An individual's decision to eat fast food, smoke, or drive a motorcycle without a helmet may help to shape the environment and preferences of others. From a population perspective, these behaviors are not solely individual affairs. In a sense, they too are infectious. Nevertheless, the relationship between an individual's illness and the population's risk of disease is far stronger and more direct in the case of real microbial infections, as opposed to metaphoric infections such as smoking. Indeed, the continued threat of microbial infections should serve to remind us about the interdependency of human health both within populations and around the globe. In an era in which diseases can hitchhike on a jet and travel around the world in hours, the prevention of disease everywhere is in the interest of everyone.

The phenomenon of emerging infections also highlights the need for a resilient and redundant health care system. Although many, if not the most, effective means of preventing infection are nonmedical, consisting of broad social and environmental interventions, medical interventions, particularly vaccination, can often prevent or blunt an epidemic as well as provide relief for those who are ill. However, the extent of the need for medical care can be difficult to predict. By definition, epidemics are illnesses in which the incidence of the disease is greater than expected.[25] Because "new" diseases are not expected, their emergence triggers an epidemic, which can spread especially rapidly in populations that lack immunity.[26] Thus emerging infections place unexpected demands on a health care system, often creating a need for a surge capacity sufficient to respond to spikes in illness. In effect, the ubiquity of infection makes clear the need to be prepared for the unexpected. It also reiterates that health care must be understood as affecting populations as a whole, not only specific individuals. Unfortunately, American health law has failed to learn these lessons.

HEALTH LAW

American health law is a messy hodgepodge, a disjointed amalgam of federal and state judge-made doctrines, statutes, regulations, and theories.[27] If there is a unifying theme to the field, and that is a big question, it is the field's focus on the laws that pertain to the relationship between health care providers, patients, and those entities that pay for care.[28] If there is a central dilemma, it is that the United States spends a greater percentage of its gross domestic product on health care than any other nation, yet unlike all other developed nations, does not guarantee health insurance to all of its citizens.[29] Indeed, in 2007, more than forty-five million Americans lacked health insurance.[30] Millions of others were underinsured. As a result, medical debt is now a major problem among both the uninsured and the insured populations.[31]

Lack of health insurance is significantly associated with poor health outcomes. According to the Kaiser Family Foundation, "health insurance affects access to health care as well as a person's financial well-being. Over 50% of uninsured adults have no regular source of health care. Worried about high medical bills, they are four times more likely to delay or forgo needed care than the insured. . . . Overall, the uninsured are also less likely to receive preventive care. . . . Researchers estimate that continuous health coverage could decrease premature mortality rates by up to 25%."[32] This alone suggests that lack of health insurance is a major problem from a population perspective.

For the most part, however, contemporary American health law has subscribed to a very different perspective. As a field, health law came of age in the late 1960s and 1970s, during the brief period between the discovery of the polio vaccine and the emergence of HIV, an era in which infectious diseases were thought to be conquered. This was also a time of great technological advances in medicine, such as the heart transplants and in vitro fertilization, and in the United States, rapid expansion of government financing for health care, through the enactment of the Medicare and Medicaid programs. It was also a time of social ferment, in which patients and regulators dared to question medical authority and the courts increasingly became involved in the business of health care.

Initially, the laws relating to health care reflected the prestige and influence of the medical profession. For example, courts deciding medical malpractice cases generally held that the prevailing standard of care was based on medical custom.[33] Likewise, at its inception, the federal Medicare program explicitly precluded federal intervention in the practice of medicine, ensuring that physicians, not the government, would establish standards of practice.[34]

Then, in the late 1960s and 1970s, a new patients' rights paradigm developed. Influenced by the constitutional rights movement of the 1960s and 1970s, the women's health movement, and the emerging field of bio-ethics,[35] it emphasized individual autonomy and the legal rights of patients.[36] Like the professional paradigm, it was also concerned with questions of quality, but it sought to replace the professionally dominated standard of care with a more patient-centered one. In this effort, the patients' rights perspective was never triumphant. The common law of medical malpractice continues to apply a professionally based standard of care. Moreover, many state tort reform statutes have underscored that standard by requiring that malpractice claims be initially submitted to expert panels.[37] Nevertheless, the patients' rights paradigm influenced the law in a variety of ways. For example, in many states the standard of care used in informed consent cases is based on the views of the reasonable patient, rather than the customary practice of providers. Likewise, the rec-ognition of a patient's right to choose end-of-life care can also be viewed as a result of the patient's right paradigm.

In the last twenty-five years, another perspective emphasizing the role and values of the market has gained prominence. This perspective arose along with the rapid rise of health care costs in the late 1970s and 1980s, as well as with the increasing dominance of market-based, antiregulatory arguments in American law and politics.[38] Borrowing the insights and methodologies of the law and economics movement, the market approach views health care as a marketable commodity.[39] The perspective places a high premium on economic efficiency, which it believes can be maximized by promoting the choices of individual parties operating under financial constraint.[40] As a result, the function of health law is viewed as "maintain-ing an open, fraud-free market in which even intractable, value-laden choices can be made, as reliably as reasonably possible, by the people most nearly affected, acting either as individuals or in groups or through selected agents."[41] Not surprisingly, the high cost of health care in the United States (no other nation spends as high a percentage of its GDP on health care)[42] is viewed by adherents of the market perspective as a sign of inefficiency and a major barrier to health care access.

Although the market and patients' rights perspectives have each been highly influential in recent decades, a fourth perspective warrants men-tion. As Rand Rosenblatt recalls, between 1960 and 1980 health law reflected a "modestly egalitarian social contract" that presupposed that society has some obligation to provide relatively equal access to health care.[43] This presumption animated a social justice paradigm that initially focused on questions relating to health care access. More recently this paradigm has emphasized the problem of racial and socioeconomic health disparities.

Despite the considerable differences in emphasis and approach between the four paradigms, it is their commonalities that stand out. Most obviously, all emphasize the importance of clinical relationships, particularly the physician-patient relationship. Thus questions of quality, cost, and access are examined primarily in relationship to individualized, clinical encounters. Second, each of these perspectives understands the goal of the health care encounter to be the care and treatment of individuals qua individuals. In effect, health care is viewed as a private, even personal, good. Likewise, illness and disease are seen as private harms.

To be sure, each of the paradigms, to different degrees and in different ways, recognizes some public dimension to health care. For example, all of the paradigms accept that society has some obligation (how much is hotly debated) to provide access to care for some who cannot otherwise afford it. The differences arise over the extent and best ways to achieve that goal. Moreover, each paradigm accepts that there are significant imbalances of information and expertise in health care and that some regulation is required to provide patients with truthful information and protect them from unsafe care. Finally, adherents of each of the paradigms, and all health law scholars and policymakers, understand that there are issues related to population health, such as disease surveillance, that justify the imposition of public duties on clinicians. But these issues are often viewed as at the periphery of if not outside the boundaries of health law proper.

Indeed, all of the paradigms and many of the doctrines, statutes, and regulations they have influenced overlook the fact that disease and illness, not only health care, can create social risks. Despite the importance of infection in shaping human history, and even the dramatic impact of HIV on American law, the dominant paradigms all treat health as primarily an individual matter. This helps to foster a health care system that is ill-suited to protect populations.

INFORMED CONSENT

Informed consent is one of the foundational doctrines of health law. Not only does it help define the relationship between patients and providers, it influences numerous other areas of health law, including the regulation of human subjects,[44] the protection of medical privacy,[45] and, as discussed in chapter 6, the constitutional rights of patients.[46]

The roots of the informed consent doctrine lie in the common law of battery and its condemnation of invasions of an individual's body without consent.[47] Today, most jurisdictions consider informed consent to be a negligence action that imposes a duty on health care providers to provide patients with material information about the risks and benefits of health care treatment options. As such, the action reflects elements of both the professional and the patients' rights perspectives. On the one hand, informed consent law presumes that providers have more knowledge and information than patients and should be obligated, as professionals, to share some of that knowledge with patients. On the other hand, informed consent accepts that the ultimate decision about treatment options should be left to patients. To further ensure that patients can exercise their choice, some courts apply a reasonable-patient standard of care, requiring providers to offer patients the information that a reasonable patient, rather than a reasonable physician, would find material.[48]

In all jurisdictions, however, informed consent focuses on clinical medical encounters (or the rights of individuals in biomedical research trials) and understates the relationship between those encounters and populations. Thus the doctrine generally demands only that health care providers, or researchers, inform individuals about risks that are relevant to their own choices, largely overlooking the risks that their choices may have on others. But, as we know, individual choices have social consequences.

To be sure, some notable cases stand apart and hold that, when patients have infectious diseases, health care providers may have a duty to provide them with information in order to protect others. A particularly interesting example is *Reisner v. The Regents of the University of California*, in which the California Court of Appeals found that a physician, treating an HIV-positive child, could be liable to the child's sexual partner for not warning either the child or her parents about her infection so that she would know to refrain from practicing unprotected sex with the plaintiff.[49] *Reisner* relied on the renowned *Tarasoff v. Regents of the University of California*,[50] which placed a limited duty on therapists to warn identifiable victims of a patient's deadly intentions.[51] To a degree, both *Reisner* and *Tarasoff* recognize that individual illnesses can have social costs and that clinicians sometimes have duties to people other than their patients.

The recognition of the social cost of disease evident in cases like *Tarasoff* and *Reisner*, however, is unusual and generally confined to relatively discrete sets of facts. For example, some courts have been unwilling to find that a physician has any duty to previously unidentified third parties.[52] And no court has imposed a general duty on clinicians to educate patients about the broad social implications of their health care decisions.

Consider, for example, the application of informed consent to the treatment of a patient with a painful ear infection, the cause of which is not yet known. Should the patient be given an antibiotic? Under traditional informed consent law, the physician must inform the patient, based on either a reasonable patient or reasonable physician standard, of the medical risks and benefits to the patient of possible antibiotic therapy. Because there is no obvious and direct harm to specific third parties, the duty to warn recognized in *Tarasoff* and *Reisner* would not require the physician to warn the patient about the social consequences of antibiotic use.

From a population perspective, however, the traditional approach to informed consent law is unsatisfactory. Although the risk that the overuse of antibiotics poses to any single patient may be trivial, the social consequences of frequent misuse are far from trivial. Excessive use of antibiotics can lead to the development of antibiotic resistant bacteria, leaving everyone in the population at greater risk from the next infection.[53] Moreover, once we recall that individual autonomy properly understood depends on the risks and opportunities that individuals have within their populations and environments, we might conclude that the contemporary approach to informed consent law, which emphasizes the physician's duty to warn only about risks to the patient, fails to protect that patient's own autonomy.

The potential impact of the individualistic bias of informed consent law, and the messages it sends about the duties of physicians to patients, may directly affect efforts to prepare for a possible influenza pandemic. For example, as the fear of an influenza pandemic first spread in 2005, reports surfaced of an upsurge in prescriptions for Tamiflu, an antiviral medication that is believed to be effective against H5N1.[54] Such private hoarding may diminish the supply of Tamiflu that would be available in the event of a pandemic. It also adds to the risk that the medication will be used inappropriately, possibly leading to the development of resistant strains of influenza.[55] Unfortunately, the law as now interpreted does not require health care providers to explain such implications to their patients. To the contrary, by teaching physicians that their primary obligation is to empower the personal choices of individual patients alone, the law may actually discourage such discussions.

The law of informed consent and the culture of practice it supports may play a similar role in the case of vaccines.[56] Vaccines are humanity's most effective weapon against some infectious diseases. They have led to the eradication of smallpox[57] and dramatic reductions in the incidence of a host of deadly infections, including polio, diphtheria, tetanus, and measles.[58] Significantly, vaccines work at a population level. By reducing the prevalence of individuals within a population susceptible to a disease, they create so-called herd immunity that reduces the risk of the disease to everyone in the community, even those who are not or cannot be vaccinated.[59]

The common law of informed consent, as applied to vaccines, has been significantly modified by federal statutes, such as the National Childhood Vaccine Injury Act, which among other things creates a modified no-fault compensation scheme for injuries resulting from certain vaccines,[60] and post-9/11 public health emergency laws that relieve manufacturers of liability for injuries caused by unlicensed vaccines used during a public health emergency.[61] These statutes are designed to address the liability fears of vaccine makers in order to encourage the development and production of vaccines. Yet, though these laws place significant limits on state tort law actions, presumably for public ends, they do not adopt a population perspective that would require manufacturers and physicians to provide patients with information about the social benefits of vaccination. As a result, these statutes accept the individualistic premises of the common law and fail to consider the importance of educating both health care providers and patients about the population effects of vaccinations.

By failing to require that the public be informed about the social importance of vaccination, informed consent law helps to perpetuate a climate in which individuals who do not perceive themselves to be at high risk for a vaccine-preventable illness, such as the seasonal flu, often chose not to be vaccinated. As a result, vaccine-preventable infectious illnesses often spread unnecessarily. Moreover, the market for many vaccines, including the influenza vaccine, is small and inconsistent, resulting in a meager manufacturing capacity.[62] This leaves the United States with a very weak manufacturing infrastructure with which to respond to the surge demands that would be created by pandemic influenza, or even a very bad year of seasonal flu. In other words, in part because the market reacts to decisions made by individuals who are informed only about and rely on their own immediate individual interests, the system lacks the resiliency necessary to respond to epidemics. True other legal mechanisms, such as government purchasing and vaccine stockpiling, can help mitigate this capacity problem and therefore are appropriately included within the government's pandemic influenza plan.[63] But the need for an emergency response is exacerbated by the law's failure to insist that patients be made aware of the social consequences of their decisions.

A population-based approach to informed consent law would seek to change this, reducing the excessive individualism of the doctrine. To be sure, the impact of such a change, unaccompanied by broader changes in legal doctrine, might be modest. As chapter 9 will discuss, contemporary tort law, including the law of informed consent, incorporates numerous individualistic premises and erects high hurdles to the legal recognition of population interests. For example, in tort cases, the plaintiff must demonstrate that the defendant's breach of duty was the cause in fact of his or her injury. As a result, unless courts adopting a population perspective also liberalize causation requirements, an issue explored in chapter 9, it will remain difficult for plaintiffs to prevail in informed consent cases based on a physician's failure to discuss the social consequences of individual health choices.

Nevertheless, even without modifying the law of causation, courts adopting a population perspective would apply cases such as *Reisner* broadly and be more open than they now are to finding that physicians have duties to inform patients about the social consequences of health decisions in those cases in which plaintiffs can demonstrate personal harm resulting from a provider's failure to warn a patient about risks to others. In addition, courts applying a population perspective would stress in their opinions the social, rather than the solitary, nature of patients' health care decisions. Given the importance of the law of informed consent to bioethics and professional norms, a new population-based legal discourse about informed consent can help alter the culture and lay the seeds for a broader understanding of the relationship between individual and social interests. In addition, a population-based informed consent law can shape a health care system that is mindful of the interdependence of health and the need to harness health care resources in ways that best protect a population's health, whether in the face of an epidemic or in the ordinary course of events.

MANAGED CARE AND CONSUMER-DRIVEN HEALTH CARE

As mentioned, despite the fact that more than forty-five million Americans do not have health insurance,[64] the United States spends more on health care than any other nation.[65] To many politicians, health economists, and health care policy scholars, the high cost of care in the United States is a glaring, if not the overriding, problem in health care today. Health care costs, after all, create enormous pressures on government budgets as well as on employers who provide health insurance benefits. Many believe that until costs can be controlled, more equitable access will be unobtainable. Indeed, the spiraling costs that have accompanied recent state efforts to expand access to care underscore the difficulty of achieving universal coverage without successful cost containment.[66]

For the last several decades, concern over the high cost of care has played a major role in shaping health law. In response to cost concerns, federal and state governments have instituted a variety of policies that have come to dominate and complicate health law. Initially many of these responses relied on traditional models of command and control regulation. For example, in the 1970s and 1980s, many states imposed legal controls on hospital prices. They also established, with federal endorsement, Certificate of Need (CON) programs that required hospitals to obtain regulatory approval before building new facilities or expanding.[67]

Since the 1980s, the market paradigm has gained influence. This has spurred policies aimed at reducing regulation and encouraging competition and market forces. To achieve greater efficiency, the market paradigm seeks to have individuals or individual entities make health care decisions based on their own resources and costs, eliminating so-called hidden cross-subsidies, which health care providers use to help pay for the cost of treating uninsured patients.[68] Of course, a health care cost looks like a cross-subsidy only if one assumes that medical care affects only the individual patient who is treated. If one adopts a population perspective and recognizes the interdependence of health, then all patients benefit to some degree from preventing or treating diseases in others. As a result, some of the cost of treating other patients properly belongs on every patient's bill and the attempt to improve efficiency by eliminating cross-subsidies becomes both illusive and counterproductive.

Still, the market paradigm's attempt to reduce or eliminate cross-subsidies is apparent in many contemporary health laws and policies. For example, since the early 1980s, Medicare has used diagnostically related groups (DRGs) to reimburse hospitals. Under this system, hospitals are paid a set amount, based on a patient's diagnosis or DRG, regardless of the actual services the patient has received. The goal is to encourage hospitals to treat patients quickly and efficiently, thereby lowering costs. But, in so doing, the system also reduces hospitals' ability to use Medicare payments to pay for the costs of treating uninsured patients.[69] True, another part of Medicare's reimbursement formula, the so-called disproportionate share program, pays more to hospitals that treat a high percentage of uninsured patients.[70] Nevertheless, the overall goal of the DRG system, and Medicare financing, is to encourage efficiency and eliminate cross subsidies.

In the late 1980s and 1990s, the market paradigm's influence became especially evident in the rise of managed care and the law that supported that development. Most simply, managed care is a form of health insurance that combines, in some form or another, the financing aspects of health insurance with delivery of care.[71] According to Peter Jacobson, "at the heart of managed care is the promise that . . . [it] could lower costs by imposing restraints on the amount of care provided without sacrificing quality of care. To achieve these goals, managed care initiated the widespread use of cost-containment practices and financial incentives to encourage physicians to limit medical treatment."[72] Managed care companies thus compete for customers, including public and employer-sponsored health care plans, by using a variety of approaches to deliver health care in a less costly manner.

Although managed care was credited with stalling health care inflation in the 1990s,[73] in recent years health care costs have begun again to escalate at a rapid rate.[74] This may be due, in part, to the development of new and costly technologies, the aging of the population, and the fact that consumers have shied away from the most aggressive cost-containment measures of managed care, such as utilization review, provoking a managed care backlash.[75] In the place of managed care, supporters of the market paradigm and the Bush administration embraced consumer-driven health care, which seeks to "increase consumer sensitivity to cost and effectiveness by making people spend their own money for health care."[76] To support this approach, in 2005 Congress granted favorable tax treatment for health savings accounts that individuals can use, when coupled with high-deductible health insurance plans, to pay for their own routine health care.[77] And, in 2007, President Bush proposed amending the Internal Revenue Code so that the current favorable tax treatment for employer-provided health insurance would be replaced by a new standard deduction for health insurance.[78] This, advocates contend, would reduce the tax-subsidy currently available to high-cost health care plans and encourage individuals and families to pay for their own less expensive coverage. During the 2008 presidential election campaign, Republican nominee Senator John McCain endorsed a similar approach.[79]

Not surprisingly, President Obama offered a starkly different prescription during his campaign for the White House. When he was a candidate, Obama promised to reform the current mix of employer-provided and public insurance plans, using a combination of individual (for children) and employer mandates, regulation of the insurance market, and government-provided subsidies to ensure that all individuals could obtain coverage.[80] He also promised to reduce health care costs by increasing prevention and modernizing the health care system. Unlike the Republicans, he did not suggest that individuals bear more of the cost of health care services they used.

Nevertheless, by building on the existing fragmented system, and by suggesting that individuals will be given a choice of health care plans (including those they already have), Obama's campaign proposals appeared to envision the type of competition between health plans that advocates of managed competition endorsed in the 1990s.[81] Although this approach presupposed a far larger role for government regulation than consumer-driven health care does, it still relies to some degree on competition between health plans to restrain health care costs. In so doing, it fails to account for the interdependence of health or the possibility of an emerging pandemic. That is because all health policies that rely on competition encourage parties (plans, individuals, and providers) to bargain and make treatment decisions based on their own short-term interests. This may be appropriate when the bargain relates to the treatment of a noninfectious condition, but it makes less sense when the bargain pertains to an infectious disease that can harm third parties. Moreover, by prompting payors and consumers to seek fewer services and to pay only for those services they personally need, competitive approaches create disincentives for payors and individuals to seek preventive care that does not lead to short-term individual benefits. And as Gregg Bloche has persuasively argued with respect to consumer driven health care, policies that prompt people to be cost-conscious may increase racial and socioeconomic health disparities.[82]

Also alarming, from a population perspective, is the fact that all market-based approaches, unless they make adjustments for the social costs of illness, may undervalue vaccination and the treatment of infectious diseases. For example, Medicare's DRG system encourages providers to perform fewer procedures and discharge patients from hospitals more expeditiously. As a result, patients may be discharged from the hospital while either still infectious or still susceptible to infectious diseases. Likewise, by reducing cross-subsidies and discouraging overconsumption of health services that may improve population health, the market approach may rob the health care system of its redundancies.[83] In each case, health care providers are left with less revenue with which to pay for the care of the uninsured[84] and maintain extra beds and supplies.[85] As a result, the United States has an increasingly fragile, though still hardly trim, health care system. This might be appropriate if health was not determined at a population level. But in a world in which infections are ubiquitous and emerging pandemics are always a threat, a lean and trim system is a dangerously unprepared system. Or, as the *Wall Street Journal* noted, "the very rules of capitalism that make the U.S. an ultra-efficient marketplace also make it exceptionally vulnerable in a pandemic. . . . Most fundamentally, the widely embraced just-in-time business practice—which attempts to cut costs and improve quality by reducing inventory stockpiles and delivering products as needed—is at odds with the logic of 'just in case' that promotes stockpiling drugs, government intervention and overall preparedness."[86]

A population-based approach to health law would question such premises and policies that have left our health care system so ill-prepared to respond to a major pandemic. Instead of assuming that health care is solely an individual concern, best left to individual bargaining, it would take account of the social risks created by inadequate and unavailable health care. As a result, it would shy away from consumer-driven health care, which emphasizes individuals and effectively discourages them from receiving routine and preventive care critical to preventing the spread of infection and protecting population health. Likewise, with respect to managed care, a population-based policy would follow the principles of the initial Health Maintenance Organization Act of 1973,[87] and require managed care companies to provide routine primary and ambulatory care, as well as emergency room treatment, ensuring that patients with potentially infectious diseases did not face obstacles to getting treatment. In addition, courts adopting a population perspective would interpret the fiduciary duties of employer-provided health plans more broadly than is done today.[88] As a result, plans would be obligated to safeguard health in addition to the economic and contract interests of the covered population.

Of course, from a population-health perspective the problem of health care costs is critical. Employers, taxpayers, and governments have every reason to be concerned about rampant inflation and spending that does not improve the health of individual patients or populations. Excessive spending that helps support layers of bureaucracy or lavish salaries for CEOs does not provide the surge capacity and resiliency necessary to protect populations against future public health emergencies. Instead, it drains budgets of health care dollars, making both taxpayers and employers less willing to provide health insurance.

Recently, policy analysts and payors have focused attention on the relationship between cost and quality and have worked to devise ways to increase knowledge about the quality of care offered at different health care institutions, especially hospitals. Some advocates of the market paradigm have endorsed the development of health quality report cards, recognizing that price competition in the absence of quality information can undermine health and even, in the long term, undermine efforts to reduce costs.[89] Others, including the Institute of Medicine, have suggested that health care providers be paid on the basis of their performance.[90] Taking up this call, the Center for Medicare Services, the federal agency that administers the Medicare program, announced in 2007 that it would no longer pay hospitals for the extra costs associated with a limited number of hospital-based adverse events.[91]

Unfortunately, for a variety of reasons, meaningful measures of quality have been hard to devise, particularly for a health care system as fragmented as the American system, where patients see different providers, operating in different institutional settings, even within short periods. Under such circumstances, it becomes difficult to attribute the health outcomes of patients to the services of particular providers. Moreover, unless quality measures are devised with care, they may discourage providers from treating the most vulnerable patients, for whom it will be more difficult to show positive outcomes.

These difficulties do not mean that efforts should not continue to assess the quality of health care providers offer. To the contrary, a population perspective would encourage such efforts. In particular, it would emphasize the importance of addressing the rates of hospital-based infections and other adverse events that have a broad population effect. A population perspective, however, would caution against imposing competition-promoting policies in the absence of effective ways of comparing quality of care. Moreover, mindful of the ubiquity of infection and the social cost of disease, a population perspective would insist that quality measures take into account not only population effects, but also the capacities of health care institutions, particularly hospitals, to prevent and respond to possible outbreaks and surges in disease.

In effect, a population perspective would place the problem of infection, microbial as well as metaphoric, front and center in the struggle to provide affordable, high-quality health care. Rather than seeing health care solely as a commodity to be bought at price-sensitive bargains, a population perspective would appreciate that health care is at least a partial public good that individual bargains may undervalue. Although this approach does not dictate a single or simple solution to the problem of health care access and inflation, it would ensure that the policies do not confuse efficiency with a lack of capacity to protect populations from future harms.

THE HEALTH SAFETY NET

The discussion so far has largely ignored the elephant in the room: the failure of the United States to provide health insurance to all of its citizens[92] Often this failure is decried from an egalitarian or distributive justice perspective. From a population perspective, it raises an additional alarm: it threatens the health of not only the uninsured (numerous studies show that health insurance status is associated with positive health)[93] but everyone else as well.[94] Individuals without insurance may delay treatment, compromising efforts to keep track of an emerging epidemic and permitting infections to remain untreated and spread in the community. In addition, the failure to compensate providers for the care ultimately provided to the uninsured creates a financial strain on providers, especially hospitals, leaving them with fewer resources to prepare for a possible pandemic.[95]

The safety net paradigm responds to the nation's failure to this point to provide a universal, positive right to health care, instead creating limited and sometimes meager programs for those who cannot otherwise afford insurance. The most notable government programs are Medicare, which provides near universal coverage for the sixty-five and older population, and Medicaid, which provides far less than universal coverage for poor children and families and disabled adults. Each of these programs has multiple gaps, many of which fail to consider the social consequences of the cessation in coverage they create. The recently created Medicare D prescription drug program (to give but one glaring example) contains a doughnut hole, or gap in coverage, that in 2008 existed between the $2,510 and $4,050 of expenses.[96] When seniors' drug costs fall within this gap they effectively lose their prescription drug insurance. This gap obviously has the potential of harming beneficiaries who may have to cut back on their medications once they fall into the hole. It can also harm others if beneficiaries discontinue antibiotic or antiviral medications, risking the development of drug resistance or the spread of infection.

The neglect of infection is also evident in the nation's ultimate safety net, the Emergency Medical Treatment and Labor Act, or EMTALA.[97] Originally enacted in 1986, as the market paradigm took hold and policies were put into place to encourage competition in the health care system, EMTALA sought to create a counterweight to market forces by creating a universal right to emergency treatment. Put most bluntly, EMTALA prohibits hospitals from dumping uninsured or otherwise undesirable patients,[98] thereby preventing them from doing precisely what the market paradigm wants hospitals to do.

Despite EMTALA's creation of a universal right to emergency treatment, the statute as written and interpreted fails to recognize the social cost of disease. Instead, EMTALA treats the obligation to the uninsured as one limited to the needs of individual patients, rather than populations. Indeed, there is substantial reason to believe that EMTALA, as it now stands, may actually complicate the nation's ability to respond to a pandemic. EMTALA's neglect of infection is easy to see. Under the act, a hospital must provide "an appropriate medical screening" to everyone who seeks treatment in an emergency room.[99] Through the screening, the hospital must determine if the individual has an "emergency medical condition." If the patient does not, the hospital's obligations under EMTALA end. The patient may be left untreated.

The statute defines an emergency medical condition, except in the case of a pregnant woman,[100] as:

(A) a medical condition manifesting itself by acute symptoms of sufficient severity (including severe pain) such that the absence of immediate medical attention could reasonably be expected to result in—

   (i)   placing the health of the individual (or, with respect to a pregnant woman, the health of the woman or her unborn child) in serious jeopardy,

   (ii) serious impairment to bodily functions, or

   (iii) serious dysfunction of any bodily organ or part.[101]

This definition, as Sara Rosenbaum and Brian Kamoie have noted, "is individual-centric, not focused on populations; that is, the emergency exam is expected to center on the individual, not whether the health of the population at large would be seriously jeopardized were the patient not stabilized or given a medical transfer."[102] As a result, if a patient has an infectious disease but is not experiencing symptoms severe enough to satisfy the statutory definition, a hospital would be perfectly free under EMTALA to release the patient without providing any treatment or even any advice about how not to spread the disease to others.

Moreover, even if the patient has an emergency medical condition within the meaning of the statute, the hospital's obligation ends once the patient is stabilized, which occurs when "no material deterioration of the condition is likely, within reasonable medical probability, to result from or occur during the transfer of an individual from a facility, or, with respect to a [pregnant woman] to deliver."[103] This definition is also individual-centric. It focuses on whether the patient's own medical condition would decline if he or she were released. The impact of a transfer or release on others is not considered by EMTALA, though it may be by state public health laws that require providers to report some infectious diseases to the state health department, which may or may not take action. But, under EMTALA, a hospital may release a patient with an infectious disease who is stable without ensuring that the patient will receive adequate follow-up care to prevent the development of drug resistance (if the patient has been put on antibiotics or antiviral medication). Nor does EMTALA require a hospital to counsel a patient who is infectious with a disease such as HIV as to the steps to take to avoid spreading the disease to others. In effect, EMTALA leaves the question of whether the patient receives necessary follow-up care and thereby whether others are endangered by the patient's illness solely to the patient, who may or may not have access to continuing care.

From a population perspective, EMTALA's greatest shortcoming is that it places the ultimate safety net in the emergency room but fails to fund the care it mandates. In 2006, the Institute of Medicine issued a report, *Hospital-Based Emergency Care: At the Breaking Point*, that presents a disturbing and, in light of a possible pandemic, terrifying portrait of the state of America's emergency rooms.[104] According to the report, the number of visits to emergency rooms increased by 26 percent between 1993 and 2003.[105] More than 91 percent of hospitals in a national survey reported that their emergency rooms were overcrowded.[106] Moreover, more than 500,000 ambulances were diverted in 2003 alone, a year in which there was no pandemic.[107] Although EMTALA is not the sole cause of overcrowding (the policies discussed earlier that aim to trim the fat out of the health care system also play a major role), it likely contributes both by requiring hospitals to provide unfunded services and by undermining social and political pressures to provide broader access to care for Americans.[108] Thus EMTALA helps to structure a hospital system that is overcrowded and lacks the surge capacity that will be required should a pandemic arise.

Policymakers have recognized that EMTALA may present problems in the event of a public health emergency. In particular, legislators and members of the federal executive branch have agreed that in an emergency, EMTALA may interfere with efforts to isolate an infectious agent, such as smallpox, in a single "hot" hospital.[109] As a result, the federal government has undertaken several initiatives that effectively permit the waiver of EMTALA's obligations during a public health emergency. For example, the Public Health Security and Bioterrorism Preparedness and Response Act of 2002 permits the secretary of the Department of Health and Human Services to waive sanctions for violations of EMTALA during a declared public health emergency.[110] This relatively narrow exception to EMTALA may, if used appropriately, be a useful tool in controlling the spread of infection and husbanding resources during a public health emergency such as a pandemic or bioterrorist incident, but it fails to address the underlying problem. Instead of developing a solution that ensures both continuing care to those who have infections and financial resources to those who treat them, the act engages in "preparedness" by creating emergency exceptions to everyday rules. In short, the act, like EMTALA itself and health law more generally, continues the illusion that epidemics are occasional and that illness is usually a private matter. A population-based approach would discard those illusions. Not only would it recommend a revision of EMTALA to ensure the treatment of patients with infections, it would emphasize the social cost of the nation's failure to pay for health care for all. In a world in which infections are common and pandemics spread around the globe in but a few hours, that failure is not only inhumane, it is dangerous.

A POPULATION-BASED HEALTH LAW

Sometimes it seems as if there are two health laws. One, public health law, focuses on the authority of government agencies charged with protecting public health as well as the rights of individuals subject to such regulations. The other, more visible health law emphasizes the relationship between health care providers, patients, and payors. Sadly, these two health laws inadequately inform the other. Thus even as attention has turned to the threat of a public health emergency, and even as preparedness efforts have been applied to the health care system, "plain old health law" remains largely oblivious of public health threats and the interdependency of the health of populations.

A population-based legal analysis would close the chasm between public health law and health law, revisiting the latter in light of the former's population perspective. Most fundamentally, a population-based approach would reject the assumption shared by all of the leading paradigms within health law: that ill health is a private matter. Instead, it would recognize the ubiquity of infection and the interdependency of population health. By so doing, it would revise existing doctrines and policies to take account of the public cost of disease. It would insist that patients and providers learn about the social consequences of treatment decisions and it would devise payment mechanisms that ensure a surge capacity sufficient to respond to an epidemic. Most important, it would recognize that providing health care to those who cannot otherwise afford it is not simply a matter of charity. Given the interdependency of health, it is a necessary component for the protection of everyone's health.

NOTES

1. This chapter is based in part on Wendy E. Parmet, *Unprepared: Why Health Law Fails to Prepare Us for a Pandemic*, 2 J. HEALTH & BIOMED. L. 157 (Issue 2) (2006).

2. Edward P. Richards, Terry O'Brien, & Katharine C. Rathbun, *Bioterrorism and the Use of Fear in Public Health*, 34 URB. LAW 685, 687–89 (2002).

3. Elin Gursky & Avani Parikh, *Some Right Jabs and Back in the Ring: Lessons Learned from the Phase I Civilian Smallpox Program*, 8 J. HEALTH CARE L. & POL'Y 162, 171–84 (2005).

4. World Health Organization, *Avian Influenza ("Bird Flu") Fact Sheet* (February 2006), http://www.who.int/mediacentre/factsheets/avian_influenza/en/index. html (last visited Nov. 15, 2008); Robert G. Webster & Elena Govorkova, *HN51 Influenza-Continuing Evolution and Spread*, 355 N. ENG. J. MED. 2174, 2174–77 (2006).

5. Homeland Security Council, *National Strategy for Pandemic Influenza,* (November 2005) (hereinafter *National Strategy*), http://www.whitehouse.gov/ homeland/nspi.pdf (last visited Nov. 4, 2006).

6. Homeland Security Council, *National Strategy for Pandemic Influenza, Implementation Plan: One Year Summary* (July 2007), http://www.whitehouse.gov/ homeland/nspi_oneyear.pdf (last visited Nov. 4, 2008); Homeland Security Council, *National Strategy for Pandemic Influenza: Implementation Plan,* 1 (May 2006) (hereinafter *Implementation Plan*), http://www.whitehouse.gov/homeland/nspi_ implementation.pdf (last visited Nov. 4, 2006); U.S. Dep't Health and Human Services, *HHS Pandemic Influenza Plan*, http://www.hhs.gov/pandemicflu/plan/pdf/ HHS PandemicInfluenzaPlan. pdf (November 2005) (last visited Nov. 4, 2008). For

a further list of federal plans and reports, see *Federal Planning and Response Activities*, http://www.pandemicflu.gov/plan/federal/index.html (last visited Nov. 4, 2008).

7. *See* Homeland Security Council, *National Strategy for Pandemic Influenza*, *supra* note 5, at 3.

8. *Id.* at 2.

9. Homeland Security Council, *Implementation Plan*, *supra* note 6, at 1.

10. *Id.* at 105–6.

11. *Id.* at 110.

12. *Id.* at 20.

13. *See* Theodore H. Tulchinsky & Elena A. Varavikova, The New Public Health: An Introduction for the 21st Century 42 (2000).

14. T. Kue Young, Population Health: Concepts And Methods 42–43 (1998).

15. Lawrence O. Gostin, *Pandemic Influenza: Public Health Preparedness for the Next Global Health Emergency*, 32 J.L. Med. & Ethics 565, 565 (2004).

16. John M. Barry, The Great Influenza: The Epic Story of the Deadliest Plague in History 4 (2004).

17. Edwin D. Kilbourne, *Influenza Pandemics of the 20th Century*, 12 Emerging Infectious Diseases 9 (2006), http://www.cdc.gov/ncidod/EID/vol12no01/05-1254.htm (last visited Dec. 14, 2008).

18. Cécile Viboud et al., *Influenza Epidemics in the United States, France, and Australia, 1972–1997*, 10 Emerging Infectious Diseases 32, 32 (2004), http://www.cdc.gov/ncidod/eid/vol10no1/02–0705.htm (last visited Dec. 14, 2008).

19. Inst. of Med., Comm. on Emerging Microbial Threats to Health, Microbial Threats to Health: Emergence, Detection and Response 26 (2003).

20. *Id.* at 25. Recently the World Health Organization and UNAIDS adopted a new methodology for estimating the incidence of HIV disease and mortality. This has led to a decline in the estimate of the number of people who are believed to have died from AIDS in 2007 to "only" 2.1 million. UNAIDS and World Health Organization, *07 AIDS Epidemic Update* 10–12 (2007), http://data.unaids.org/pub/EPISlides/2007/2007_epiupdate_en.pdf (last visited Nov. 4, 2008). This will presumably lower WHO's overall estimate of the number of deaths due to infectious disease.

21. Inst. of Med., *supra* note 19, at 23.

22. *Id.* at 2.

23. Betsey McCaughey, *Unnecessary Deaths: The Human and Financial Costs of Hospital Infections* 1–2 (2d ed. 2006), http://www.hospitalinfection.org/rid booklet.pdf (last visited Nov. 3, 2008).

24. David Woodward & Richard D. Smith, *Global Public Goods and Health*, *in* Global Public Goods for Health: Health Economic and Public Health Perspectives 10–13 (Richard Smith et al. eds, 2003).

25. Medline Plus, Medical Dictionary, http://www.nlm.nih.gov/medline plus/mplusdictionary.html (type "epidemic" into search term) (last visited Sept. 10, 2006).

26. Richard M. Krause, *Introduction to Emerging Infectious Diseases: Stemming the Tide*, *in* EMERGING INFECTIONS 7 (Richard M. Krause ed., 1998).

27. Mark A. Hall, *The History and Future of Health Care Law: An Essentialist View*, 41 WAKE FOREST L. REV. 347, 350 (2006).

28. *Id.* at 360.

29. Timothy Stoltzfus Jost, *Reflections from the Experts: Why Can't We Do What They Do? National Health Reform Abroad*, 32 J.L. MED. & ETHICS 433, 433 (2004).

30. U.S. Census Bureau, *Health Insurance Coverage: 2007*, http://www.census.gov/hhes/www/hlthins/hlthin07/hlth07asc.html (last visited Jan. 17, 2009).

31. The Access Project, *The Consequences of Medical Debt; Evidence from Three Communities* (February 2003), http://www.accessproject.org/downloads/med_consequences.pdf (last visited Nov. 4, 2008).

32. Kaiser Comm'n on Medicaid and the Uninsured, Kaiser Family Foundation, *The Uninsured and the Difference Health Insurance Makes*, http://www.kff.org/uninsured/upload/1420_10.pdf (last visited Nov. 3, 2008).

33. E. Haavi Morreim, *Cost Containment and the Standard of Medical Care*, 75 CALIF. L. REV. 1719, 1725 (1987).

34. PUB. L. NO. 89–97, 102(a), 70 STAT. 290, 291 (1965), *codified at* 42 U.S.C. 1395.

35. Patricia Illingworth & Wendy E. Parmet, *What and Why Autonomy?*, *in* ETHICAL HEALTH CARE 74–78 (Patricia Illingworth & Wendy E. Parmet eds., 2005).

36. Mark A. Hall & Carl E. Schneider, *Where is the "There" in Health Law? Can It Become a Coherent Field?*, 14 HEALTH MATRIX 101, 102 (2004).

37. BARRY R. FURROW ET AL., HEALTH LAW 353 (2d ed. 2000).

38. Clark C. Havighurst, *I've Seen Enough! My Life and Times in Health Law and Policy*, 14 HEALTH MATRIX 107, 115 (2004).

39. Philip Lee et al., *Health Care in America: A New Generation of Challenges: Politics, Health Policy and the American Character*, 17 STAN. L. & POL'Y REV. 7, 29 (2006).

40. Rand E. Rosenblatt, *The Four Ages of Health Law*, 14 HEALTH MATRIX 155, 155–56 (2004).

41. Havighurst, *supra* note 38, at 110.

42. Uwe E. Reinhardt, Peter S. Hussey, & Gerard F. Anderson, *U.S. Health Care Spending in an International Context*, 23 HEALTH AFFAIRS 3, 10–11 (May–June 2004).

43. Rosenblatt, *supra* note 40, at 155.

44. 45 C.F.R. § 46.109(b); 45 C.F.R. §. 46.116 (2005).

45. 45 C.F.R. §§ 164.508–510 (2005).

46. *E.g.*, Cruzan v. Director, Missouri Dep't of Health, 497 U.S. 261, 269–70 (1990).

47. FURROW ET AL. *supra* note 37, at 311.

48. *E.g.*, Canterbury v. Spence, 464 F.2d 772 (D.C. Cir. 1972); Cobbs v. Grant, 502 P.2d 1, 11 (Cal. 1972).

49. 37 Cal. Rptr.2d 518 (Cal. Ct. App. 1995).

50. 551 P.2d 334 (Cal. 1976).

51. 37 Cal. Rptr.2d at 520–21.

52. *E.g.*, Hawkins v. Pizarro, 713 So. 2d 1036, 1038 (Fla. Dist. Ct. App. 1998).

53. David Atkins, Joanna Siegel, & Jean Slutsky, *Making Policy When the Evidence Is in Dispute: Good Health Policy Making Involves Consideration of Much More than Clinical Evidence*, 24 HEALTH AFFAIRS 102, 110 (Jan.–Feb. 2005).

54. *E.g.*, Delthia Ricks, *Patients' Fear Boosts Antiviral Sales*, NEWSDAY, Mar. 17, 2006, at A05.

55. Denise Grady & Gina Kolata, *Avian Flu: The Uncertain Threat*, N.Y. TIMES, Mar. 28, 2006, at F1.

56. Wendy E. Parmet, *Informed Consent and Public Health: Are They Compatible When It Comes to Vaccines?*, 8 J. HEALTH CARE L. & POL'Y 71, 107–10 (2005).

57. Donald A. Henderson, *Eradication: Lessons from the Past*, 48 MORBIDITY & MORTALITY WKLY REP. 16 (1999), http://www.cdc.gov/mmwr/preview/mmwr html/su48a6.htm (last visited Nov. 7, 2008).

58. *See* Parmet, *supra* note 56, at 93.

59. INST. OF MED., FINANCING VACCINES IN THE 21ST CENTURY: ASSURING ACCESS AND AVAILABILITY 27 (2004).

60. *See* 42 U.S.C. §§ 300aa-1-34 *et seq.* (2003).

61. Public Readiness and Emergency Preparedness Act, Pub. L. No. 109–148, 119 Stat. 2818 (2005).

62. TIM BROOKES, A WARNING SHOT: INFLUENZA AND THE 2004 FLU VACCINE SHORTAGE 24 (2005).

63. *See* Homeland Security Council, *Implementation Plan*, *supra* note 5, at 104–05.

64. U.S. Census Bureau, *supra* note 30.

65. Uwe E. Reinhardt, Peter S. Hussey, & Gerard F. Anderson, *supra* note 42, at 10, 11.

66. Alice Dembner, *Healthcare Cost Increases Mass. Budget Dominate Debate— Controlling Them Said Key to Keeping Universal Coverage*, BOSTON GLOBE, Mar. 26, 2008, at A12 (describing high cost of Massachusetts health care reform and stress it is placing on efforts to expand coverage).

67. Lauretta Higgins Wolfson, *State Regulation of Health Facility Planning: The Economic Theory and Political Realities of Certificates of Need*, 4 DEPAUL J. HEALTH CARE L. 261, 266–67 (2001).

68. Rosenblatt, *supra* note 40, at 155–56.

69. Steven Golub, *The Role of Medicare Reimbursement in Contemporary Hospital Finance*, 11 AM. J.L. MED. 501, 519 (1986). For an early analysis of DRGs, see J. Timothy Phillips & Don E. Wineberg, *Medicare Prospective Payment: A Quiet Revolution*, 87 W. VA. L. REV. 13 (1984).

70. Dean M. Harris, *The Future of Medicare, Post Great Society and Post Plus-Choice Legal and Policy Issues: Beyond Beneficiaries: Using the Medicare Program to Accomplish Broader Public Goals*, 60 WASH. & LEE. L. REV. 1251, 1290 (2003).

71. PETER D. JACOBSON, STRANGERS IN THE NIGHT, LAW AND MEDICINE IN THE MANAGED CARE ERA 8 (2002).

72. *Id.*

73. Federal Trade Comm'n & Dep't of Justice, *Improving Health Care: A Dose of Competition—Executive Summary, reprinted in* 31 J. HEALTH POL. POL'Y & L. 437, 439 (2006).

74. Michael A. Fletcher, *Rising Health Costs Cut into Wages, Higher Fees Squeeze Employers, Workers,* WASH. POST, Mar. 24, 2008, at A01; Katharine Levit et al., *Inflation Spurs Health Spending in 2000,* 21 HEALTH AFFAIRS 172, 172 (2002).

75. Paul B. Ginsburg, *Competition in Health Care: Its Evolution over the Past Decade,* 24 HEALTH AFFAIRS 1512, 1515–16 (2005).

76. Timothy S. Jost & Mark A. Hall, *The Role of State Regulation in Consumer-Driven Health Care,* 31 AM. J.L. & MED. 395, 395 (2005).

77. Pub. L. No. 108–173 (2003).

78. Robert D. Reischauer, *Perspective—Benefits with Risks: Bush's Tax-Based Health Care Proposals,* 356 N. ENG. J. MED. 1393, 1393 (2007).

79. McCain-Palin, *The Truth about the McCain-Palin Health Care Plan,* http:// www.johnmccain.com/Informing/Issues/19ba2f1c-c03f-4ac2-8cd5-5cf2edb527cf .htm (last visited Nov. 8, 2008).

80. Obama-Biden, *Healthcare,* http://www.barackobama.com/issues/health-care/index.php (last visited Nov. 8, 2008). For a discussion of the various plans put forth by the 2008 presidential candidates, see Jonathan Oberlander, *Presidential Politics and the Resurgence of Health Care Reform,* 275 N. ENG. J. MED. 2102 *passim* (2007).

81. *E.g.,* Alain C. Enthoven, *The History and Principles of Managed Competition,* 12 HEALTH AFFAIRS 24, 24–48 (1993).

82. M. Gregg Bloche, *Consumer-Directed Health Care and the Disadvantaged: If the Consumer-Directed Model Prevails in the Marketplace, Class and Race Disparities Will Probably Worsen,* 26 HEALTH AFFAIRS 1315, 1320–22 (2007).

83. Deanna Bellandi, *Healthcare Industry Gets Clean Bill of Health: Predictions of Economic Ills Haven't Been Realized,* 28 MODERN HEALTHCARE 68 (1998).

84. INST. OF MED., AMERICA'S HEALTH CARE SAFETY NET: INTACT BUT ENDANGERED (2000).

85. *See* Vickie J. Williams, *Fluconomics—Preserving our Hospital Infrastructure during and after a Pandemic,* 7 YALE J. HEALTH POL'Y L. & ETHICS 99, 108–09 (2007) (discussing the impact of DRGs on hospital financing in the event of an influenza pandemic).

86. Bernard Wysocki Jr. & Sarah Lueck, *Just-in-Time Inventories Make U.S. Vulnerable in a Pandemic,* WALL STREET JOURNAL, Jan. 12, 2006, at A1.

87. Health Maintenance Organization Act of 1973, Pub. L. 93–222 (codified at 42 U.S.C. §§ 300e *et seq.* (1996)).

88. 29 U.S.C. § 1104(a). *See* Pegram v. Herdrich, 530 U.S. 211 (2000) (interpreting ERISA's fiduciary duties as to not apply to decisions by managed care plans to create economic incentives to withhold medical care).

89. Federal Trade Comm'n & U.S. Dep't of Justice, *supra* note 73, at 462.

90. COMM. ON QUALITY OF HEALTH CARE IN AMERICA, INST. OF MED., NAT. ACAD. OF SCI., CROSSING THE QUALITY CHASM: A NEW HEALTH SYSTEM FOR THE

21ST CENTURY 17, 181–208 (2001). For an analysis of pay for performance, see William M. Sage & Dev N. Kalyan, *Horses or Unicorns: Can Paying for Performance Make Quality Competition Routine?* 31 J. HEALTH POL'Y POL. & L. 531, 533–53 (2006).

91. Meredith B. Rosenthal, *Perspective—Nonpayment for Performance? Medicare's New Reimbursement Rule*, 357 N. ENG. J. MED. 1573, 1573–575 (2007).

92. Kaiser Commission on Medicaid and the Uninsured, *supra* note 32.

93. Laura D. Hermer, *Private Health Insurance in the United States: A Proposal for a More Functional System*, 6 HOUS. J. HEALTH L. & POL'Y 1, 62 (2005) (reviewing studies).

94. Mark A. Rothstein, *Are Traditional Public Health Strategies Consistent with Contemporary American Values?*, 77 TEMP. L. REV. 175, 179 (2004).

95. Elizabeth A. Weeks, *After the Catastrophe: Disaster Relief for Hospitals*, 85 N.C.L. REV. 223 (2006).

96. Kaiseredu.org, *Prescription Drug Benefit under Medicare*, http://www.kaiseredu.org/topics_im.asp?id = 131&imID = 1&parentID = 66 (last visited Nov. 4, 2008).

97. 42 U.S.C. § 1395dd (1986).

98. Sara Rosenbaum & Brain Kamoie, *Finding a Way through the Hospital Door: The Role of Emtala in Public Health Emergencies*, 31 J.L. MED. & ETHICS 590, 591 (2003).

99. 42 U.S.C. § 1395dd(a)(2006).

100. *See* 42 U.S.C. § 1395dd(e)(1)(B)(2006).

101. 42 U.S.C. § 1395dd(e)(1)(A)(2006).

102. Rosenbaum and Kamoie, *supra* note 98, at 592.

103. 42 U.S.C. §1395dd(e)(3)(A)(2006).

104. *See* INST. OF MED., HOSPITAL-BASED EMERGENCY CARE AT THE BREAKING POINT 5 (2006), http://newton.nap.edu/catalog/11621.html (last visited Oct. 11, 2008).

105. *Id.* at 1.

106. *Id.* at 3.

107. *Id.*

108. *See id.* at 2.

109. *See* Rosenbaum & Kamoie, *supra* note 98, at 594–95.

110. Public Health Security and Bioterrorism Preparedness and Response Act of 2002, Pub. L. No. 107–188, § 143(b)(3) (codified at 42 U.S.C. § 1320b-5(2004)).

CHAPTER 9

Tort Law: A Population Approach to Private Law

Tort is a haphazard public health strategy.

—Robert L. Rabin, *The Tobacco Litigation:
A Tentative Assessment*

A SBESTOS, CIGARETTES, lead paint, and guns. In recent decades privately initiated tort litigation about each of these dangerous products and others has captured the headlines, occupied courtrooms, and provoked a heated debate about the role of tort law in protecting public health. On one side of the debate, critics of the tort system, such as Peter Huber, the author of *Galileo's Revenge*, bemoan junk science and cry out against the high cost of frivolous litigation.[1] On the other side, trial lawyers and some public health advocates contend that tort law is a critical tool for promoting population health.

This chapter uses population-based legal analysis to engage that debate and explore tort law's role in protecting population health, assessing contemporary tort theory from a population perspective, critiquing tort law, and suggesting doctrinal reforms. The chapter concludes by reaffirming tort law's importance to population health.

INJURY PREVENTION AND TORT LAW—
THE THEORETICAL LANDSCAPE

Put most simply, tort law is the field of civil (noncriminal) law that determines the rights and responsibilities that individuals and organizations, including corporations, owe one another.[2] In contrast to the law of contracts, in which rights and responsibilities flow primarily from private agreements, in tort law responsibilities arise from and are shaped by social, especially legal, norms. On the other hand, tort actions are private in that they are generally initiated by private parties who seek compensation. Hence tort law has both public and private characteristics. In essence, it lies at the intersection of private and public law.[3] Thus tort law is an especially apt domain of private law in which to apply population-based legal analysis, which emphasizes public health and the role of populations.

But do torts scholars agree? Do they see tort law as embodying the key tenets of population-based legal analysis, including the importance of populations and the promotion of public health? Or do they view it through a prism of individual rights and private interests, seeing it as relatively unconcerned about the values and issues that are central to population-based legal analysis?

Scholars disagree about the answers to these questions and the relationship between tort law and population health. All tort scholars concede that tort law seeks to compensate injured parties, but they have conducted a heated debate about its other aspirations. On one side of this debate have been those, such as George Fletcher, who emphasize tort law's moral foundations and believe that it seeks to affirm principles of corrective justice.[4] Although these principles may derive from or reflect social goals, scholars adhering to this view tend to emphasize individual rights over the well-being of populations. From a population perspective, this view of tort law is, of course, highly problematic because it both ignores the critical value of population health and neglects the role that populations play as subjects and objects of the law.

Not all scholars, however, see tort law as primarily individualistic and disinterested in population health. For example, law and economics scholars, such as Guido Calabresi[5] and Richard Posner,[6] argue that tort law is and ought to be properly concerned with achieving an optimal distribution between the costs of accidents and the costs of accident avoidance. To them, questions about population health, framed as questions of deterrence of injuries, are central to tort law. Moreover, because law and economics scholars prioritize social welfare over individual claims, they share with the population perspective a concern for the well-being of groups and a disdain for an inflexible individualism. As we shall see, this has led both judges and scholars who adopt a law and economics approach to advocate for certain changes in tort doctrine (such as a relaxation of the causation requirement) that a population-based approach would also recommend.[7]

Nevertheless, the law and economics view of tort law diverges from a population perspective in many critical ways. First, though the law and economics approach accepts that preventing injuries is a critical goal of tort law, it treats maximizing welfare, rather than protecting population health, as tort law's highest objective.[8] As a result, its advocates believe that tort law should deter preventable injuries or deaths only when doing so maximizes welfare.[9] (Other more progressive law and economics proponents, however, argue that so-called strict liability should nevertheless be imposed on certain defendants, such as the manufacturers of goods, on the theory that they can best bear and spread the cost of injuries.)[10] This, of course, is the teaching of the so-called Hand formula, negligence law's version of the cost-benefit analysis, which holds that a defendant is negligent only when he or she has failed to take precautions that would cost less than the cost of the plaintiff's injury discounted by its probability of occurrence.[11] Likewise it is the clear implication of risk-utility analysis, the term applied to the form of cost-benefit analysis used in product liability cases, thus moving that area of tort law closer to negligence law.[12]

In contrast, a population-based approach would consider the reduction of injuries as tort law's chief goal, rejecting the subordination of population health to economic efficiency. That does not mean, of course, that population-based legal analysis denies that trade-offs are necessary. Informed by humanity's experience with epidemics, population-based legal analysis is neither naïve nor utopian; it recognizes that death and injury are inevitable. Moreover, population-based legal analysis accepts that resources are scarce and that hard, indeed tragic, choices are inevitable. This means that tort law must necessarily be mindful of the unintended, potentially deleterious consequences of legal rules that aim to protect population health. For example, a tort rule that holds physicians liable for failing to perform diagnostic tests may have the unintended effect of increasing the number of patients who are given false positive results and consequently subjected to unnecessary and even risky additional tests.[13] But a population-based tort law would be far less willing than law and economics theorists to accept readily preventable injuries on the grounds of economic efficiency. In effect, rather than focusing on the trade-offs between human injuries and aggregate welfare, a population-based approach would emphasize the trade-offs among and between different threats to the health of different populations, thereby avoiding many of the utilitarian pitfalls for which the law and economics approach has rightly been castigated.[14]

The reliance by the law and economics approach on cost-benefit analysis reveals another critical distinction between it and population-based legal analysis. In tort cases, compensable injuries must always be assigned dollar values in order to calculate and award damages. The law and economics approach goes further, however, treating the conversion of human injury and death into dollars not simply as a crude but necessary tool for the award of damages, but rather as a fundamental component of the determination of a defendant's liability. Thus the Hand formula and similar tests for liability require that the plaintiff's injury be converted into dollars so that it can be measured against the cost of prevention to determine if the defendant is liable.

Such a monetization of injury and death is, of course, a hallmark of cost-benefit analysis as it is applied in the regulatory arena. In tort law, its use for the ascertainment of liability is problematic for several reasons. First, as critics have suggested, the conversion of human pain, injury, and death into dollars is to some degree incompatible with the value and meaning we give to human health.[15] As a result, it clashes with the norms and values of a population approach and should be used only when it is essential to do so (for the calculation of damages), and not to determine liability. Second, the conversion process is suspect because it gives a false aura of certainty, offering the illusion of specificity where none is available.[16] In fact, none of the methods used to determine the dollar value of health or injury prevention, including revealed preference studies, which seek to determine the dollar value that people place on certain risks and actuarial assessments, can offer a fully satisfactory answer to the question of how we much we value life and the avoidance of injury or disease.[17] This is in part because such valuations inevitably accept the existing distribution of wealth so that the value of the life of a poor person is viewed as less than that of a wealthy one.[18] It is also because such valuations inevitably ignore the population effect of injuries and premature deaths; losses that are felt not only by individuals and their families but also by broader populations. Finally, the conversion process generally ignores the critical fact that individual preferences are themselves at least partially socially determined.[19]

In a world in which government does not protect public health, life may well be nasty, brutish, and short, and the early death of a child or a young adult may be accepted as merely the way of the world. In contrast, if population health is cherished and safeguarded by the law, lives will be longer and premature death may be considered a monumental loss, not only to the individual plaintiff and his or her immediate family (who may be subject to compensation under tort law), but more broadly to a larger population.

In addition, the law and economics approach often ignores the fact that the costs of preventing accidents (or the benefits gained from permitting accidents) are themselves a function of the social order. Consider, for example, a products liability case in which the question is whether a product was defective in design. The Products Liability Restatement adopts a law and economics perspective by imposing a risk-utility or cost-benefit test as the primary means for deciding whether there is a design defect.[20] One component of that test requires consideration of whether, at the time of the product's design, a reasonable alternative design existed.[21] That question, however, accepts the existing technology and the costs associated with it as a given, unaffected by the law. Yet legal interventions designed to promote health and safety can potentially have the effect of "pushing" new technologies.[22] Thus to say that a safer design is not economically feasible because of its cost is to forget that new technologies may be developed and costs may fall once more safety is required by law.

Another stark difference between the law and economics approach to tort law and a population-based approach concerns the treatment of subpopulations and the recognition that dangerous activities can have a disparate effect on different groups. Because the law and economics approach sees tort law as striving to maximize aggregate welfare, it can be blind, at least in the hands of its more market-loving adherents, to the disparate impact that various activities, such as dumping hazardous waste, may have on distinct and often vulnerable populations. In contrast, because the population perspective considers an activity's impact not simply on the aggregate population, but also on multiple, contingent, and varying populations, it would find the trade-off of one population's health for greater wealth for the overall population to be quite problematic.

Likewise, as discussed, the law and economics approach fails to consider the full social costs of accidents. Although scholars such as Guido Calabresi have paid considerable attention to the costs of accidents and have recognized accidents as a social problem, they have not fully appreciated the social or public dimensions of preventable death and injury.[23] A population perspective recognizes that an individual's illness or death does not affect only that individual or even the individual's immediate family members (who may be compensated by tort law through loss of consortium or wrongful death actions). Preventable illness and premature death have broader, ripple effects on communities. Consider, for example, the impact on a neighborhood when a child is killed by a stray bullet. Although many of these social costs cannot be readily quantified, they are nevertheless real and help shape the experiences of populations and the environment in which risks are determined. A population-based approach would consider these very important but often neglected social costs and recognize that preventable injuries and death are population harms that tort law must aim to reduce.

Injury Prevention and Tort Law— the Doctrinal Environment

From a population perspective, tort law should seek to protect the health of populations. To do so, it must understand both how populations experience and determine risk. Contemporary tort doctrine, however, frequently overlooks the importance of populations, focusing instead on the injuries, rights, and duties of individuals. By so doing, it impedes law's ability to promote the health of both populations and the individuals it supposedly serves.

Numerous tort doctrines and rules evidence a stark individualism that undermines the law's ability to deter accidents, even to the degree suggested by a cost-benefit analysis. For example, the defense of assumption of risk permits defendants to escape liability for otherwise hazard-creating activity by focusing on the explicit or implicit consent of individual plain-tiffs to the risk, generally disregarding both the social factors that helped to create the plaintiff's so-called consent as well as the risks that broader populations face.[24] Early in the twentieth century, employers often used this defense successfully to escape liability to injured workers on the the-ory that workers chose or assumed the hazards associated with the work-place.[25] Although worker compensation laws have largely extinguished this use of the assumption of risk defense,[26] and many state courts have rejected it for activities of significant public import,[27] the idea that plaintiffs should bear individual responsibility for the injuries they suffer, despite the circumstances they face and the social costs of the defendant's actions, continues to permeate tort law, especially in the application of comparative fault. For example, cigarette manufacturers have at times attempted to escape liability on the theory that an ill or dead plaintiff knew about and chose the risk of smoking.[28]

Assumption of risk and related doctrines presuppose that individuals develop and exercise truly free and autonomous choices apart from the social environment they inhabit. Although some courts have recognized that individuals cannot make free choices when they are addicted,[29] courts more often forget that individual preferences are largely determined by population-wide factors, including not only the advertising and marketing campaigns of defendants, but also the social norms of the individual's peer groups.[30] By assuming that someone who engages in a risky behavior in a social environment or population that normalizes or entices that behavior has chosen and accepted the risks of the behavior is to ignore the popula-tion nature of risks and retard tort law's ability to deter injury-provoking behavior.

A similar disregard for population impacts and the interdependency of risk is evident in many applications of tort law's no-duty-to-rescue rule. Put most bluntly, this rule posits that individuals have no general obliga-tion to act affirmatively to protect others from harm.[31] Thus someone who walks down the street and sees an unfamiliar child lying on the road bleeding to death is under no legal obligation (except in a few states that have codified a duty to rescue)[32] to come to the child's assistance or even to call 911. In this respect, tort law, like constitutional law, treats actions differently than omissions and protects negative rather than positive rights.

A voluminous literature debates the no-duty-to-rescue rule.[33] Exceptions to the rule, however, are numerous and important. For example, in *Tarasoff v. Regents of the University of California*, discussed in chapter 8, the court held that a mental health therapist had a duty to inform the identifiable intended victim of a patient's violence of the threat the patient posed.[34] Limitations of space preclude a full discussion of either that case or other judicially created exceptions to the no-duty rule. For our purposes it is enough to point out that despite the many exceptions to the no-duty rule, and the undeniable difficulties that would ensue were it abandoned wholesale,[35] the rule demonstrates individualism's pervasive and problematic influence on tort law. By privileging the individual's right to refuse to engage in an easy rescue over the well-being or even life of an injured or dying victim, tort law disregards the interdependency of human health and the importance of population-based factors. In so doing, it endorses the view that individuals have no obligation to protect the health of others; a view that, as we have seen, can easily travel from the confines of common law courtrooms to public law.

Although the no-duty-to-rescue rule undoubtedly offers the clearest rhetorical example of tort law's failure to protect population health, its direct impact is likely modest. Fortunately, bleeding children do not frequently lie on the road waiting for rescue. In the more typical case, the no-duty rule has only a limited impact both because of myriad judicially created exceptions and because the plaintiff can identify some action by the defendant, rather than a failure of action, as the cause of his or her injury. Thus, in a motor vehicle case, the plaintiff can point to the driver's negligent driving of the car (an action) rather than the defendant's failure to brake (an inaction). Likewise, although a car maker has no duty to act to protect third parties, it does have a duty to manufacture its cars in such a way that third parties are not injured by the car's design.[36] Hence the no-duty rule's importance relates more to its rhetorical impact than its direct legal consequences.

The reach of tort law's causation requirement, however, is not so limited. As scholars have noted, the demand that plaintiffs establish that defendants factually and proximately cause their own injury creates a significant barrier to tort law's ability to protect and promote public health. As Richard Abel has suggested, the causation requirement is "inconsistent with probabilistic theories of causation," theories that are central to epidemiology and a population perspective.[37] Ironically, as the next section more fully describes, this inconsistency has only grown as tort law has come to rely more and more on epidemiological evidence.

INDIVIDUALIZED CAUSATION

The idea that defendants should be liable only for those injuries they cause is one of the most fundamental and enduring ideas in tort law.[38] Reflecting tort law's concerns for corrective justice, the individual causation requirement bespeaks a primitive but powerful notion that an individual defendant's right of action should be limited only when it would harm another. To put it another way, causation provides the rationale for stating that an injured victim has a claim on a particular defendant, as opposed to any other human being or collectivity. In this sense, causation is closely connected with the no-duty-to-rescue rule. If I have no duty to stop another from being harmed, then I can have no liability to that individual unless and until I have affirmatively acted in such a way as to harm that individual.

Despite its deep tradition and intuitive appeal, the causation requirement has long been seen as at odds with other putative goals of tort law, including deterrence. If, as the instrumentalists and law and economics scholars argue, tort law seeks to reduce the costs of accidents to an economically efficient level, then it makes little sense to require defendants to internalize only the costs of those accidents that plaintiffs can prove the defendants caused.[39] This is so for two interrelated reasons. First, from any instrumentalist perspective (including population-based), law's focus should be less on individual cases than on social consequences. Hence, if a defendant engages in an activity that is known to increase the risk of harm to one or more populations, it is inappropriate to permit that defendant to ignore the external costs of the activity and escape liability simply because no individual plaintiff can establish that the defendant caused his or her own injury.[40]

More pragmatically, as the instrumentalists have long recognized, in our increasingly complex environment, plaintiffs often face insurmountable problems in trying to prove causation. A hundred and fifty years ago, when the bread and butter tort case involved railroad accidents or other injuries that occurred quickly through physical contact, it was relatively simple to show that the defendant's action caused the plaintiff's injury. In a more complex world, in which toxic chemicals and other hazards are understood to have long-term diffuse and disparate effects over broad populations, and in which we understand that the determinants of disease and injury are almost always multifactorial, the relationship between the defendant's action and any one plaintiff's injury cannot be established merely on intuition or eyewitness testimony. Indeed, as discussed, the most potent determinants of a disease or injury are often those that are distal and incidental, observable only by comparing the incidence of a disease or injury in one population to that in another population which is not exposed to that variable.[41] In such cases, it is often difficult, if not impossible, to establish the linkage that courts frequently demand between the plaintiff's injury and the defendant's activity.

Moreover, even if epidemiological studies demonstrating such relationships exist, and they frequently do not,[42] they are not well designed to establish the type of individual causation traditionally demanded by tort law.[43] For example, epidemiological studies may determine that a particular chemical increases the risk of lung cancer in exposed populations by a factor of two. That does not mean, however, that the chemical increased the probability that any one exposed individual will have the disease by a factor of two.[44] Likewise, one cannot know from epidemiological studies alone that a chemical with an incidence ratio (defined as the incidence rate of a disease in an exposed population divided by the incidence rate of the disease in an unexposed population) of only 1.5 failed to make it more likely than not that a particular plaintiff became ill because of the exposure. For multiple reasons, there can be no quick and easy (never mind definitive) way to jump from population-based studies to individual causation. As a result, the individual causation requirement, referred to sometimes as the specific causation requirement, makes it difficult for plaintiffs to prevail when the determinants of disease are remote and discernable only at a population level. And, for that very reason, the individual causation requirement undermines tort law's ability to deter many preventable sources of disease and injury.

In the middle of the twentieth century, when the instrumentalist law and economics approach to tort law was at its apogee, multiple doctrinal developments seemed to relax the specific causation requirement to better equip tort law to deter preventable injuries and disease. For example, in the oft-discussed case of *Sindell v. Abbott Laboratories*, the California Supreme Court adopted a market share approach to causation that permitted a plaintiff who was injured by diethylstilbestrol (DES) to recover from defendant manufacturers based upon their share of the DES market, without proving that the particular defendants manufactured the dose of DES that harmed her.[45] Other courts soon followed suit and enunciated their own version of the market share approach in DES cases.[46] This seemed to portend a recognition, aligned with a population perspective, that the law should hold defendants liable for imposing preventable health risks to populations even when individual plaintiffs cannot readily show which defendant caused the injury. However, though the market share approach relaxed individual notions of causal responsibility, it did not negate the fundamental requirement that the plaintiff demonstrate that her injuries were caused by DES. Instead, as a population perspective would counsel, the market share approach stretched earlier notions of joint liability to permit a plaintiff to dispense with demonstrating the link between a particular defendant's product and his or her own disease.

Regrettably, in the twenty-five years since the courts adopted market share liability in DES cases, they have been strongly reluctant to expand the use of that approach to cases involving other products, albeit with some exceptions such as lead paint.[47] Courts adopting population-based legal analysis would likely reverse this trend and be far more willing to apply a market share or similar approach that holds defendants at least proportionally liable for the disease or injuries their actions create in a population, even if a particular plaintiff cannot establish that it was more likely than not that the injury or disease would not have occurred but for the defendant's actions.[48] In other words, causation requirements should be reformed to deter the injuries caused to populations.

A population approach to tort law would also take a liberal attitude toward using class actions and case consolidations to help make complex tort actions economically feasible for plaintiffs to bring, and to overcome some of the difficulties of establishing specific causation. After all, although epidemiological evidence cannot establish individualized causation, it is well suited to determine the risk a particular agent or product presents to an exposed population. If that population constituted the plaintiff class, then theoretically the problems of determining individualized causation could dissolve as the court focused only on whether the defendant's actions harmed the plaintiff class.[49] In recent years, however, the high costs and questionable outcomes associated with some infamous mass tort cases, such as those involving asbestos[50] and the Dalkon Shield,[51] provoked a backlash that led to congressional action making it more difficult to bring class action cases in state courts that are believed to be far friendlier to plaintiffs than the federal courts are.[52] In addition, the Supreme Court in *Amchem Products, Inc. v. Windsor* held that class actions are inappropriate when individual cases raise distinct issues of law and fact.[53] As a result, class actions are now onerous to bring in tort cases that present difficult questions of individual causation. Thus the relationship between class actions and individualized causation has been reversed. Rather than serving as a reason for using the class action, the individualized causation requirement has now come to impede class actions.[54] This would change if a population-based approach to the individualized causation requirement were followed.

In recent years, actions brought by state officials on behalf of their states have offered another possible end-run around the individualized causation requirement. For example, in the late 1990s, state attorneys general began to bring litigation against the tobacco companies to recoup state health care costs attributable to tobacco-related illnesses. Because these recoupment actions were brought by states, which represented the public writ large, the states argued that they did not have to show that the tobacco companies caused any one individual's illness, rather, that the states could rely on statistical and epidemiological evidence to establish the probable costs to the state health insurance programs.[55] (The states also hoped to avoid assumption of risk and comparative fault defenses.)

The theory that the states could avoid the individualized causation requirement was never tested in the courts because the states entered into a Master Settlement Agreement (MSA) with the tobacco companies.[56] The effect of that settlement on population health is questionable. As Stephen Sugarman notes, "many public health experts believe that the behavioral measures agreed to in the MSA (such as an end to billboard advertising and certain magazine advertising)—despite their aim of changing social norms around smoking—are too narrow in their reach and as a result have had, and will continue to have, little impact on smoking and health."[57] The

MSA did, however, lead to a rise in the price of cigarettes, which does retard the use of cigarettes, especially by young people.[58] In addition, the MSA spurred other public tort actions, including public nuisance actions, against other manufacturers or sellers of other hazardous products, such as guns.[59] To date, these efforts have mostly been stymied, both by state and federal statutory impediments,[60] as well as by the courts' reluctance to dispense with notions of individual responsibility and individual causation.[61]

Indeed, with certain exceptions, tort law's individual causation requirement "remains remarkably resilient."[62] Paradoxically, its strength rests in part on its supposed embrace, rather than rejection, of epidemiology, a methodology that focuses on populations not individuals. The following section describes that embrace and further discusses how courts have misused epidemiology, thereby undermining tort law's capacity to protect populations.

Daubert and the Embrace of Epidemiology

In the mid-twentieth century, epidemiology appeared to offer a solution to the problem of proving individualized causation. In cases in which the causal relationship between an agent manufactured or released by the defendant and the plaintiff's injury was neither readily apparent nor intuitively obvious, epidemiological evidence could be used to demonstrate an association between the agent and the type of injury the plaintiff experienced.[63] Moreover, by using the Bradford Hill criteria, which include the strength and consistency of a statistical association, its specificity, its temporal sequence, and its biological plausibility, epidemiologists could go further and make an inference as to whether an association between a particular agent, such as tobacco smoke, and an illness within a population, such as lung cancer, was causal.[64] This might have opened the door to a greater appreciation of population health, moving tort law closer to a population perspective.

That did not happen. Instead, as courts became more receptive to the use of epidemiological evidence and more willing to relax the individualized causation requirement, the industries most threatened by tort litigation responded. But rather than challenge the relevance of epidemiological evidence, these critics argued that tort law had gone astray because it had come to rely on poor epidemiological evidence, which critics decried as junk science. As Thomas McGarity has noted, this argument used the popular appeal of science to defend industries that threatened public health and safety.[65] In so doing, it followed the playbook first drafted by the tobacco industry in the 1950s and 1960s, when it defended tobacco's safety by questioning the reliability of scientific evidence demonstrating an association between tobacco and a host of human ailments.

Industry's assault on the use of epidemiological evidence in the courtroom received an enormous boost in 1993 in the Supreme Court's seminal decision in *Daubert v. Merrell Dow Pharmaceuticals, Inc.*[66] In *Daubert* the plaintiffs alleged that the drug Bendectin caused birth defects. The question specifically before the high Court was whether courts should apply the *Frye* rule that required expert testimony to be based on generally accepted principles and practices.[67] In an opinion by Justice Blackmun, the Court found *Frye* at odds with the liberal spirit of the *Federal Rules of Evidence*. The Court then went on to say that, in the absence of *Frye*, trial judges must ensure "that any and all scientific testimony or evidence admitted is not only relevant, but reliable."[68] Hence, judges must determine "at the outset" whether "the reasoning or methodology underlying the testimony is scientifically valid and . . . whether that reasoning or methodology properly can be applied to the facts in issue."[69] To do that, the Court suggested, the trial court should consider whether the theory or technique the expert would rely on has been subject to peer review and publication, the potential rate of error, and the existence and "maintenance of standards controlling the technique's operation."[70] In short, federal trial courts were charged to be the gatekeepers of scientific testimony and to weed out junk science.

In subsequent cases, the Supreme Court reaffirmed and extended its mandate to the trial courts. In *General Electric Co. v. Joiner*,[71] the Supreme Court held that lower courts should critically examine not only an expert's methodology but also whether the expert's conclusions are actually supported by the studies cited. In effect, the Supreme Court required the trial court to serve as the ultimate peer reviewer. Later, in *Kumho Tire Co. v. Carmichael*,[72] the Supreme Court applied *Daubert* to the expert testimony of engineers and other technical experts.

The influence of the *Daubert-Kumho-Joiner* trilogy has been both remarkable and paradoxical. On the one hand, these decisions and the 2000 amendments to the *Federal Rules of Evidence* that codified them[73] have directed the spotlight onto epidemiology, prompting efforts to educate lawyers and judges in epidemiology and biostatistics.[74] As a result, these cases have adopted and strengthened the call of population-based legal analysis to utilize epidemiology in legal analysis (interestingly, courts seldom apply *Daubert* to forensic evidence presented by prosecutors in criminal cases).[75] On the other hand, from a population-based perspective, much of the post-*Daubert* use of epidemiological evidence has been troubling.

Critics have pointed to several problems with the courts' use of the *Daubert* trilogy in tort cases. First, rather than interpreting *Daubert* and its progeny as simply requiring federal judges to review the reliability of epidemiological evidence, some courts, following the Supreme Court's lead in *Joiner*,[76] have required plaintiffs to introduce *Daubert*-worthy epidemiological evidence to establish causation,[77] particularly when defendants introduce their own epidemiological evidence to discredit general causation.[78] In effect, the trilogy has been read as if to say that only peer-reviewed epidemiological evidence can establish causation, turning epidemiological evidence from a tool plaintiffs can use to a necessity they must use, despite the fact that epidemiology cannot prove individual causation.[79]

As commentators have noted, the demand that plaintiffs produce reliable epidemiological evidence that can pass the *Daubert* test can be extremely burdensome. In most cases, the potentially hazardous substance at issue simply has not been the subject of any epidemiological study,[80] never mind a study large and thorough enough to meet the reliability criteria the Court put forward in *Daubert*. Indeed, in the absence of regulations requiring potential defendants to finance such studies, they have little reason to do so. Plaintiffs, on the other hand, often lack the resources necessary to underwrite epidemiological studies that can survive *Daubert* challenges. As a result, the requirement that plaintiffs produce reliable epidemiological studies often bars a plaintiff's action, even when animal or toxicology studies suggest that the product at issue can cause the type of harm the plaintiff experienced.[81]

In addition, many courts have used epidemiological studies in an artificially wooden and misleading way.[82] For example, some courts have held that the relative risk associated with exposure to the agent must be 2.0 or greater for the plaintiff to meet the burden of demonstrating that the agent caused the illness.[83] The rationale for this ruling is that unless there is a relative risk of 2.0 or greater, it is not more probable than not that the agent caused the plainiff's illness. But, as discussed, population-based data should not be used in this way to reach conclusions about individual causation. Indeed, the relative risk may tell us next to nothing about factors that make the plaintiff especially vulnerable to or immune from the agent's harmful impact.[84] An agent can cause less than half the cases in a population, but still have caused an individual's case. Conversely, a toxic agent can cause more than half of the cases of disease within a population but not the individual plaintiff's. In addition, a low relative risk may hide the fact that the agent accelerates the onset of a disease, causing people (perhaps even the plaintiff) to become sick at a younger age than they otherwise would.[85] In short, a relative risk of less than 2.0 may undermine a plaintiff's claim of specific causation, but does not refute it in the simplistic way that some courts, acting as peer reviewers in their *Daubert* gate-keeping roles, presume.

More disturbing has been the tendency among judges to apply *Daubert* in a way that might be described as corpuscular, subjecting each piece of evidence to a rigorous review for its reliability and relevance.[86] This approach, which rejects testimony based on small studies that do not meet the test of statistical significance, is troubling, first because it treats conventions of statistical significance as if they established clear criteria for determining which studies were worthwhile and which were not. In fact, though the various tests for statistical significance are critical tools for interpreting a particular study and appreciating its limitations, the conventions used to distinguish a statistically significant study from an insignificant one are simply that, conventions. Moreover, these conventions are purposefully designed to ensure "a categorical advantage to the null hypothesis," because scientists prefer to risk false negatives rather than false positives.[87]

The preference of epidemiological conventions for false negatives makes perfect sense given that science is a process aimed at furthering the accumulation of knowledge; individual studies are used not to reach definitive conclusions but to pave the way for additional research. Scientists, after all, seldom reach their conclusions based upon a single study;[88] they would not reject the conclusion that smoking causes health problems based on the fact that one initial study failed a test of statistical significance. Rather they would look at all of the information available, even from small studies, and use their understanding and even intuitions[89] to develop contingent conclusions about the course of future research and after substantial research has been concluded whether the weight of the evidence points in a particular direction.[90]

The corpuscular approach the courts have used in the wake of *Daubert* rejects this weight of the evidence approach, inviting judges instead to reject any piece of evidence that on its own does not meet the reliability tests the courts have applied. As a result, plaintiffs are required to present a type and quality of epidemiological evidence that is often lacking, even when expert epidemiologists might concur that the agent at issue likely causes disease and even when other, nonepidemiological evidence gives strong support for that conclusion. The effect is to magnify plaintiffs' burden of proof beyond the traditional preponderance of the evidence standard typically used in civil cases.[91] Although this higher standard may make sense if our primary concern is the cost of nonmeritorious tort claims to industry, it makes little sense if preventing harm is one of tort law's primary goals, as it is under a population approach. Thus a population-based approach to tort law would firmly reject the corpuscular interpretation of *Daubert*. It would not demand that plaintiffs produce evidence that is neither practically nor scientifically plausible to produce. Moreover, as noted a population-based approach would relax demands for specific causation, prompting courts to expand the market share and like approaches to hold defendants responsible when plaintiffs can show through the weight of credible epidemiological or other empirical evidence that more likely than not the defendant's activities have increased the incidence of disease or injury in a population of which the plaintiff is a member. Although it may well make sense to reduce defendant's liability in such cases take into account the fact that the defendant's activities were not the only cause of disease in the population (in effect relying on principles of comparative fault), a population approach to tort law would not permit defendants to wholly escape liability simply because each plaintiff would have trouble showing that the defendant's action caused his or her injury.

IN THE REAL WORLD

The discussion thus far has argued that neither tort theory nor doctrine adopts a population perspective that places a high value on the prevention of disease and injuries. To the contrary, both tort theory and doctrine (especially if we treat *Daubert* and progeny as if they were a part of tort doctrine) reveal a stark individualism that discounts the full social costs of preventable harms and places a high hurdle on those who seek to hold defendants liable for actions or inactions that threaten population health. Ironically, these hurdles are the highest in mass and toxic tort cases in which large numbers of people are harmed by the defendant's actions. Not surprisingly, it is in these cases that the population approach would bring the greatest reform, abandoning unrealistically strict requirements for epidemiological evidence and specific causation.

Given the ongoing debate, however, it is still worth asking whether tort law can or does have any positive effect on population health. Perhaps not surprisingly, empirical research has yet to provide a clear or definitive answer to that question. Although the body of empirical research on tort law is growing, much of it has focused on describing the nature and outcomes of claims,[92] or the impact of particular tort reforms.[93] Rarer and far more difficult to construct are studies analyzing tort law's deterrent effect. Nevertheless, after reviewing studies focused on product liability law, Michael Moore and Kip Viscusi conclude that "product recalls and litigation adversely affect the wealth of manufacturers. . . . It is clear from these results that the potential stock market losses from defects in product design and manufacture provide enormous incentives for safety."[94] On the other hand, the same authors question whether tort law has a substantial deterrent effect with respect to mass torts, where the long latency period and difficulties establishing causation may impede the tort system's ability to assess liability.[95]

Other scholars have reached similarly mixed conclusions. For example, after acknowledging the limitations of empirical studies on the subject, Gary Schwartz concluded that tort law may have some deterrent effect, but probably less than the law and economics approach to the subject presumes.[96] How much less is unknown.

Perhaps one of the reasons it is so difficult to assess tort law's impact on the health of populations is that tort law does not exist in a vacuum. To

understand tort law's true impact on the health of populations, it is important to appreciate its interrelationship with other areas of law as well as
with the larger political and legal culture.

From the perspective of public health advocates and plaintiffs' lawyers,
tort law is important not only because it deters and provides compensation
but also because it offers a vehicle for learning about and garnering attention to public health issues that would otherwise go unnoticed. For example, tobacco industry documents that became public in the course of
tobacco litigation helped change public attitudes, and thereby the political
agenda, about cigarettes.[97] Likewise, individual lawsuits filed when Ford
Explorers with Firestone tires rolled over, killing and injuring passengers,
received media attention and sparked an investigation by the National
Highway Transportation Safety Administration that ultimately led to the
recall of the tires.[98] Thus tort law can sometimes promote population
health not through direct deterrence, but by creating the political conditions that prompt regulatory action. Likewise, the financial threat civil litigation poses may lead industries to compromise and accept regulations
they would otherwise fight tooth and nail with the hope (or promise) that
the regulation might preempt their tort liability.[99] Thus it was under threat
of crippling liability that the tobacco industry entered into (and finally
walked away from) discussions to permit the Food and Drug Administration to regulate cigarettes.[100]

These observations suggest a different way of thinking about tort law
and population health. As we have seen, from a population-based perspective, contemporary tort doctrine is sorely wanting. It is riddled with an
individualism that makes it difficult for the field to recognize, never mind
to promote, population health. Moreover, with its emphasis on individual
plaintiffs, individual causation, and individual responsibility, tort law may
even corrode a population-based perspective. For example, the Institute of
Medicine, in its influential report on medically induced injuries, *To Err Is
Human,* suggested that, because of its focus on bad actors and its tendency
to place blame on individuals, tort law may discourage health-care providers from working together to develop system-wide approaches to reducing
medical error.[101] More fundamentally, tort law may offer the false promise
of a private solution to very population-based problems.

A population approach to tort law would reject the excessive individualism that permeates tort discourse today. Instead, it would place a greater

value than current doctrine or theory does on the social cost of disease and injury. It would also recognize the social factors that influence the choices that plaintiffs make as well as the fallacy of the action-inaction distinction. Moreover, though valuing epidemiology, it would respect it as a scientific method designed to increase understanding of the determinants of death and disease, not as a minefield for the unwary plaintiff. And most important, it would liberalize and relax the requirement that plaintiffs prove specific causation.

In the end, however, population-based legal analysis would not seek to remake tort law into a field of public law. Rather, it would recognize that because tort law seeks to provide individuals with compensation as well as with a way to redress their own, very personal grievances, the field must inevitably consider not only the health of populations but also the interests and needs of individuals within affected populations. But by articulating the importance of population health and safety, and providing individuals and classes with a way to learn about, expose, and seek greater regulation of possible risks, a population-based tort law can play an important, albeit imperfect, role in protecting and promoting public health.

NOTES

1. PETER W. HUBER, GALILEO'S REVENGE: JUNK SCIENCE IN THE COURTROOM (1991).

2. *See* WILLIAM L. PROSSER, HANDBOOK OF THE LAW OF TORTS 1–2 (4th ed. 1971) (noting the difficulty in defining tort law and offering some attempts at a definition).

3. For a discussion of the relationship between public and private law, see Daniel A. Farber & Philip P. Frickey, *In the Shadow of the Legislature: The Common Law in the Age of the New Public Law*, 89 MICH. L. REV. 875, 888–906 (1991).

4. George P. Fletcher, *Fairness and Utility in Tort Theory*, 85 HARV. L. REV. 537, 550, 573 (1972).

5. GUIDO CALABRESI. THE COSTS OF ACCIDENTS: A LEGAL AND ECONOMIC ANALYSIS *passim* (1970).

6. Richard A. Posner, *A Theory of Negligence*, 1 J. LEGAL STUD. 29, 32–33 (1972).

7. Donald G. Gifford, *The Challenge to the Individual Causation Requirement in Mass Products Torts*, 62 WASH. & LEE L. REV. 873, 881–83 (2005).

8. CALABRESI, *supra* note 5, at 26–28.

9. WILLIAM M. LANDES & RICHARD A. POSNER, THE ECONOMIC STRUCTURE OF TORT LAW 16–19 (1987).

10. CALABRESI, *supra* note 5, at 39–67. For a discussion of the different schools of law and economics, see James R. Hackney, Jr., *Law and Neoclassical Economics: Science, Politics, and the Reconfiguration of American Tort Law Theory*, 15 LAW & HIST. REV. 275 *passim* (1997).

11. United States v. Carroll Towing Co., Inc., 159 F.2d 169, 173–74 (2d Cir. 1947).

12. RESTATEMENT (THIRD) OF TORTS: PRODUCTS LIABILITY § 1 cmt. a (1998).

13. *See* Eric E. Fortess & Marshall B. Kapp, *Medical Uncertainty, Diagnostic Testing, and Legal Liability*, 13 L. MED. & HEALTH CARE 213, 214–17 (1985) (discussing Helling v. Carey, 519 P.2d 981 (Wash. 1974) (holding an ophthalmologist liable for failing to screen a patient under forty for glaucoma despite the fact that such screening was not the established professional custom).

14. For a fuller development of such criticisms as well as an argument as to why tort law should focus on the tradeoffs between injuries, see Kenneth W. Simons, *Tort Negligence Cost-Benefit Analysis and Tradeoffs: A Closer Look at the Controversy* 15–17 (Boston Univ. Sch. L. Working Papers Series, Pub. L. & Leg. Theory Working Paper No. 08–15, 2008) (forthcoming in LOY. L.A. L. REV.), http://www.bu.edu/law/faculty/scholarship/workingpapers/2008.html (accessed October 10, 2008).

15. William E. Nelson, *Teaching Torts: The Moral Perversity of the Hand Calculus*, 45 ST. LOUIS L.J. 759, 760–61 (2001).

16. *See* Simons, *supra* note 14, at 14–15.

17. *See, e.g.*, Douglas A. Kysar, *It Might Have Been: Risk, Precaution, and Opportunity Costs* 25–36 (Cornell Legal Studs. Research Paper No. 06–023, 2006), http://papers.ssrn.com/sol3/papers.cfm?abstract_id=927995 (last visited Dec. 14, 2008).

18. Nelson, *supra* note 15, at 760.

19. *See* chapter 7, *supra*.

20. RESTATEMENT (THIRD) OF TORTS, *supra* note 12, at § 2 cmt. d.

21. *Id.* at § 2 cmt. F (1998).

22. *See, e.g.*, Nicholas A. Ashford & Robert F. Stone, *Liability, Innovation, and Safety in the Chemical Industry, in* THE LIABILITY MAZE: THE IMPACT OF LIABILITY LAW ON SAFETY AND INNOVATION, 367, 377–78 (Peter W. Huber & Robert E. Litan eds., 1991).

23. CALABRESI, *supra* note 5, at 307–08.

24. RESTATEMENT (SECOND) OF TORTS §§ 496A-496G (1965). For a broad treatment of assumption of risk, see Stephen D. Sugarman, *The Assumption of Risk*, 31 VAL. U.L. REV. 833 *passim* (1997).

25. MARC A. FRANKLIN, ROBERT L. RABIN & MICHAEL D. GREEN, TORT LAW AND ALTERNATIVES 489 (8th ed. 2006).

26. Lawrence M. Friedman & Jack Ladinsky, *Social Change and the Law of Industrial Accidents*, 67 COLUM. L. REV. 50, 69–71 (1967).

27. *E.g.*, Tunkl v. Regents of Univ. of Cal., 383 P.2d 441, 443–47 (Cal. 1963) (rejecting express assumption of risk defense in a malpractice case against hospital).

28. Horton v. American Tobacco Co., 667 So.2d 1289, 1293 (Miss. 1995).

29. Rose v. Brown & Williamson Tobacco Corp., 809 N.Y.S.2d 784, 791–93 (Sup. Ct. N.Y. 2005).

30. *See* chapter 7, *supra*.

31. Restatement (Second) of Torts, *supra* note 24, at § 314.

32. For a discussion of Good Samaritan statutes and a list of state laws that codify this doctrine, see Nancy Levit, *The Kindness of Strangers: Interdisciplinary Foundations of a Duty to Act*, 40 Washburn L.J. 463, 466–67 (2001).

33. *E.g.*, Leslie Bender, *A Lawyer's Primer on Feminist Theory and Tort*, 38 J. Legal Educ. 3, 33–36 (1988); William M. Landes & Richard A. Posner, *Salvors, Finders, Good Samaritans, and Other Rescuers: An Economic Study of Law and Altruism*, 7 J. Legal Stud. 83 (1978); Saul Levmore, *Waiting for Rescue: An Essay on the Evolution and Incentive Structure of the Law of Affirmative Obligations*, 72 Va. L. Rev. 879 (1986).

34. Tarasoff v. Regents of Univ. of Cal., 551 P.2d 334, 342–49 (Cal. 1976).

35. *See* Ernest J. Weinrib, *Case for a Duty to Rescue*, 90 Yale L. J. 247 (1980).

36. MacPherson v. Buick Motor Co., 111 N.E. 1050, 1053–54 (N.Y. 1916).

37. Richard L. Abel, *A Critique of Torts*, 37 U.C.L.A. L. Rev. 785, 792 (1990).

38. Gifford, *supra* note 7, at 933.

39. *Id.* at 877–81 (describing the instrumentalist critique of causation).

40. *See* William Meadow & Cass R. Sunstein, *Causation in Tort: General Populations vs. Individual Cases* (John M. Olin L. & Econ. Working Paper No. 360 2d Series, 2007), http://www.law.uchicago.edu/academics/publiclaw/index.html (last visited May 5, 2008).

41. Geoffrey A. Rose, The Strategy of Preventive Medicine 60–61 (1992).

42. Mark Geistfeld, *Scientific Uncertainty and Causation in Tort Law*, 54 Vand. L. Rev. 1011, 1015 (2001).

43. *See* Meadow & Sunstein, *supra* note 40, at 2–7.

44. Sander Greenland & James M. Robin, *Epidemiology, Justice and the Probability of Causation*, 40 Jurimetrics J. 321, 321–25 (2000).

45. Sindell v. Abbott Labs., 607 P.2d 924, 935–38 (Cal. 1980).

46. *E.g.*, Hymowitz v. Eli Lilly & Co., 539 N.E. 2d 1069, 1078 (N.Y. 1989).

47. Gifford, *supra* note 7, at 903–04. *But see* Thomas v. Mallett, 701 N.W.2d 523 (Wis. 2005) (applying risk contribution theory applicable in DES cases to manufacturers of lead paint).

48. A rich and voluminous literature discusses market share liability and other approaches that courts can use to assess partial culpability in such situations. *See, e.g.*, Michelle Adams, *Causation and Responsibility in Tort and Affirmative Action*, 79 Tex. L. Rev. 643, 677–96 (2001); Thomas C. Galligan, Jr., *The Risks and Reactions to Underdeterrence in Torts*, 70 Mo. L. Rev. 691, 714–21 (2005); David Rosenberg, *The Causal Connection in Mass Exposure Cases: A 'Public Law' Vision of the Tort System*, 97 Harv. L. Rev. 851, 866–69 (1984); Elizabeth A. Weeks, *Beyond Compensation: Using Torts to Promote Public Health*, 10 J. Health Care L. & Pol'y 27, 52–55 (2007).

49. *See* Robert L. Rubin, *The Third Wave of Tobacco Tort Litigation*, *in* Regulating Tobacco 176, 179–83 (Robert L. Rabin & Stephen D. Sugarman eds., 2001).

50. *E.g.*, In re Eastern and Southern Dists. Asbestos Litigation, 772 F. Supp. 1380 (E.D.N.Y. 1991).

51. In re Northern Dist. Cal. "Dalkon Shield" IUD Prods. Liability Litigation, 521 F. Supp. 1188 (N.D. Cal. 1981).

52. Class Action Fairness Act of 2005, Pub. L. No. 109–2, 119 Stat. 4 (2005).

53. 521 U.S. 591 (1997).

54. Gifford, *supra* note 7, at 897; Donald G. Gifford, *The Death of Causation: Mass Products Torts' Incomplete Incorporation of Social Welfare Principles*, 41 WAKE FOREST L. REV. 943, 994–96 (2006).

55. Gifford, *The Death of Causation*, *supra* note 54, at 997–1000.

56. Stephen D. Sugarman, *Comparing Tobacco & Gun Litigation*, *in* SUING THE GUN INDUSTRY 196, 217–18 (Timothy D. Lytton ed., 2005).

57. *Id.* at 218.

58. Frank J. Chaloupka et al., *Tax, Price and Cigarette Smoking: Evidence from the Tobacco Documents and Implications for Tobacco Company Marketing Strategies*, 11 TOBACCO CONTROL: AN INT'L J. 62 (Supp. 1 2002).

59. Sugarman, *supra* note 56, at 220.

60. Protection of Lawful Commerce in Arms Act, Pub. L. No 109–92; 119 Stat. 2095 (2005); *see also* FLA. STAT. § 790.331 (2006); N.C. Gen. Stat. § 14–409.40 (2006); Ohio Rev. Code Ann. § 2305.401 (2006); Ariz. Rev. Stat. § 12–714 (2006).

61. *E.g.*, Hamilton v. Beretta U.S.A. Corp., 750 N.E. 2d 1055, 1067 (N.Y. 2001) (rejecting a market share argument for liability, holding that an individual must show which individual manufacturer caused the injury).

62. Gifford, *supra* note 7, at 933.

63. *E.g.*, Allen v. United States, 588 F. Supp. 247 (D. Utah 1984) (accepting epide-miological evidence to establish that atomic testing caused plaintiffs' cancers), *rev'd on other grounds*, 816 F.2d 1417 (10th Cir. 1987).

64. Richard Doll & A. Bradford Hill, *Smoking and Carcinoma of the Lung*, 2 BRIT. MED. J. 739 (1950). Other criteria include whether there is a dose-response relation-ship, the coherence of the statistical relationship, and whether there is experimental and analogical support for the relationship.

65. Thomas O. McGarity, *Our Science Is Sound Science and Their Science is Junk Science: Science-Based Strategies for Avoiding Accountability and Responsibility for Risk-Producing Products and Activities*, 52 U. KAN. L. REV. 897, 901 (2004).

66. 509 U.S. 579 (1993).

67. *Id.* at 585–86 (citing Frye v. United States, 293 F. 1013 (D.C. Cir. 1923)).

68. *Id.* at 589.

69. *Id.* at 592–93.

70. *Id.* at 592–94.

71. 522 U.S. 136 (1997).

72. 526 U.S. 137 (1999).

73. U.S.C.S. Fed. Rules Evid. R. 702 (2006).

74. *E.g.*, FEDERAL JUDICIAL CENTER, REFERENCE MANUAL ON SCIENTIFIC EVI-DENCE *Preface* v (2d ed. 2000).

75. Margaret A. Berger, *The Supreme Court's Trilogy on the Admissibility of Expert Testimony*, *in* Federal Judicial Center, *supra* note 74, at 9, 30–32.

76. 522 U.S. at 144–47.

77. Geistfeld, *supra* note 42, at 1012–13.

78. *E.g.*, Norris v. Baxter Healthcare Corp., 397 F.3d 878, 882 (10th Cir. 2005).

79. WILLIAM BRAITHWAITE ET AL., EPIDEMIOLOGY IN DECISION-MAKING 16 (1999). For a discussion of the inability of epidemiology to establish individualized causation, see Meadow & Sunstein, *supra* note 40, at 1–7.

80. Geistfeld, *supra* note 42, at 1014.

81. *E.g.*, Hollander v. Sandoz Pharms. Corp., 289 F.3d 1193 (10th Cir. 2002) (rejecting evidence of differential diagnosis and animal studies in absence of epidemiological studies).

82. David Egilman, Joyce Kim, & Molly Biklen, *Proving Causation: The Use and Abuse of Medical and Scientific Evidence Inside the Courtroom—An Epidemiologist's Critique of the Judicial Interpretation of the Daubert Ruling*, 58 FOOD & DRUG L.J. 223, 224 (2003).

83. *Id.* at 224; Jan Beyea & Daniel Berger, *Scientific Misconceptions among Daubert Gatekeepers: The Need for Reform of Expert Review Procedures*, 64 LAW & CONTEMP. PROBS. 327, 353 (Spring/Summer 2001); Michael D. Green, D. Michael Freedman, & Leon Gordis, *Reference Guide on Epidemiology* in FEDERAL JUDICIAL CENTER, *supra* note 74, at 333, 384 n.140 (citing cases).

84. Greenland & Robin, *supra* note 44, at 324–28.

85. Egilman, Kim, & Biklen, *supra* note 82, at 230.

86. McGarity, *supra* note 65, at 922.

87. Daniel J. McGarvey & Brett Marshall, *Making Sense of Scientists and "Sound Science": Truth and Consequences for Endangered Species in the Klamath Basin and Beyond*, 32 ECOLOGY L.Q. 73, 100 (2005).

88. *Id.* at 75.

89. Beyea & Berger, *supra* note 83, at 328.

90. Sheldon Krimsky, *The Weight of Scientific Evidence in Policy & Law*, 95 AM. J. PUB. HEALTH S-129 (2005).

91. Lucinda M. Finley, *Guarding the Gate to the Courthouse: How Trial Judges Are Using Their Evidentiary Screening Role to Remake Tort Causation Rules*, 49 DEPAUL L. REV. 335, 336–37 (1999).

92. *E.g.*, Deborah Jones Merritt & Kathryn Ann Barry, *Is the Tort System in Crisis? New Empirical Evidence*, 60 OHIO ST. L.J. 315 (1999); Theodore Eisenberg et al., *Juries, Judges, and Punitive Damages: An Empirical Study*, 87 CORNELL L. REV. 743 (2002).

93. *E.g.*, Geoffrey Christopher Rapp, *Doctors, Duties, Death and Data: A Critical Review of the Empirical Literature on Medical Malpractice and Tort Reform*, 26 N. ILL. U.L. REV. 439 (2006) (surveying the empirical literature on medical malpractice).

94. MICHAEL J. MOORE & W. KIP VISCUSI, PRODUCT LIABILITY ENTERING THE TWENTY-FIRST CENTURY: THE U.S. PERSPECTIVE 26 (2001).

95. *Id.* at 31–38. For further discussion of the deterrent effect of tort law, see Margo Sclanger, *Second Best Damage Action Deterrence*, 55 DEPAUL L. REV. 517, 520–37 (2006).

96. Gary T. Schwartz, *Empiricism and Tort Law*, 2002 U. ILL. L. REV. 1067, 1068. *See also* Gary T. Schwartz, *Reality in the Economic Analysis of Tort Law: Does Tort Law Really Deter?*, 42 U.C.L.A. L. REV 377, 390–422 (1994) (summarizing empirical evidence about the deterrent effect of tort law with respect to several types of injuries).

97. Lynn Mather, *Theorizing about Trial Courts: Lawyers, Policymaking and Tobacco Litigation*, 23 LAW & SOC. INQUIRY 897, 913–33 (1998).

98. Bill Vlasic, *Tire Recalls, Tragedies Tax Ford, Firestone and Public; Global Crisis Ensnares Companies, Feds in Safety Nightmare*, DETROIT NEWS, Sept. 3, 2000, at A1 (noting that reporters unearthed problems with Firestone tires after noticing that several lawsuits were pending, media reports then led to a federal recall of the tires).

99. *E.g.*, Jill R. Baniewicz, *Is Hamilton v. Accu-tek a Good Predictor of What the Future Holds for Gun Manufacturers?*, 34 IND. L. REV. 419, 440 (2001) (positing that the loss of a mass tort action made the gun industry willing to accept greater federal regulation).

100. Robert A. Kagan & William P. Nelson, *The Politics of Tobacco Regulation in the United States, in* REGULATING TOBACCO 11, 23 (Robert L. Rabin & Stephen D. Sugarman eds., 2001).

101. INST. OF MED., TO ERR IS HUMAN: BUILDING A BETTER HEALTH CARE SYSTEM 112 (Linda T. Kohn et al. eds., 2000).

CHAPTER 10

Globalizing Population-Based Legal Analysis

Someone who has TB in India can infect you here. They cough, maybe they are working at an airport, the germs slither onto the plane, then you get on the plane, and you are infected.

—Archbishop Desmond Tutu, *HIV/AIDS and the Global Community: We Can Be Human Only Together*

IT IS BANAL BUT TRUE to say that we live in a global age. Advances in communication technology (especially the Internet) and travel have combined with the integration of markets and the spread of capitalism to knit the world in new ways. This integration, or globalization as it is widely called, can create novel risks for population health, both by increasing health disparities around the world and by facilitating the spread of disease-causing vectors, either microbial or man-made. On the other hand, globalization also has the potential to promote population health, both by supporting the diffusion of health-promoting interventions and technologies and by highlighting the interdependency of population health. In either case, globalization creates new challenges and opportunities for population-based legal analysis. This chapter looks at some of those challenges and opportunities.

A GLOBAL POPULATION

In discussions of international public health, two seemingly contradictory facts stand out. First, as Allyn L. Taylor has observed, there has been an increase in the "number and the scale of transboundary public health concerns. . . ."[1] Second, despite the growing interdependence of the world's populations, enormous and potentially growing disparities exist between the health status and needs of different populations around the world. In a global era, a population perspective requires recognition of both interdependency and distinction.

Consider first the phenomenon of global interdependence. To a significant degree, it has always existed. The Black Death of the fourteenth century traveled from the steppes of Asia along trade routes to Italy and ultimately throughout Europe.[2] Likewise, the Spanish conquest in the New World in the fifteenth century began a migration of germs between the Eurasian and American continents.[3] In the nineteenth century, cholera epidemics traveled from the Indian subcontinent to cities around the world.[4] These epidemics helped spur the International Sanitary Conference of 1851, the first international effort to control the spread of disease through diplomacy.[5]

Today, of course, travel is both faster and more frequent than ever, exacerbating the risks that emerging or re-emerging infections will rapidly proliferate around the globe.[6] Although Yersinia pestis (the microorganism that is believed to have been the cause of the Black Death) traveled in the fourteenth century at the speed of horses and sails, HIV and SARS spread in the twentieth and twenty-first centuries with the swiftness of jet planes. Likewise, dramatic increases in the international trade of food supplies have increased the risk that food-borne diseases will traverse the planet.[7] In a global era, an infection in any region of the globe can rapidly be transplanted to any other region. This is the danger that Laurie Garrett warned of in 1994 in her frighteningly named but prescient book, *The Coming Plague*.[8]

The health risks created by globalization are not limited to infectious diseases that spread from the developing world to the developed world. Globalization instead affects almost all determinants of health. Moreover, the trajectory of travel is multidirectional. Although some diseases such as

HIV or dengue fever may emerge from the developing world and later pose a risk to populations in developed nations, other health threats such as tobacco or fast food migrate in the other direction.[9] In addition, global environmental problems, such as climate change and the depletion of the ozone layer, arise from activities that occur all over the world, from the cutting of the rain forests to excessive reliance on carbon-based fuels, exacerbating a broad array of public health problems, including asthma and malaria.[10] Indeed, climate change has the potential to affect almost all aspects of human health. Moreover, by altering the economies and influencing the cultures of the entire world, globalization necessarily influences myriad social determinants of health and therefore can be expected to have powerful, if not fully understood, impacts on all of the planet's populations.[11] In that critical sense, by interconnecting the world's economies and cultures, globalization has necessarily increased the health interdependency of every human population on the planet.

Health Disparities

Interdependency does not imply uniformity. Likewise, the fact that health threats can spread rapidly around the world does not mean that all populations face the same degree of all or most risks. Rather, enormous disparities and differences exist alongside interconnection and interdependence.[12]

Whether or not globalization has increased health disparities, as many critics contend,[13] there can be little doubt that great disparities and distinctions continue despite the homogenizing effects of globalization. Most notable and alarming has been the divergence between life expectancy in sub-Saharan Africa, which fell after 1990 primarily because of the HIV/ AIDS epidemic, and life expectancies elsewhere, which have generally continued to rise.[14] According to Barry Levy and Victor Sidel, a female infant born in Japan can expect to live to be eighty-five years old; in contrast, a female infant born in Sierra Leone can expect to live only thirty-six years.[15] Looking at somewhat broader populations, in 2003, the World Health Organization (WHO) reported that life expectancy for women in the developed world was seventy-eight years; for men in sub-Saharan Africa life expectancy was only 46 years of age.[16]

Other health statistics also reveal stark differences in the health status of populations in different nations. In particular, infant mortality rates vary dramatically around the globe. According to the WHO, a child born in Sierra Leone "is three and half times more likely to die before its fifth birthday than a child born in India, and more than a hundred times more likely to die than a child born in Iceland or Singapore."[17] Nineteen of the twenty countries with the highest mortality rate for children under five are in Africa; the only nation in that group outside of Africa is Afghanistan.[18]

Although the disparity in health status between nations in sub-Saharan Africa and the developed world is particularly great, it is not the only notable regional disparity. For example, since the demise of the Soviet Union, adult mortality has declined in some of the former Soviet-bloc nations, such as Hungry and Poland, but not in others, such as Russia.[19] There are also wide differences in child mortality rates between nations within Central America and the Caribbean region,[20] and in adult mortality rates in nations within the Eastern Mediterranean.[21]

Within nations, males and females also experience different health outcomes. In much of the world, the child mortality rate is higher for males than for females, but in some nations in Asia, including India, China, Nepal, and Pakistan, the reverse is true.[22] Among adults, men and women face different rates of risk for many health conditions, and in some regions, mortality rates have fallen for women, but not for men.[23]

As was discussed in chapter 1, the health of populations also varies by wealth and socioeconomic status. Interestingly, between relatively rich countries, differences in per capita GDP do not seem to be associated with health outcomes, but "within a rich country, there is a strong relationship between measures of socio-economic status and health."[24] This gradient appears to run from the very top of the socioeconomic ladder to the very bottom.[25] According to John Lynch and George Kaplan, "the general pattern of better health among those socioeconomically better off is found across time periods, demographic groups, most measures of health and disease, and various measures of socioeconomic position."[26]

In the United States, at least, race is also an important variable distinguishing the health of populations. For example, from 1998 to 2000, the infant mortality rate for blacks in the United States was fourteen per thousand live births; for whites and Hispanics it was six.[27] Black Americans also face higher rates than whites do of death from heart disease, cancer,

HIV, and many other diseases.[28] Likewise, Latinos face a higher risk of dying of diabetes than non-Hispanic whites do, yet generally have lower infant mortality rates.[29] Other notable distinctions exist within and between ethnic and minority groups.

It is beyond the scope of this chapter to recount all of the critical distinctions in health within and among groups around the planet. Nor can this chapter seek to explain all of the possible reasons for such disparities, a task that has been very central to much recent public health scholarship.[30] Rather, the point here is a simple but critical one at the heart of the population perspective: disparities can and do coexist with interdependence. Although globalization has increased the influence that events in any one region of the world may have on the health of people elsewhere, it has not erased the sharp distinctions that mark the health experiences of various populations. Indeed, to a significant degree, globalization has increased those distinctions by exacerbating economic differentials and promoting social dislocations that can jeopardize the health of vulnerable populations.

Globalization has also increased the possibility that risks that disparately affect one population will spread to other populations. In an era of increasing travel and contact between diverse populations, the health risks that propagate under the conditions faced by vulnerable populations can eventually reach beyond those populations, creating dangers for others. Thus, as Archbishop Tutu's quotation suggests, the diseases that most frequently affect disadvantaged populations in poorer nations may now threaten privileged populations in wealthy countries. Conversely, because actions in the United States and the rest of the developed world can have more deleterious impacts on poorer populations than wealthy ones, it becomes essential that decision makers in the developed world consider the implications of their decisions on nondomestic populations. Hence, a population-based analysis of the law must necessarily appreciate not only the local but the distinctive and global impact of law.

At the same time, globalization highlights another central aspect of the population perspective: populations are socially constructed and overlapping. Although it is common and often helpful to think about the characteristics of populations in traditional ways, thus focusing on disparities based on gender, race, ethnicity, or religion, for public health purposes, these characteristics are merely variables that can be used to define and understand population dynamics. Individuals, it must be remembered, are members of multiple populations. Moreover, the defining characteristics of populations can and do change, depending on the questions asked and the health conditions under discussion.

Globalization necessarily challenges traditional and commonplace definitions of populations. Old boundaries, such as those between the countries of Western Europe or between the United States and Asia, may be less critical and possibly have less explanatory power than they once would have. At the same time, globalization creates the possibility of new, worldwide populations, defined not by their region, but instead by shared cultures, occupations, or exposures. Thus the population of McDonalds' eaters can no longer be assumed to include only people living in the United States or even in the developed world. Likewise, YouTube viewers form a worldwide population that exhibits both agency and explanatory power. The challenge is to notice and appreciate the role and health of these new populations while recalling the needs and circumstances of more traditional, but too-often neglected, groups.

INTERNATIONAL HEALTH LAW

With the advent of globalization and the recognition of the interdependency of populations around the world with respect to health, new attention has been given to the role that international law and international institutions, such as the WHO and the International Monetary Fund, play with respect to population health. Although a full review of how these laws affect the health of the world's varied populations is well beyond the scope of this chapter, a brief discussion of the role of the relationship of population health to international law (which consists of international treaties, customary international law, general principles of law, and non-binding resolutions and advisories, known as soft law) is critical to understanding the challenges facing a globalized population-based legal analysis.

Just as global interdependency with respect to health predates globalization, so too do efforts to use law to protect populations from global threats. But as David Fidler notes, before the nineteenth century, these efforts were generally taken unilaterally by individual states.[31] In 1851, as tensions between trade, the spread of cholera epidemics, and the burdens of quarantines grew, France hosted the first International Sanitary Conference, which aimed to produce a treaty to clarify the role of quarantine in international trade. During the next few decades, until the dawn of World War II, several more such conferences were held and several conventions negotiated.[32]

In the years immediately following World War II, the locus of international legal efforts to protect public health moved to the United Nations system, and in particular the establishment of WHO, whose constitution states that "the enjoyment of the highest attainable standard of health is one of the fundamental rights of every human being without distinction of race, religion, political belief, economic or social condition. . . . The health of all peoples is fundamental to the attainment of peace and security and is dependent upon the fullest co-operation of individuals and States."[33] According to Allyn Taylor, the WHO has a "constitutional directive to act as the 'directing and co-ordinating'" authority on international health matters.[34] It is an authority that the WHO has not always seized. Nevertheless, in 2005, in the wake of the SARS epidemic and concerns about the weakness of international surveillance, as well as the impact of disease on global travel, the WHO's legislative body, the World Health Assembly, revised the International Health Regulations (IHR) to apply broadly to any public health risk, rather than, as previously the case, only specified communicable diseases. The new regulations call on states, among other things, to enhance their surveillance capacities and notify the WHO within twenty-four hours of any "public health emergency of international concern" in their territory.[35] In addition, the IHR provide parameters for the application of health criteria to travelers. Significantly, the regulations require states to treat travelers "with respect for their dignity, human rights and fundamental freedoms and minimize any discomfort or distress associated with" the application of health measures.[36] They also make clear that actions taken shall be "applied in a transparent and non-discriminatory manner."[37]

The World Health Assembly has also taken the lead in developing an International Framework Convention on Tobacco Control (IFCTC), in which the signatory parties recognize "that the spread of the tobacco epidemic is a global problem with serious consequences for public health that calls for the widest possible international cooperation."[38] The treaty calls for states to develop tobacco control strategies that reach both the supply and the demand side of the equation. However, most of the specifics are left to the signatory states.[39] This first international agreement focusing on a noninfectious health threat thus evidences both the potential and the limitations of relying on international legal agreements for protecting populations from noninfectious diseases. Indeed, by leaving specifics to individual nations, the treaty reflects the reality that despite the global nature of health threats, legal interventions are still primarily left to the purview of individual nations.

In many ways, both the IHR and the IFCTC are the international equivalent of traditional state public health laws, such as those that establish boards of health or authorize surveillance and quarantine.[40] As such, these laws reflect, in an international dimension, the conflicts and dilemmas that exist domestically between core public health laws and the interests and liberties of individuals and groups.[41] As in the domestic context, a population-based analysis of international health laws must appreciate not only their purported goals, but also their actual (empirically verifiable) impact on different populations. Thus, for example, the restrictions on travel permitted by the IHR must be assessed to determine both whether they are applied disparately to distinct populations and whether they are used in such a way as to actually reduce the spread of infectious diseases. Of course, as in the domestic context, a population-based analysis of such laws must be mindful of their impact not only on the negative liberties of individuals, but also on populations' positive liberty. As always, a population approach questions whether the conflict between the rights of individuals and the health interest of populations is as inevitable or central to international public health law as is often thought.

Core international health laws are not, of course, the only international laws that affect the health of populations. Nor are they the only ones that should be subject to a globalized population-based legal analysis. Of particular interest are treaties and laws that establish the world's international trading system, particularly those that establish and enforce the World Trade Organization (WTO), or those established by regional treaties such as the North American Free Trade Association (NAFTA). A full discussion of this vast and complex set of international treaties and legal rulings is not possible here, but it is critical to note that international trade laws, like domestic laws affecting commerce, can have a profound and disparate impact on the health of populations. Moreover, as is true in the domestic arena, imperatives for free trade can conflict with and undermine efforts by states to protect the health of their populations.[42] This risk is especially great under the WTO system, which applies not only to laws that operate at the border, but also and more broadly to laws, including health laws, that operate within a nation.[43] Or, to put it another way, the WTO like the dormant commerce clause does not apply only to laws that discriminate against or block commerce, but as well to laws that burden or have an effect on commerce.

Just as the Supreme Court has historically permitted states to burden interstate commerce to protect health and safety, international trade laws generally contain some provisions to permit states to limit free trade in order to protect the health of their populations.[44] For example, the General Agreement on Tariffs and Trade (GATT), which forms part of the WTO system, makes clear that states may adopt and enforce measures necessary to protect health provided such measures do not discriminate or serve as a disguise for protectionism.[45] Likewise, the WTO's Agreement on the Application of Sanitary and Phytosanitary Measures permits states to impose health-based restrictions on trade in food items, but restrictions (other than the merely provisional) that are more protective than the standards promulgated by competent international bodies must be based on a valid risk assessment.[46] Not surprisingly, as in domestic law, the question of whether a restriction that purports to protect public health is a valid health measure can be a contentious one. For example, in the important *Beef Hormone Case,* the European Union (EU) argued that the precautionary principle should apply and that it should have the authority to ban beef raised with growth-promoting hormones despite the lack of scientific evidence establishing a risk. The WTO Appellate Body disagreed and held that though the EU could choose to adopt a more protective standard than is provided for in international codes, it could not forego a risk assessment.[47] Recently, similar questions have arisen in a case challenging the EU's decision to ban genetically modified food.[48]

By permitting nations to burden trade in order to protect the health of their populations as long as such burdens are based on scientific evidence, the WTO system seems to adopt (perhaps more so than has the United States Supreme Court in its own commerce clause jurisprudence[49]) two key aspects of population-based legal analysis: an appreciation for the importance of population health as a valid governmental goal and a reliance on scientific and empirical evidence. However, in other critical ways, the WTO system appears wanting from a population perspective. Perhaps most important, by granting the international free trade system jurisdiction over domestic health laws, and by requiring evidence of a health impact to justify restrictions on trade, the WTO implicitly prioritizes trade over population health.

In addition, as many commentators have noted, several aspects of the WTO system have had detrimental effects on the health of populations in poorer countries. For example, the strong protections for intellectual property created by the Agreement on Trade-Related Aspects of Intellectual Property Rights (TRIPS) has limited the availability in the developing world of lifesaving pharmaceuticals, particularly antiretroviral drugs used to treat HIV/AIDS.[50] Although the Doha Declaration permits nations to issue compulsory licenses to make patented pharmaceuticals available for public health emergencies, the practical impact in poor nations without a robust pharmaceutical industry has been called into question. In response, WTO member nations eventually agreed to allow developing nations to import generic drugs under limited circumstances.[51] Critics, however, continue to argue that the flexibilities afforded in the new agreement are not enough to ensure affordable access to lifesaving medications in poor nations.[52] If so, the TRIPS system that protects intellectual property, supposedly to encourage inventiveness and the development of life-saving drugs, neglects disparities and overlooks the fact that a policy which may, theoretically, benefit one population (those in the developed world who will have access to the drugs that will be developed) can harm the health of other populations. In a sense, though purporting to recognize the value of population health abstractly, TRIPS disregards the distinctive environments and circumstances that different populations face.

INTERNATIONAL HUMAN RIGHTS LAWS

If trade laws exemplify the challenge that international law may pose for population health, many commentators argue that, in contrast, international human rights laws provide a model for using law to ensure the conditions in which populations may be healthy.[53] As George Annas has noted, the modern international human rights movement and international human rights law developed in the aftermath of the horrors of World War II. According to Annas, the Nuremburg Trials, which helped to provide the foundations for human rights law, were "held on the premise that there is a higher law of humanity, derived from natural law rules based on an understanding of the essential nature of humans."[54]

The formative document of international human rights law is the Universal Declaration of Human Rights (UDHR), adopted by the General Assembly of the United Nations in 1948. Although it is not a treaty with the force of law, the UDHR articulates the essential premise that all individuals, across the globe, are entitled to a basic array of rights. Many of these rights are similar to those found in the U.S. Constitution. However, Article 25 of the UDHR goes further in suggesting the importance of health, specifically stating that "everyone has the right to a standard of living adequate for the health and well-being of himself and of his family, including food, clothing, housing, and medical care and necessary social services, and the right to security in the event of unemployment, sickness, disability, widowhood, old age or other lack of livelihood in circumstances beyond his control."[55]

Many of the rights expressed as aspirations in the UDHR were affirmed in two subsequent international treaties. The International Covenant on Civil and Political Rights (ICCPR) compels states to respect civil and political rights, many of which are quite similar to the negative rights guaranteed by the U.S. Constitution.[56] In contrast, many of the rights appearing in the International Covenant on Economic, Social and Cultural Rights (ICESCR) have the characteristic of so-called positive rights that have for the most part not been recognized by courts in the United States as constitutionally guaranteed.[57] As a result, it is not surprising that the United States has failed to ratify the ICESCR.

Despite this failure, the ICESCR along with the WHO Constitution and other international human rights conventions, such as the Convention on the Rights of the Child,[58] establish a framework for the recognition of rights relating directly to population health. Most important, Article 12 of the ICESCR provides that states recognize "the right of everyone to the enjoyment of the highest attainable standard of physical and mental health."[59] To realize such rights, states further commit to take steps necessary for

(a) The provision for the reduction of the stillbirth-rate and of infant mortality and for the healthy development of the child;
(b) The improvement of all aspects of environmental and industrial hygiene;
(c) The prevention, treatment and control of epidemic, endemic, occupational and other diseases;
(d) The creation of conditions which would assure to all medical service and medical attention in the event of sickness.[60]

In 2000, the Committee on Economic, Social and Cultural Rights issued General Comment 14, which aims to explicate and expand upon rights articulated in Article 12: the "right to health is closely related to and dependent upon the realization of other human rights . . . including the rights to food, housing, work, education, human dignity, life, non-discrimination, equality, the prohibition against torture, privacy, access to information, and the freedoms of association, assembly and movement."[61] Comment 14 continues by noting the importance of decision making by an affected population.[62] It also provides a long list of legal obligations that states are required to fulfill under the covenant. Among these are protecting clean air and water, adopting legislation, and taking measures to ensure equal access to health services. Perhaps most important from a population-based perspective, Comment 14 requires states to give "sufficient recognition to the right to health in the national political and legal systems."[63]

Despite the strong affirmative language, the actual legal requirements created by the covenant are tempered by the fact that it states that signatory nations agree to take steps "to the maximum of [their] available resources with a view to achieving progressively the full realization of the rights recognized."[64] In other words, the hard-law rights provided for in the covenant are not traditional liberal rights, not fully enforceable trumps. On the other hand, General Comment 3 argues that the ICESCR imposes on states "a minimum core obligation to ensure the satisfaction of, at the very least, minimum essential levels of each of the rights" protected by the covenant and that that obligation exists "irrespective" of the availability of resources.[65] This suggests that the ICESCR has created some essential core of positive rights.

Although the rights created by the covenant are not fully enforceable, they are nonetheless important. First, they can help illuminate the nature of the interests recognized and provide a powerful source of legitimacy for claims made against states on behalf of those interests. Second, the international human rights framework provides for a variety of mechanisms, official and unofficial, for reporting on and monitoring nations' fidelity to international human rights.[66] Although such mechanisms may lack teeth, they highlight and reinforce the importance of the goals articulated in human rights documents.

In addition, courts around the world rely increasingly on international human rights as persuasive sources of authority.[67] For example, in the oft-cited *Grootboom* case, the Constitutional Court of South Africa looked to international law and particularly the ICESCR in discussing the South African government's constitutional obligations to provide access to shelter.[68] Even in the United States, one of the nations most resistant to the incorporation of international law into domestic law, several Supreme Court justices have begun to cite international human rights principles and have even debated the merits of doing so.[69]

The positive rights articulated in the ICESCR and General Comment 14 can also provide a model for the recognition through law of positive, population-based interests, thereby helping dispel the assumption, common in the United States at least, that liberty is purely individualistic and negative. For example, the ICESCR explicitly recognizes that individuals are embedded in families, communities, and cultures. Thus, though all individuals have rights as individuals, their relationship with the state must be understood with an appreciation of their membership in various populations. And, as noted, General Comment 14 asserts the importance of decision making by affected populations.

International conventions also recognize the particularity of diverse populations. For example, the Convention on the Rights of the Child sets forth specific obligations on states with respect to children, recognizing the distinct needs and circumstances of that population.[70] Likewise, the Convention on the Elimination of All Forms of Discrimination against Women condemns discrimination against women, yet also recognizes the particular needs and circumstances of women.[71] And the recently ratified Convention on the Rights of Persons with Disabilities requires states to protect the rights of all persons with disabilities, including specifically children and women with disabilities.[72]

Perhaps even more remarkable from a U.S. perspective, international human rights laws explicitly recognize rights, such as education and the control of disease, whose realization requires affirmative actions and interventions on the part of states and nonstate actors. Thus the Convention on the Rights of Persons with Disabilities mandates a long list of affirmative steps that states must take, which include providing reasonable accommodations, accessible information, accessible transportation, education, independent living, and "awareness-raising."[73] Conceptualizing and recognizing a right to these social goods can open the door for using law to improve the health of populations. At the same time, this conceptualization offers the possibility of diminishing, if not extinguishing, the purported conflict between individual rights and population health protection assumed by the conventional view.[74] According to Wendy Mariner, the human right to health framework "lays out the entire spectrum of legal tools at our disposal. It not only parallels the types of health laws in the United States, but also reminds us that human rights include both freedoms and entitlements."[75]

It is precisely for this reason that many scholars and activists, following in the footsteps of Jonathan Mann and the insights he developed in response to the HIV epidemic,[76] have turned to international human rights law as a vehicle for protecting the health of populations, particularly vulnerable populations. Sofia Gruskin and Paula Braveman argue that "[a] human rights lens brings attention not only to the technical and operational aspects of health-related interventions but also to the civil, political, economic, social and cultural factors that surround them."[77] In essence, the human rights framework accords with population-based legal analysis not only in prioritizing the health of populations, but also in recognizing that achieving it depends on interventions that take account of the complex environments in which populations reside. A question emerges: what are the distinctions between the health and human rights framework and population-based legal analysis?

COMPARING POPULATION-BASED LEGAL ANALYSIS WITH INTERNATIONAL HUMAN RIGHTS

As suggested, international human rights law provides a lens that shares many characteristics with population-based legal analysis: concern for the health of populations, a recognition of the complementarity of rights and health, an awareness that individuals are situated within populations and that their health is affected by their environment, an appreciation of the distinct needs of vulnerable populations, and an understanding that positive legal interventions can play an important and at times essential role in securing the health of populations. In addition, the international human rights perspective helps highlight the global nature of population health and law.

Despite these strong similarities, important differences remain between population-based legal analysis and the international human rights framework. First, populaiton-based legal analysis is a legal theory, a tool that can be used to analyze and critique law, including international and domestic law as well as legal discourse. In contrast, the international human rights framework lies at the juncture between positive law, ethical theory, and political activism. It thus draws much of its strength from political mobilization and grassroots movements, whereas population-based legal analysis remains more focused on opinions of judges as well as the teachings of scholars and legal professionals. On the other hand, the legitimacy and strength of the international human rights movement depend significantly on the recognition of the values the movement articulates in formal legal documents (including hard-law treaties and soft-law resolutions and advisories) as well as the impact of those documents in the real world. As a result, the movement is vulnerable when governments, as is all too often the case, fail to recognize or respect the rights agreed upon in international law documents. In contrast, because it is more purely a branch of legal theory and criticism that does not draw its legitimacy from the articulation of its norms in ratified legal documents, population-based legal analysis can remain more comfortably outside of and apart from positive law.

More generally, by emphasizing and relying on rights, the human rights movement draws upon a tradition strongly influenced by Kantian ethics that prioritizes individuals and esteems their essential, and universal, individuality and autonomy.[78] Perhaps as a result, in its formative years, the human rights movement tended to emphasize the rights of individuals. As a result, as Benjamin Meier has noted, despite the broad language in General Comment 14, human rights discussions about health have, for the most part, focused on the right of individuals to medical care, rather than broad-based rights to protection of population health.[79]

Nevertheless, as noted, the human rights movement has also had a long tradition of recognizing so-called collective rights. Thus the United Nations Charter speaks of the "principle of equal rights and self-determination of *peoples*."[80] Likewise, Article 27 of the ICCPR states that "ethnic, religious, or linguistic minorities . . . shall not be denied the right, in community with the other members of their group, to enjoy their own culture, to profess and practice their own religion, or to use their own language."[81] Other international treaties and conventions create rights specific to vulnerable populations, such as women, children, or people with disabilities.[82] Moreover, scholars working within the framework have sought to expand, explore, and reconcile these collective rights with the universality and individuality of human rights.[83] In so doing, they have touched on and considered tensions reminiscent of those that arise domestically when protection of population health appears to clash with individual rights.[84]

Despite these important similarities, distinctions remain between the recognition of collective rights by the international human rights movement and the role of populations in population-based legal analysis. Because the international human rights movement remains a rights-based movement, it necessarily focuses on rights and asks, with respect to collectivities, whether and how they can be rights-bearers much as individuals can be. In population-based legal analysis, however, the role of populations is far more pervasive, and that of traditional rights less privileged. Populations are not simply entities that may or may not be entitled to rights. They are instead the fundamental subjects and objects of the law. All legal issues are subject to analysis from a perspective that considers the impact of populations qua populations on the topic at hand as well as the topic's impact on varied populations.

In addition, though the international human rights movement grants an important role to particular groups, the groups or collectivities are, for the most part, traditionally recognized, demographically identifiable groups, such as children, women, people with disabilities, or ethnic minorities. A population-based approach to law is, of course, also concerned about these and other vulnerable groups, and pays particular attention to the ways in which governmental interventions aimed at promoting health have a disparate impact on them. Yet, the concept of population used by a population-based approach to law is far broader and encompasses many populations beyond those typically discussed. As noted in chapter 3, population-based legal analysis recognizes that populations are epidemiologically created constructs and that the designation of different populations depends solely on the variables one seeks to analyze. Hence, population-based legal analysis may focus its concern on a population defined as children who drink soft drinks at school or children who drink soft drinks only at home. Such a construct generally lies outside the bounds of human rights discourse. Yet, only by recognizing the existence and influence of such epidemiologically defined, nontraditional populations can the law begin to take account of how social determinants influence populations and affect the risks faced by the individuals within the populations.

The discussion of epidemiology points to another critical distinction between population-based legal analysis and international human rights discourse. Although scholars and activists who use and speak the language of human rights law rely on a wide variety of scientific and technical disciplines, including epidemiology, to define and measure the attainment of those rights,[85] the concept of human rights is not an empirically verifiable construct. Instead, human rights are fundamentally transcendent notions, ideals that build and rely on widely shared ethical norms. Science may help to implement them, or tell us when they are wanting, but science cannot tell us anything about the nature of human rights as such. Indeed, one can well imagine a human rights movement or discussion in which empirical verification is considered either irrelevant or even problematic. After all, in some sense, the entire idea of human rights is that they ought to exist and be respected no matter the state of scientific understanding and technology.

In contrast, population-based legal analysis relies on epidemiology, biostatistics, and empirical verification. Although the idea of valuing population health can be articulated and defended by moral reasoning without recourse to science, empirical reasoning is needed both to define populations and their critical characteristics and to determine whether particular legal interventions promote or thwart the health of the relevant populations. For population-based legal theory, empiricism is not simply a useful tool to be used or not to promote the good; it is an essential and defining element and methodology of the construct. Without empiricism, population-based legal analysis cannot judge laws, it can only offer hypotheses. Hence it may lack some of the moral clarity and organizing power of human rights discourse. Yet, given the shifting nature and complexity of the threats facing the multiplicity of human populations, the humility and contingency of this approach is a virtue that should not be discounted.

A Globalized Approach

Seventy years have passed since the Supreme Court abandoned its traditional police power jurisprudence and dethroned public health from its central role in American law.[86] Given the health threats that potentially face the world today, from pandemic influenza to HIV and bioterrorism, it may be tempting to look back to that earlier age and urge a resurrection of the police power in the name of protecting the health of populations. But such nostalgia can have no place in any serious effort either to promote the health of populations or to reinsert a population perspective into the center of legal analysis.

In a globalized world in which an increasingly critical population is the population of the whole, quaint legal tools such as police power that rely on the sovereignty of a single subdivision of a single nation cannot begin to respond adequately to many of the varied risks at hand. Nor, indeed, can the law of any single nation-state. Instead, local, national, and international legal systems must each be recognized as having a critical role in influencing and protecting the health of populations.[87] As a result, to have a beneficial effect on population health, population-based legal analysis must necessarily be global. At the same time, the population perspective must take cognizance of and apply not only to those international health laws that facially affect the health and well-being of populations, but also to the vast array of other laws, including trade and human rights laws, that have the potential to broadly affect populations by influencing social determinants of health.

In undertaking this task, population-based legal analysis draws on and borrows from other legal perspectives, including international human rights law, that share many of its objectives. But learning from those paradigms does not undermine the importance of developing population-based legal analysis as an independent construct that can be used to criticize and analyze both domestic and international law. In a world in which the pace of change is rapid, travel and migration are constant, and the world is ever more connected even though the lives of people are ever more different, a legal paradigm that emphasizes the dynamism and multiplicity of global populations, the importance of empirical verification, and the centrality of promoting the well-being of populations to law is more essential than ever.

NOTES

1. Allyn L. Taylor, *Governing the Globalization of Public Health*, 32 J. L. MED. & ETHICS 500, 500 (2004).

2. J. N. HAYS, THE BURDENS OF DISEASE: EPIDEMICS AND HUMAN RESPONSE IN WESTERN HISTORY 39–40 (1998).

3. *Id.* at 62–77.

4. *Id.* at 135–36.

5. David P. Fidler, *The Future of the World Health Organization: What Role for International Law?*, 31 VAND. J. TRANSNAT'L L. 1079, 1083–84 (1998). For a further discussion of emerging infections, see chapter 8, *supra*.

6. Mitchell L. Cohen, *Changing Patterns of Infectious Disease*, 407 NATURE 762, 765 (2000); David P. Fidler, *Return of the Fourth Horseman: Emerging Infectious Diseases and International Law*, 81 MINN. L. REV. 771, 775–98 (1997); World Health Organization, *Travel by Air: Health Considerations*, http://whqlibdoc.who.int/publications/2005/9241580364_chap2.pdf (last visited Nov. 18, 2008).

7. Fidler, *supra* note 6, at 797–98.

8. LAURIE GARRETT, THE COMING PLAGUE: NEWLY EMERGING DISEASES IN A WORLD OUT OF BALANCE (1994).

9. Taylor, *supra* note 1, at 500.

10. *Id.* For a further discussion of the impact of climate change on global health, see Lisa Heinzerling, *Climate Change, Human Health, and the Post-Cautionary Principle*, 96 GEO. L.J. 445, 447, 452 (2008).

11. Benjamin Mason Meier, *Employing Health Rights for Global Justice: The Promise of Public Health in Response to the Insalubrious Ramifications of Globalization*, 39 CORNELL INT'L L.J. 711, 712–13 (2006).

12. *See* Jennifer Prah Ruger, *Normative Foundations of Global Health Law*, 96 GEO. L.J. 423, 430–31 (2008). Ruger argues that reduction of these disparities should be a central aim of what she terms global health law.

13. *Compare* Benjamin Mason Meier & Larisa M. Mori, *The Highest Attainable Standard: Advancing a Collective Human Right to Public Health*, 37 COLUM. HUM. RTS. L. REV. 101, 104–105 (2005) (arguing that modernization has exacerbated disparities in health between rich and poor) *with* Brian Goesling & Glenn Firebaugh, *The Trend in International Health Inequality*, 30 POPULATION & DEVELOPMENT REV. 131, 133 (2004) (arguing that inequality between countries peaked in the mid-twentieth century and life expectancies have converged between countries, but also noting that other scholars disagree).

14. Goesling & Firebaugh, *supra* note 13, at 134.

15. Barry S. Levy & Victor W. Sidel, *Introduction, in* SOCIAL INJUSTICE AND PUBLIC HEALTH 5, 7 (Barry S. Levy & Victor W. Sidel eds., 2006).

16. WORLD HEALTH ORGANIZATION, THE WORLD HEALTH REPORT 2003 4 (2003), www.who.int/whr/2003/en/Chapter1-en.pdf (last visited Nov. 18, 2008).

17. *Id.* at 8.

18. *Id.*

19. *Id.* at 18.

20. *Id.* at 11.

21. *Id.* at 17.

22. *Id.* at 8.

23. *Id.* at 14–17.

24. Michael Marmot & Ruth Bell, *The Socioeconomically Disadvantaged, in* Levy and Sidel, *supra* note 15, at 25, 29.

25. *Id.* For a further discussion of the socioeconomic gradient, see chapter 1, *supra*.

26. John Lynch & George Kaplan, *Socioeconomic Position, in* SOCIAL EPIDEMIOLOGY 13 (Lisa F. Berkman & Ichiro Kawachi eds., 2000).

27. Levy & Sidel, *supra* note 15, at 7.

28. Carol Easley Allen & Cheryl E. Easley, *Racial and Ethnic Minorities, in* Levy & Sidel, *supra* note 15, at 46, 50.

29. *Id.*

30. *See, e.g.*, Nancy Krieger, *Discrimination and Health, in* Berkman & Kawachi, *supra* note 26, at 36–68 (proposing explanations for racial disparities); Lynch & Kaplan, *supra* note 26, at 13–30 (discussing and proposing explanations for socioeconomic disparities).

31. Fidler, *supra* note 5, at 1083.

32. *Id.* at 1084; Lawrence O. Gostin, *World Health Law: Toward a New Conception of Global Health Governance for the 21st Century*, 5 YALE J. HEALTH POL'Y L. & ETHICS 413, 414 (2005).

33. World Health Organization Constitution, July 24, 1946, 62 Stat. 2679, 14 U.N.T.S. 185.

34. Taylor, *supra* note 1, at 504.

35. Fifty-Eighth World Health Assembly, Art. 6, International Health Regulations (2005) (2d ed. 2008), http://who.int/csr/ihr/IHR_2005_en.pdf (last visited Nov. 18, 2008).

36. *Id.* at Art. 32.

37. *Id.* at Art. 42.

38. World Health Organization, *WHO Framework Convention on Tobacco Control*, May 21, 2003, http://www.who.int/tobacco/framework/WHO_FCTC_english.pdf (last visited Nov. 10, 2008).

39. *Id.* at Art. 5.

40. *See* chapter 2, *supra.*

41. *See* chapter 5, *supra.*

42. *See* chapter 4, *supra.*

43. Jan Bohanes, *Risk Regulation in WTO Law: A Procedure-Based Approach to the Precautionary Principle*, 40 COLUM. J. TRANSNAT'L L. 323, 325 (2002).

44. David P. Fidler & Martin S. Cetron, *International Considerations, in* LAW IN PUBLIC HEALTH PRACTICE 168, 184 (Richard A. Goodman et al. eds., 2d ed. 2006).

45. World Trade Organization, *Understanding the WTO: Standards and Safety*, http://www.wto.org/english/thewto_e/whatis_e/tif_e/agrm4_e.htm (last visited Nov. 18, 2008).

46. Fidler & Cetron, *supra* note 44, at 184–85.

47. Bohanes, *supra* note 43, at 335–36 *citing* Appellate Body Report, *European Communities—Measures Concerning Meat and Meat Products (Hormones)*, T/DS26/AB/R (Jan. 16, 1998).

48. *Panel Report, European Communities—Measures Affecting the Approval and Marketing of Biotech Products*, WT/DS292/17 (Sept. 29, 2006).

49. *See* chapter 4, *supra.*

50. *E.g.*, Brook K. Baker, *Arthritic Flexibilities for Accessing Medicines: Analysis of WTO Action regarding Paragraph 6 of the Doha Declaration on the TRIPS Agreement and Public Health*, 14 IND. INT'L & COMP. L. REV. 613, 617 (2004); Uche Ewelukwa, *Patent Wars in the Valley of the Shadow of Death: The Pharmaceutical Industry, Ethics, and Global Trade*, 59 U. MIAMI L. REV. 203, 207 (2005).

51. World Trade Organization, *Implementation of Paragraph 6 of the Doha Declaration on the TRIPS Agreement and Public Health*, http://www.wto.org/English/tratop_e/trips_e/implem_para6_e.htm (last visited Nov. 10, 2008); Baker, *supra* note 50, at 636–56.

52. Baker, *supra* note 50, at 636–56.

53. *E.g.*, Wendy K. Mariner, *Law and Public Health: Beyond Emergency Preparedness*, 38 J. HEALTH L. 247, 270–76 (2005).

54. George J. Annas, *The State of Security: Human Rights and Post 9/11 Epidemics*, 38 J. HEALTH L. 319, 322 (2003).

55. Universal Declaration of Human Rights, G.A. Res. 271A, Art. 25, U.N. GAOR, 3d Sess., 1st plen. mtg., U.N. Doc. A/810 (Dec. 12, 1948).

56. International Covenant on Civil and Political Rights, G.A. Res. 2200A (XXI), U.N. GAOR, Supp. No. 16, U.N. Doc. A/6316 (Dec. 16, 1966).

57. *See* chapter 6, *supra.*

58. Convention on the Rights of the Child, G.A. Res. 44/25 (1989), U.N. GAOR, 44th Sess., U.N. Doc. A/Res/44/25 (Nov. 20, 1989).

59. International Covenant on Economic, Social and Cultural Rights, G.A. Res. 2200A (XXI)(1966), Art. 12, 21 U.N. GAOR Supp. No. 16, U.N. Doc. A/6316 (Dec. 16, 1966).

60. *Id.*

61. U.N. Comm. on Econ., Soc. & Cultural Rights [CESCR], *General Comment No. 14: The Right to the Highest Attainable Standard of Health*, U.N. Doc. E/C. 12/2000/4 (Aug. 11, 2000).

62. *Id.*

63. *Id.*

64. *Id.* at Art. 2; International Covenant on Economic, Social and Cultural Rights, Art. 12, *supra* note 59.

65. CESCR, *General Comment 3: The Nature of States Parties Obligations*, U.N. Doc. E/1991/23 (Dec. 14, 1991). For further commentary on the ICESCR, see CESCR, *Maastricht Guidelines: Substantive Issues Arising in the Implementation of the International Covenant on Economic, Social and Cultural Rights*, 24th Sess., U.N. Doc. E/C. 12/2000/13 (Oct. 2, 2000); U.N. Econ. & Soc. Council [ECOSOC], Comm'n on Human Rights, *Limburg Principles on the Implementation of the International Covenant on Economic, Social and Cultural Rights*, U.N. Doc. E/CN. 4/1987/17 (1987).

66. Sofia Gruskin & Paula Braveman, *Addressing Social Injustice in a Human Rights Context*, *in* SOCIAL INJUSTICE AND PUBLIC HEALTH, *supra* note 15, at 405, 408.

67. *See* Michael Kirby, *International Law: The Impact on National Constitutions*, 21 AM. U. INT'L L. REV. 327, 329–32 (2006).

68. Government of the Republic of South Africa v. Grootboom, 2000 (11) BCLR 1169.

69. *E.g.*, Hamdan v. Rumsfeld, 548 U.S. 557, 760–61 (2006) (Stevens, J., plurality opinion); Lawrence v. Texas, 539 U.S. 558, 576 (2003); *The Relevance of Foreign Legal Materials in U.S. Constitutional Cases: A Conversation between Justices Antonin Scalia and Justice Stephen Breyer*, 3 INT'L J. CONST. L. 519 (2005).

70. Convention on the Rights of the Child, *supra* note 58.

71. Convention on the Elimination of All Forms of Discrimination against Women, G.A. Res. 34/180, U.N. Doc. A/RES/34/180 (Dec. 18, 1979).

72. Convention on the Rights of Persons with Disabilities, G.A. Rees. 61/106, U.N. GAOR, 61st Sess. U.N. Doc. A/Res/61/106 (Dec. 13, 2006).

73. *Id.* at Arts. 2, 8, 9, 24, 25, 26, & 27.

74. *See* chapter 5, *supra.*

75. Mariner, *supra* note 53, at 276.

76. Jonathan M. Mann, *Medicine and Public Health, Ethics and Human Rights*, 27 HASTINGS CTR. RPT. 6, 6–13 (1997).

77. Gruskin & Braveman, *supra* note 66, at 410.

78. Jerome J. Shestack, *The Philosophical Foundations of Human Rights*, 20 HUM. RTS. Q. 201, 215–16 (1998).

79. Meier, *supra* note 11, at 753–56. *See also* Benjamin Mason Meier, *Advancing Health Rights in a Globalized World: Responding to Globalization through a Collective Human Right to Public Health*, 35 J.L. MED. & ETHICS 545, 550 (2007).

80. U.N. Charter Art. 55, http://www.un.org/aboutun/charter/ (last visited Nov. 18, 2008) (emphasis added).

81. International Covenant on Civil and Political Rights, *supra* note 56, at 11–23.

82. *See* Convention on the Elimination of All Forms of Discrimination against Women, *supra* note 72, at 212–19; Convention on the Rights of the Child, *supra* note 59; Convention on the Rights of Persons with Disabilities, *supra* note 72.

83. *See, e.g.*, Ruth L. Gana, *Which 'Self'? Race and Gender in the Right to Self-Determination as a Prerequisite to the Right to Development*, 14 Wis. Int'l L.J. 133, 137–53 (1995); Michael R. Geroe & Thomas K. Gump, *Hungary and a New Paradigm for the Protection of Ethnic Minorities in Central and Eastern Europe*, 32 Colum. J. Transnat'l L. 673, 674–84 (1995).

84. *See* chapter 5, *supra*.

85. *See, e.g.*, Alicia Ely Yamin, *Defining Questions: Situating Issues of Power in the Formulation of a Right to Health under International Law*, 18 Hum. Rts. Q. 398, 426 (1996) (noting the work of NGOs in documenting violations of the right to health).

86. *See* chapter 2, *supra*.

87. David P. Fidler, *A Globalized Theory of Public Health Law*, 30 J. L. Med. & Ethics 150, 152 (2002).

CHAPTER 11

The Future of Population-Based Legal Analysis

Often a new paradigm emerges, at least in embryo, before a crisis has developed far or been explicitly recognized.

—Thomas S. Kuhn, *The Structure of Scientific Revolutions*

THIS BOOK BEGAN with the common law maxim, *salus populi suprema lex*. Its meaning is simple: the well-being of the community is the highest law. The maxim helps remind us of why we have law. Law exists not only to vindicate the interests and rights of individuals, nor simply to empower officials, but also to promote and ensure the well-being of populations. Central to that objective is promoting and enhancing population health. Only when that is secured can the well-being and interests of both individuals and the populations they form be realized.

Population-based legal analysis is an approach to legal reasoning, analysis, and decision making that is inspired by the vision of *salus populi*. It seeks to enable law to fulfill its mission of promoting the health of all populations, thereby providing communities and individuals with the chance to pursue their own vision of the good life. As the preceding chapters have explained, population-based legal analysis assists law in this mission by applying public health's population perspective to legal analysis. In so doing, it recognizes the promotion of population health as a legal norm and helps law appreciate the role that populations play as both objects and subjects of the law. In addition, it adopts the epistemology and methodologies of public health, especially epidemiology, for legal analysis and decision making. In doing so, population-based legal analysis improves law's capacity to serve as an effective tool for the protection and promotion of population health.

The application of population-based legal analysis to the many diverse and pressing health problems that populations confront today, from obesity to emerging infections, has revealed the poverty of contemporary American legal analysis. Population-based legal analysis has exposed the hyperindividualism that infects much of contemporary American discourse, uncovering critical insights into the relationship between individuals, populations, and legal doctrines. Key among these insights is that the choices individuals exercise and the health risks they face are determined, to a large degree, by the environments they experience and the populations they comprise. Also important is the prevention paradox, which suggests that laws that have only a modest impact on a broad population may have a greater effect on human health and well-being than laws that target, often coercively, so-called high-risk individuals. And perhaps most crucial is the recognition that both the positive and negative rights of individuals are often conducive, if not essential, to securing the health of the populations they form. As a result, the conflict between population health and the interests of individuals is neither as deep nor as enduring as the conventional view holds.

Unfortunately, in the early years of the twenty-first century, American law often seems either to neglect its own mission to protect population health or to see that mission as requiring the suppression of individual rights. Thus American law oscillates between libertarianism and authoritarianism, in either case assuming that we can have our liberty, or our health, but not both.[1] Population-based legal analysis teaches that this notion is false, indeed, dangerous. It undermines the law's capacity to protect population health while eviscerating myriad other constitutional norms, including separation of powers, federalism, equal protection, and due process.

Thus the challenge we face today is to recognize the importance of population health to law without permitting the protection of public health to serve as an excuse to undermine the rule of law. To do this, we need to incorporate a true population perspective into law, so that the fear of health threats and the cry of public health are not exploited or misused, but rather, that population health is enhanced by a legal discourse and jurisprudence that appreciates how law can help lay the conditions for people to be healthy. To do this, law must embrace a sophisticated understanding of public health's relationship to law. It must recognize the diversity and constructed nature of populations and eschew the belief in a single, totemic public. It must also take note of the ways that environments and population-level determinants affect the health of diverse groups. Finally, it must be more open to and learned about empirical inquiry and reasoning. Law and lawyers must appreciate the value of what is known, as well as what cannot be known, about law's impact on the material world as well as the factors that improve and threaten population health.

Can this be done? Can a population-based approach to law take hold and become one of the commonly accepted approaches used by lawyers, jurists, and policymakers? Can the law value population health without falling prey to the exploitation of public health fears? In a decade in which public health law has largely focused on preparedness, the jury is still out.[2] There is reason for both optimism and concern.

The Legal Climate

Despite the puzzling persistence of the conventional view,[3] there are several reasons to be hopeful about the prospects of a population approach to the law in the United States. Some have been discussed, at least in passing, in the preceding chapters. Each deserves brief comment here.

Perhaps the most pressing reason for optimism is the wide recognition of the impoverished state of much of contemporary legal discourse, especially as it relates to public health. As discussed earlier, contemporary American law, especially constitutional law, is notable both for its inconsistent attentiveness to the critical issues and problems diverse populations face, as well as for its frequent disregard of the empirical world. In addition, American legal discourse is obviously and excessively individualistic. It generally overlooks the deep connections between individuals and multiple populations and fails to appreciate the impact of populations and environments in shaping people's lives. As a result, legal decisions by courts but also by legislatures frequently disregard the health of populations. And when they purport to address that concern, they are too quick to defer to public health officials or the legislature and too ready to assume the necessity of and sanction highly coercive actions. As a result, American public law secures neither population health nor individual rights. Yet, as the threats to population health become increasingly complex, and the dangers of excessive individualism are clearly exposed, for example, by the financial panic of 2008, public law's failure to fulfill its basic mission may become more evident and less tenable, whetting the desire for a new and more effective approach.

Our private law is also in dire straights for it largely neglects the importance of population health. Indeed, the field of private law most relevant to public health threats—tort law—appears increasingly incapable of responding adequately to the complex risks, from global warming to reemerging infections, from toxic chemicals to medical injuries, that populations face today. Moreover, whatever ability tort law has to protect the health of populations is now threatened by a tort reform movement that seems more bent on slamming the courthouse door than on using the law to deter readily preventable injuries. Eventually not only legal critics but injured populations may demand true reform.

For the most part, academic discourse has also generally failed to provide legal decision makers with the tools needed to make law more responsive to the complex problems different populations face. Although legal scholarship is in many ways flourishing, and has introduced a wide array of new voices, disciplines, insights, and critical perspectives, including the perspectives of various subpopulations and identity groups, academic writings have also become increasingly removed from the work of everyday lawyers, jurists, and legislators. Indeed, it appears that courts today rely less than they did in the past on legal scholarship.[4] This suggests a need and an opening for a new approach, such as that population-based legal analysis offers, that is both theoretically grounded and practically useful.

Moreover, signs of change are in the air. One is the growth of international human rights law and the partnership it has spawned between scholars and activists. As discussed in chapter 10, international human rights law is not simply a body of binding law; it is a movement that has engaged activists, scholars, and jurists around the globe. This provides it with an exciting potential to bridge the gap between theory and praxis. Moreover, the international human rights movement shares many of the values and insights of the population perspective. Most critical, it places a high value on population health and recognizes the complementary relationship between rights and health. It also has been attentive to both the importance and distinctiveness of multiple populations, especially traditionally vulnerable populations. And, as discussed in chapter 10, the international human rights framework has not only helped change the debate about issues affecting the health of populations around the world, but has also influenced the content of domestic law in many jurisdictions. Thus it offers an important vehicle to reinvigorate law and help lay the foundations for a fuller adoption of a population perspective.

The recent renaissance of public health law is also cause for both optimism and alarm. For many decades, at least in the United States, the close connections between public health and law were frequently overlooked. Both theorists and jurists lost sight not only of the fact that promoting population health is one of law's goals, but also the many ways in which population health has helped shape law.

Today, in the wake of new public health problems, such as HIV, bioterrorism, and the threat of pandemic influenza, and thanks to the dedication of and dialogue between a diverse group of practitioners, policymakers, and scholars, public health law is reemerging as a vibrant and increasingly active field of law. Books such as Lawrence Gostin's *Public Health Law: Power, Duty, Restraint*[5] and *Law in Public Health Practice* edited by Richard Goodman and his colleagues,[6] as well as a plethora of scholarly articles, have helped shine the spotlight on public health law and highlight a long list of critical public health law issues. Some have gone even further and explored the theoretical justifications for and key attributes of public health law. Although these works vary enormously in both their content and their vantage points, they have all brought attention to the importance of population health and the key role that law can and should play in safeguarding it. And, to different degrees, many of these works have adopted, or at least explored, different components of the population perspective.

Public health law has also grown in the world of practice. In the United States alone, major foundations, such as the Robert Wood Johnson Foundation, have supported initiatives to advance and modernize the field.[7] The CDC has established a Public Health Law Program (PHLP) whose "primary goal" is to "enhance the public health system's legal preparedness to address emerging threats, chronic diseases, and other national public health priorities and to improve use of law to support program activities."[8] And a professional organization, the Public Health Law Association (PHLA), was formed with a mission of "promoting healthy people and healthy communities through dialogue, partnerships, education and research in public health law."[9] Unfortunately, PHLA's continuing struggles to become financially secure reaffirm public health law's fragile status in the legal profession.[10]

Still, evidence of the reemergence of public health law is apparent both domestically and internationally. For example, the World Health Congress has revised and modernized the International Health Regulations and has led the way in global tobacco control.[11] In the United States, as discussed, the federal government has emphasized law's role in protecting the nation against bioterrorism as well as naturally occurring infections.[12] In addition, states have undertaken a wide variety of measures to address problems such as obesity, tobacco, and HIV/AIDs. Likewise, cities and local governments have attempted to use their regulatory authority in novel ways to address new public health threats, such as that posed by trans-fats.[13] Although some of these efforts are well advised and some are not, they all exemplify a renewed realization by public health practitioners that law can be used affirmatively to enhance the health of populations.

Nevertheless, the renewed focus on public health law does not assure either the adoption of a population perspective or the advancement of population health. Although public health law's reemergence has helped establish law's importance to public health, it has not consummated the adoption of a true population perspective either within the reemerging field or more broadly. Rather, in many ways, it has ignored critical aspects of the population perspective.

According to one of its leading theorists, Lawrence Gostin, public health law is the "study of the legal powers and duties of the state, in collaboration with its partners (e.g. health care, business, the community, the media, and academe), to assure the conditions for people to be healthy (to identify, prevent, and ameliorate risks to health in the population) and the limitations on the power of the state to constrain the autonomy, privacy, liberty, proprietary, or other legally protected interests of individuals for the common good."[14] As David Fidler points out, Gostin's definition applies solely to public health law within a nation-state.[15] However, even when it is expanded to accommodate its global dimensions, public health law is both narrower than and different from population-based legal analysis. Although both enterprises put protection of population health at the forefront of their concern, public health law remains focused, as Gostin's definition suggests, on core public health laws that governments use either directly or indirectly to promote the health of populations, as well as on the legal principles that guide the reach of such laws. Hence public health law emphasizes government powers and the limits placed on them. This perspective leads, almost inevitably, to the conventional view with its supposition that the interests of the public (as represented by the government) and individuals are necessarily in opposition. But, as we have seen repeatedly, the population perspective questions that premise and reveals the many ways in which the interests of individuals and populations are complementary.

In addition, though most practitioners and theorists working in public health law are sensitive to the multiplicity of populations, the field tends to reify populations into a singular public. As we have seen, this ignores the constructed and changing nature of populations. It also allows legal decision makers to disregard or discount the different circumstances distinct subpopulations face. And, once again, it helps reinforce the conventional view by framing the debate as if the restraint on an individual is critical to the security of the public. The result, not surprisingly, is a worrisome toleration for assertive government authority, an increasing willingness to sacrifice individual rights, and a growing disdain for judicial oversight and legal remedies that check the actions of public health officials, actions that are invariably taken in the name of protecting the public.[16]

Nevertheless, despite the profound differences between public health law and population-based legal analysis, the former's revival can certainly help plant the seeds for population-based legal analysis. Indeed, both public health law and population-based legal analysis share a common mission: to use law to promote the health and well-being of the world's many populations. Working together, supporters of each, even when they disagree, can highlight the importance of population health to law and law to population health. They can also stimulate research on and analysis of how the law protects, and fails to protect, the health of populations. And they can introduce into legal discourse the reasoning and methodologies of public health.

ADOPTING A POPULATION PERSPECTIVE

Protecting and promoting population health is both a demanding and an elusive goal for the law. In the face of the infinite diversity of the world's populations, the breathless expansiveness of human health, and the inevitability of death, the quest to use law to promote the health of all populations is daunting. Certainly, population health can never be secured. It can, however, be enhanced. And law, when viewed and applied through a population perspective, can help to achieve that enhancement. Indeed, law is essential for that enhancement.

Adopting a population-based legal analysis can help law fulfill its population health mission. It can also enrich the law. It can anchor legal discourse to the critical but often undervalued legal norm—population health—and thereby restore both law's legitimacy and its relevance as a practical tool. In addition, by focusing attention on the diversity and importance of populations, population-based legal analysis can help law shed the unrealistic and corrosive individualism that has pervaded much of contemporary American jurisprudence. And by incorporating the methodologies of public health into legal analysis, including empiricism and probabilistic reasoning, population-based legal analysis can help legal decision makers make sense of complex scientific evidence, freeing them from the dual but divergent dangers of skepticism and deference.

In addition, by reminding us of the complex interdependency between populations and individuals, and by embracing the contingent and changing lessons of empiricism and probabilistic reasoning, population-based legal analysis can nurture our legal imaginations. By altering the focus of our analysis, it can help us change how we think about, practice, and teach the law, leading us to see alternatives to the endless, sterile, and frequently dangerous debates about the conflict between the rights of the individual and the public's health. By forcing us to remember population effects and to recall the role that population-level factors play in determining the preferences individuals form and the risks they face, population-based legal analysis can remind us that rights can be complementary as well as conflicting, and that liberty can be positive as well as negative. In short, by incorporating the population perspective into law, population-based legal analysis can advance *salus populi* without eroding the rights of the populations and individuals that the law is called to serve.

NOTES

1. This view was especially apparent in the post-9/11 public health preparedness efforts of the Bush administration. *See* George J. Annas, Wendy K. Mariner, & Wendy E. Parmet, *Pandemic Preparedness: The Need for a Public Health—Not a Law Enforcement/National Security Approach,* American Civil Liberties Union (Jan. 14, 2008), http://www.aclu.org/pdfs/privacy/pemic_report.pdf (last visited Nov. 5, 2008).

2. For a discussion of some recent public health preparedness activities, see chapter 8, *supra.* For an overview of what has been termed *public health legal preparedness,* see Georges C. Benjamin & Anthony D. Moulton, *Public Health Emergency Legal Preparedness: A Framework for Action,* 36 J. L. MED. & ETHICS 13, 13–14 (Spec. Supp. 2008).

3. *See* chapter 5, *supra.*

4. Adam Liptak, *When Rendering Decisions Judges Are Finding Law Reviews Irrelevant,* NEW YORK TIMES, Mar. 19, 2007, at A-8.

5. LAWRENCE O. GOSTIN, PUBLIC HEALTH LAW: POWER, DUTY, RESTRAINT (2d ed. 2008); LAW IN PUBLIC HEALTH PRACTICE (Richard A. Goodman et al. eds., 2d ed. 2006).

6. Richard A. Goodman et al., *supra* note 5.

7. *E.g.,* Robert Wood Johnson Foundation, *What We Fund: Public Health,* http://www.rwjf.org/publichealth/approach.jsp (last visited Nov. 5, 2008).

8. Richard A. Goodman et al., *Law and Public Health at CDC,* 55 MORBIDITY & MORTALITY WKLY REP. Supp. 02, 29, 29–33 (Dec. 2006).

9. Public Health Law Association, *About PHLA,* http://www.phla.info/about phla.htm (last visited Nov. 5, 2008).

10. This discussion is based on my personal knowledge as a member of PHLA's board of directors.

11. *See* chapter 10, *supra.*

12. *See* chapter 5, *supra.*

13. *E.g.,* 24 RCNY Health Code Reg. § 81.08 (2006) (New York City regulation barring food service establishments from serving foods with trans fat).

14. Lawrence O. Gostin, *A Theory and Definition of Public Health,* 10 J. HEALTH CARE L. & POL'Y 1, 1 (2007).

15. David P. Fidler, *A Globalized Theory of Public Health Law*, 30 J. L. MED. & ETHICS 150, 152 (2002). Gostin would appear to agree. His recent works have emphasized the global dimensions of public health law. *See* Gostin, *supra* note 5, at 229–83.

16. For example, the Model State Emergency Health Powers Act provides broad immunity for state officials who take actions against individuals during a so-called public health emergency. *See* The Center for Law and the Public's Health at Georgetown and Johns Hopkins Universities, *The Model State Emergency Health Powers Act*, Art. 804 (Dec. 21, 2001), http://www.publichealthlaw.net/MSEHPA/MSEHPA2.pdf (last visited Nov. 5, 2008).

TABLE OF U.S. CASES

INDEX